CHRISTIAN INITIATION

THE
REFORMATION
PERIOD

Some Early Reformed Rites of
Baptism and Confirmation and
Other Contemporary Documents

J.D.C. Fisher

HillenbrandBooks

Chicago / Mundelein, Illinois

In an effort to better serve scholars and students,
pages 1–271 have been reproduced exactly as they appeared in
the original 1970 edition of *Christian Initiation: The Reformation Period.*
No changes have been made to the original folios;
therefore, the pagination and footnotes from the original edition
have been preserved.

First published in 1970 as part of the Alcuin Club Collections No. 51 by
S.P.C.K., Holy Trinity Church, Marylebone Road, London, N.W.1.

Reprinted by arrangement with The Alcuin Club, The Parsonage, 8 Church
Street, Spalding PE11 2PB, London.

CHRISTIAN INITIATION: THE REFORMATION PERIOD: THE EARLY
REFORMED RITES OF BAPTISM AND CONFIRMATION © 2007 Archdiocese of
Chicago: Liturgy Training Publications, 1800 North Hermitage Avenue,
Chicago IL 60622; 1-800-933-1800, fax 1-800-933-7094, e-mail
orders@ltp.org. All rights reserved. See our Web site at www.LTP.org.

On the cover: Martin Luther, façade of the Berlin Cathedral, Berlin, Germany
© The Crosiers: Father Gene Plaisted, osc.

Hillenbrand Books is an imprint of Liturgy Training Publications (LTP) and
the Liturgical Institute at the University of Saint Mary of the Lake (USML).
The imprint is focused on contemporary and classical theological thought
concerning the liturgy of the Catholic Church. Available at bookstores
everywhere, through LTP by calling 1-800-933-1800, or visiting
www.ltp.org. Further information about the **Hillenbrand Books** publishing
program is available from the University of Saint Mary of the
Lake/Mundelein Seminary, 1000 East Maple Avenue, Mundelein IL 60060;
847-837-4542, on the Web at www.usml.edu/liturgicalinstitute, or e-mail
litinst@usml.edu.

Printed in the United States of America.

Library of Congress Control Number: 2006932566

ISBN 978-1-59525-017-9

HCIRP

Contents

Foreword to the Hillenbrand Classics Edition

John Douglas Fisher's collection of Reformation-era Christian
initiation texts, like its predecessor volume, *Christian Initiation:
Baptism in the Medieval West*,[1] is a classic work, still widely consulted
as an important and indispensable resource by all who wish to study
the history and theology of Christian initiation in Protestant
Christianity in that formative period of the sixteenth century. How
fortunate, then, that the editors of Hillenbrand Books have decided
to bring this back into print and so make it more easily accessible
to a new generation of scholars and students.

    As a Reformation-era collection of liturgical texts for Baptism,
Private Baptism, and Confirmation in English this volume remains
one of its kind. It is a thorough compendium of sources and offers the
reader the most pertinent texts for the Lutheran (including the relevant
German *Kirchenordnungen*), Reformed, and Anglican traditions. If its
lack of a detailed treatment of the Anabaptist movement is a weakness,
and it is, it must be said that such lack reflects the attitudes of liturgical
scholarship at the time it was written. That is, Fisher's primary
interest, of course, was in the development of the 1549 and 1552
editions of the *Book of Common Prayer* in service to liturgical reform in
England, and so, was naturally much more inclined to deal with those
liturgical-textual traditions that came to have some bearing on that.

    In addition to this potential weakness, the contemporary
reader needs to be aware of and cautious of other areas where
contemporary scholarship has surpassed Fisher's work. For example, in
treating Martin Luther's first *Taufbüchlein* of 1523 (pp. 6–16), Fisher
provides as a comparative text the 1497 *Magdeburg Agenda*, which
tends to give the impression that Luther himself was rather creative in
his adaptation of the Western medieval baptismal rites. More recent
scholarship, however, has demonstrated that Luther also followed the
probably Prussian *Agenda communis*, which appeared in various
editions from 1505 to 1520. An analysis of this *Agenda* suggests that
Luther's first *Taufbüchlein* was more of a *translation* of late medieval

---

1 (London: SPCK, 1965; reprinted by Chicago: Hillenbrand Books, 2004).

Latin rites into German than a creative adaptation of those rites.[2] In a very real sense, then, his first *Taufbüchlein* was simply the late medieval Latin baptismal rite in German translation and, except for the use of German, anyone presenting their child for baptism according to this rite would have experienced little that was different from the previous rites which had been in use. Indeed, there is not even any mention that this rite should be done in the context of public worship. Similarly, with regard to Luther's retention of infant baptism, Fisher repeats the former common critique that this was an inconsistency due to his emphasis on faith alone (see pp. 4–5), a critique based on an inadequate understanding of Luther's own theology.

There is also to be noted a similar Anglo-Catholic sort of bias against the Reformed theologians, Zwingli and Calvin, and the initiation rites that they produced, and one needs always to balance Fisher's comments with representative scholars of the Reformed tradition itself. And, of course, Fisher compiled this collection long before the more recent positive assessments of Reformed baptismal practice and theology by contemporary liturgical scholars.[3]

With these caveats in mind, this volume is still to be commended to a wide readership. Not only are there translations of texts here that simply cannot be found elsewhere, but Fisher's provision of the texts for the baptism and confirmation rites of the 1549 *Book of Common Prayer*, followed by Martin Bucer's *Censura* of those rites, which are then also followed immediately by the 1552 revisions, is a superb example of the kind of textual study that Fisher offers. I am delighted that this volume, along with his *Christian Initiation: Baptism in the Medieval West* and *Confirmation Then and Now*,[4] are back in print and I commend Hillenbrand Books for undertaking this project.

Maxwell E. Johnson
University of Notre Dame

---

2 See Kent Burreson, "The Saving Flood, The Medieval Origins, Historical Development, and Theological Import of the Sixteenth-Century Lutheran Baptismal Rites" (PhD Dissertation, University of Notre Dame, 2002), 89–91.

3 Confer Hughes Oliphant Old, *The Shaping of the Reformed Baptismal Rite in the Sixteenth Century* (Grand Rapids: Eerdmans, 1992). See also James F. White, *Protestant Worship: Traditions in Transition* (Louisville: Westminster/John Knox Press, 1989); and Nathan Mitchell, "Reforms: Protestant and Catholic," in *The Oxford History of Christian Worship*, ed. Geoffrey Wainwright and Karen Westerfield Tucker (New York: Oxford University Press, 2006), 307–50.

4 (London: SPCK, 1978; reprinted by Chicago: Hillenbrand Books, 2004).

Preface to the First Edition

The main object of this book is to supply an English version of some of the better-known rites of baptism and confirmation, produced by the Reformers, and of certain other documents which throw light on the circumstances in which these rites were compiled and used. Some of these documents have been included because they express the viewpoint of the conservatives, who, content with the old Latin services, resisted the Reformers' innovations. Limitation of space has compelled me to omit altogether the relevant portions of certain works which I should have preferred not to ignore, such as Richard Ryce's *The Right Institution of Baptism*, the Scottish *Directory*, the *Westminster Confession*, and the services of baptism and confirmation in the *Book of Common Prayer* of 1662. The commentary has been kept as brief as possible in order to let the documents speak for themselves, and to leave the reader to form his own conclusions. Where it seemed desirable, I have altered the spelling of words and punctuation in the works quoted, in order to obtain a measure of consistency throughout the book.

The extent of my indebtedness to others may be gauged from the bibliography at the end. Of the books and articles there listed, justice demands that I specially mention here the works of F. E. Brightman, W. Lockton, S. L. Ollard, W. D. Maxwell, and A. C. Repp. My warmest thanks are also due to the Reverend Dr. G. J. Cuming for much useful advice as to the content of this book, and for reading it through in typescript, and to Mr. A. Marks for assistance in the work of translating some of the German texts.

Finally, I must express my gratitude to the Committee of the Alcuin Club for encouraging me to write this book, and for accepting it for their 1969 Collection.

Acknowledgments

Thanks are due to the following for permission to quote from copyright sources:

The Alcuin club: *The Rationale of Ceremonial 1540–1543*, by C. S. Cobb; *Visitation Articles and Injunctions of the Period of the Reformation*, by W. H. Frere and W. M. Kennedy.

Basil Blackwell & Mott Ltd.: *The Reformation Writings of Martin Luther*, by Bertram Lee Woolf.

The editor of *Church Quarterly Review:* an article entitled "The Age of Confirmation," by W. Lockton, which appeared in the issue of April 1925.

Concordia Publishing House, St. Louis, MO.: *Confirmation in the Lutheran Church*, by A. C. Repp.

Darton, Longman & Todd Ltd. and Newman Press, Westminster, MD: *Sacraments and Worship*, edited by P. F. Palmer.

The Faith Press Ltd.: *The Liturgical Portions of the Genevan Service Book*, by W. D. Maxwell.

The Westminster Press, Philadelphia: *Baptism: Foundations for Christian Unity*, by Dale Moody.

Abbreviations

C.R.   *Corpus Reformatorum,* ed. C. G. Bretschneider. Halle 1834.

C.S.E.L.   *Corpus Sciptorum Ecclesiasticorum Latinorum.* Vienna 1866.

Mansi   *Sacrorum Conciliorum nova et amplissima collectio, in qua . . .
              ea omnia . . . exhibentur quae J. D. Mansi evulgavit.* Florence
              1759–98.

P. G.   *Patrologiae Cursus Completus, series Graeca,* ed. J. P. Migne.
              Paris 1857.

P. L.   *Patrologiae Cursus Completus, series Latina,* ed. J. P. Migne.
              Paris 1844.

Other Books by J.D.C. Fisher

Christian Initiation: Baptism in the Medieval West
(Hillenbrand Books, 2004)

Christian Initiation: Confirmation Then and Now
(Hillenbrand Books, 2005)

About the Author

Canon J.D.C. Fisher was born in 1909. He spent his whole working life as a parish priest as the vicar of St. John the Baptist in Hove, Sussex, England, while pursuing scholarly research and writing in his spare time. He is the author of two other Hillenbrand Books editions: *Christian Initiation: Confirmation Then and Now*, and *Christian Initiation: Baptism in the Medieval West*. He contributed to *The Dictionary of Liturgy and Worship* (Macmillian, 1972) and *The Study of Liturgy* (Oxford University Press, 1978). Canon Fisher died in 1996.

Maxwell E. Johnson holds a PHD in Liturgical Studies from the University of Notre Dame. He is currently a professor of Liturgical Studies at the University of Notre Dame. His research interests are in the origins and development of early Christian liturgy and in the history and theology of the rites of Christian initiation. His 1999 book, *The Rites of Christian Initiation: Their Evolution and Interpretation* (Collegeville: Pueblo), was chosen by the Alcuin Club, England, as its 1999 selection. Dr. Johnson is the author and/or editor of several books, including *The Prayers of Sarapion of Thmuis* in the Orientalia Christiana Analecta monograph series published by the Pontifical Oriental Institute in Rome, and over fifty articles in scholarly and pastoral-theological publications. Recent publications include *Images of Baptism* (Chicago: Liturgy Training Publications, 2001), and as editor and contributor, *Between Memory and Hope: Readings on the Liturgical Year* (Collegeville: Pueblo, 2000). Recent books include, as co-author with Paul F. Bradshaw and L. Edward Phillips, *The Apostolic Tradition, Attributed to Hippolytus of Rome*, Hermeneia Commentary Series (Minneapolis: Augsburg Fortress Press, 2002), and *The Virgin of Guadalupe: Theological Reflections of an Anglo-Lutheran Liturgist* (Lanham: Rowman & Littlefield, 2002). He is an editorial consultant for *Worship*, a member of The North American Academy of Liturgy, and Societas Liturgica.

BAPTISM

1. *Luther and Baptism*

A study of the baptismal rites of the Reformers begins inevitably with the first *Taufbüchlein*, or Baptismal Booklet, of Luther, published in 1523. Three years earlier it appears that Luther still regarded the contemporary Latin rite of baptism with some favour, because in his *Babylonian Captivity*, published in 1520, he wrote, in the style of St Peter,

Blessed be the God and the Father of our Lord Jesus Christ who of his rich mercy has preserved at least this one sacrament in his church unspoiled and unspotted by man-made ordinances, and made it free to all races and classes of men; nor has he allowed it to be suppressed by foul money-grubbing and ungodly monsters of superstition.[1]

But the doctrine of justification by faith, as Luther expounded it, necessitated some modification of the then traditional doctrine of baptism. He laid great emphasis on the divine promise or word, without which baptism could not be a means of grace or a sacrament:

The first point about baptism is the divine promise, which says: "He that believeth and is baptized shall be saved." This promise is far superior to all the outer shows of works, vows, orders, and whatever else men have introduced. Our entire salvation depends on this promise; and we must be watchful to keep our faith in it, knowing without any hesitancy of mind that, once we have been baptized, we are saved.[2]

Whereas the Church during the Middle Ages had precisely defined the trinitarian formula to be recited by the officiant at every baptism, and had ordered the parochial clergy frequently to teach it to their parishioners in case they had to baptize in sudden emergency,[3] Luther considered that the form of baptism was of far less importance than the faith of the person to be baptized:

The truth is that no matter in what words baptism is administered, as long as it is not in a human name but in the Lord's name, it surely saves. Indeed I have no doubt that any one who receives it in the name of the Lord, even if the ungodly minister were not to give it in his

---

[1] *Reformation Writings of Martin Luther*, tr. Bertram Lee Woolf, I (London 1952), p. 254.
[2] Ibid., p. 255.
[3] For example, see Council of Constance (1300), c. 6; Mansi 25.30f; Synod of Salisbury (c. 1217), c. 20; F. M. Powicke and C. R. Cheney, *Councils and Synods with other documents relating to the English Church*, II, vol. 1 (Oxford 1964), p. 68.

3

name, would be truly baptized in the Lord's name. For the virtue of baptism lies not so much in the faith or practice of the administrator as in that of the recipient.[1]

In Luther's opinion the traditional doctrine of baptism so emphasized the divine activity in the sacrament as to leave insufficient room for the subjective response which was necessary if the benefits of the sacrament were to be effectively received. Duns Scotus, for instance, had said:

A sacrament of the New Law by virtue of the act performed confers grace, in such a way that there is not required in it a good impulse of the heart which may deserve grace, but it suffices that the recipient place no obstacle in the way.[2]

Later, in 1530, the *Augsburg Confession* was to contain a condemnation of the schoolmen for teaching that the sacraments conferred grace as a result of the act performed without a good impulse in the user of them (*ex opere operato sine bono motu utentis*), on the ground that this implied that justification could be received by means of a ceremony without a good impulse of the heart, that is to say, without faith.[3] How far Luther was fair to those whom he criticized is a question which cannot be entered into here; but what is quite evident is that he put a new emphasis on the subjective element in the reception of the sacraments. The efficacy of the sacrament, he said, depended on faith in the divine word of promise:

Thus, baptism justifies nobody, and gives advantage to nobody; rather, faith in the word of promise to which baptism was conjoined, is what justifies, and so completes, that which the baptism signified. Faith is the submission of the old self and the emersion of the new self.[4]

The sacraments are not fulfilled by the ritual, but only when they are believed ... They must be called efficacious, however, in the sense that, when faith is indubitably present, they most assuredly and effectively impart grace.[5]

So great an emphasis on the need for faith in the recipient of the sacraments would seem to make Luther's retention of infant baptism inconsistent, and even indefensible. He defended the practice thus:

On this matter I agree with everyone in saying that infants are helped by vicarious faith: the faith of those who present them for baptism. The word of God, whenever uttered, is powerful enough to change the

---

[1] Woolf, op. cit., p. 261.
[2] *Comm. in Sent. IV*, d. 1, q. 6, n. 10; see J. Pohle, *The Sacraments*, ed. A. Preuss (St Louis and London 1946), pp. 137f.
[3] Art. 13, n. 18; cited by Pohle, op. cit., p. 136; see B. Leeming, *Principles of Sacramental Theology* (London 1956), pp. 5–15.
[4] Tr. Woolf, op. cit., p. 263.   [5] Ibid., p. 264.

hearts even of the ungodly, and these are not less unresponsive and incapable than any infant. Further, all things are possible in response to the prayers of a believing church when it presents the infant, and this is changed, cleansed, and renewed, by their infused faith.[1]

In his *Greater Catechism* he defended infant baptism on the ground that

it is not of the utmost importance whether he who is baptized has faith or not, for this will not make the baptism wrong: everything depends on God's word and command ... For my faith does not make the baptism, but receives baptism ... We bring the child in the belief and hope that it has faith, and pray God to give it faith; but we do not baptize it on this account, but solely because God has commanded it.[2]

Thus in order not to contradict his assertion that the sacraments could not confer grace unless there were faith in the recipients, Luther was forced to contend that in some sense infants could have faith. But his argument is not wholly convincing, and seems to attribute to the baptism of an infant an objective efficaciousness inconsistent with what he said elsewhere about the necessity of personal faith.[3]

[1] Ibid., p. 271.
[2] *Primary Works*, ed. H. Wace and C. A. Buckheim (London 1896), pp. 138f.
[3] See Leeming, op. cit., pp. 68ff.

2. *Luther's First Taufbüchlein*

In 1523, deciding that the times required an order of baptism in the vernacular, Luther published his *Taufbüchlein* as a model of a baptismal liturgy suitably reformed, but without any intention that it should be followed to the letter in all Churches which accepted his reforms. The motives which inspired the compiling of this rite are given in its Epilogue.

EPILOGUE

Martin Luther to all Christian readers
grace and peace in Christ our Lord.

While I see and hear every day how even with carelessness and little reverence, not to mention, with frivolity, the high, holy and comfortable sacrament of baptism is treated in the case of little children, one cause of which I consider is the fact that those who stand by (*the font*) understand nothing of what is spoken and performed, it seems to me not only useful but also necessary that baptism be administered in the German tongue. And therefore I have put into German what hitherto took place in Latin, that is, to baptize in German, so that the sponsors and bystanders may be moved much more to faith and to a more earnest reverence, and the priests who baptize should have much more care for the hearers.

But in Christian sincerity I beg all and singular who baptize, hold children[1] or stand by to take to heart this excellent work and the great seriousness which belongs to it. For here you hear in the words of these prayers how pitifully and earnestly the Christian church here treats the little child, and with sure undoubting words confesses before God that he is possessed by the devil and is a child of sin and disfavour, and carefully prays for help and grace through baptism that he may become a child of God.

Therefore you shall remember that it is by no means a light matter to act against the devil, and not only to drive him from the little child, but also to load the little child up to the neck with so mighty and lifelong a foe; that it is very necessary to assist the poor little child with

[1] I.e., godparents.

6

your whole heart and a strong faith, and earnestly to pray that God, according to the tenor of this prayer, would not only deliver him from the power of the devil, but also strengthen him that he may gallantly resist him in life and in death. And I am concerned that people turn out so ill after baptism for the reason that our care for them has been so cold and indifferent, and we have prayed for them with so little earnestness at their baptism.

Now remember also that in baptism the least importance attaches to these external things, namely, breathing under the eyes, signing with the cross, placing salt in the mouth, putting spittle and clay on the ears and nose, anointing with oil the breast and shoulders, and signing the top of the head with chrism, vesting in the christening robe, and giving a burning candle into the hand, and whatever else there is that men have added to embellish baptism. For certainly without all such things baptism may take place, and they are not the kind of devices that the devil shuns or avoids. He despises much greater things than these. Here is earnestness required.

But take care that you are present in right faith, that you listen to God's word and earnestly join in the prayers. For when the priest says, "Let us Pray", he exhorts you to pray with him. All the sponsors also and those who stand there should also say to God in their hearts the words of his prayer. Therefore the priest should say these prayers very distinctly and slowly, so that the sponsors can hear and understand them, and the sponsors with one accord pray with the priest in their hearts, and bring the need of the little child with all earnestness before God, with all their power set themselves against the devil on behalf of the child, and show that they regard it as a serious matter and no small thing so far as the devil is concerned.

Therefore it is also very proper and right that drunken and coarse ministers be not allowed to baptize, and that such people be not accepted for sponsors, but decent, chaste, earnest, devout priests and sponsors should be provided, that they may handle the matter with earnestness and right faith, so that the holy sacrament may not be made a laughing-stock for the devil and insult may not be offered to God, who therein sheds the overflowing and infinite riches of his grace upon us, and God himself calls it a new birth, whereby we are freed from all the tyranny of the devil, delivered from sin, death and hell, and become children of life and heirs of all God's good things and his own children and brothers of Christ. O dear Christians, let us not so carelessly regard and treat so unspeakable a gift. For baptism is our only comfort and sure entry into all God's good things and into the communion of all the saints. So help us God. Amen.

However I have not so far wished to make considerable alterations in the order of baptism, which I might well allow could be improved, because it has had careless authors who did not realize sufficiently the glory of baptism.

But in order to be gentle with tender consciences, I am allowing it to remain unchanged, so that they may not complain that I wish to institute a new baptism, and find fault with those previously baptized, as if they were not rightly baptized. For, I said, man-made additions are not important, provided that baptism itself is administered with God's word, with a right faith and earnest prayer. Now we trust you to God. Amen.

Next follow in parallel columns the order of baptism found in a Magdeburg *Agenda* of 1497, and that in Luther's *Taufbüchlein*, published in Wittenberg in 1523. The former has been edited by Gustav Kawerau in C. E. Luthardt, *Zeitschrift für kirchliche Wissenschaft und kirkliches leben* (Leipzig, vol. 10, 1889), pp. 421ff. An example of a baptismal liturgy in use in Germany on the eve of the Reformation, it was the principal source of Luther's rite. The German text of the *Taufbüchlein* may be read in A. L. Richter, *Die Evangelischen Kirchenordnungen* (Weimar 1846), pp. 7ff, and in E. Sehling, *Die Evangelischen Kirchenordnungen des XVI Jahrhunderts*, I (Leipzig 1902), pp. 18ff. An English translation by P. Z. Stronach, revised by U. S. Leupold, is found in *Luther's Works*, vol. 53 (Philadelphia 1965), pp. 96–103.

In the footnotes we have indicated other rites of baptism, contemporary or earlier, which include in substantially the same form the prayers found in the Magdeburg *Agenda*. The following is an explanation of the abbreviations used, the editions being given in the bibliography at the end:

Gel.   The Gelasian Sacramentary (7th century)
Ordo 11   Ordo Romanus XI (7th and 8th centuries)
Ordo 50   Ordo Romanus L (German, 10th century)
Fulda   Sacramentarium Fuldense Saeculi X
R1487   Rituale Romanum (secundum consuetudinem romanae curiae), the first printed edition, 1487
R1520   Rituale Romanum (secundum curiam romanam), 1520
Sarum   Manuale ad usum percelebris ecclesiae Sarisburiensis
Bamb.   Agenda secundum imperialem ecclesiam et dyocesim Bambergensem, 1491
Strasb.   Die Strassburger Taufordnung von 1513, ed. G, Kawerau in Luthardt, op. cit., X
Magd.   a Magdeburg Agenda of 1497

MAGDEBURG, 1497

Here begins the order for catechising a catechumen.
And first in front of the church are set the males on the right and the females on the left;[1] and the presbyter breathes on the face of the infant three times,[2] saying:

Come out of him, unclean spirit, and give place to the Holy Spirit.

Then the presbyter shall ask the name of the infant, making a cross on the forehead and heart of the infant, saying the names, N. and N., and taking note of their sex and numbers:

Receive the sign of God the Father almighty, and of the Son and of the Holy Spirit both on thy forehead and on thy heart.

Take to thee the faith of the heavenly precepts. So conduct thyself that thou canst now be a temple of God, and having entered the church of God, rejoice to know that thou hast escaped the snares of death. Flee from idols: spurn images: worship God the Father almighty and Jesus Christ, his Son, who with the Father and the Spirit.[3]

Almighty and eternal God, Father of our Lord Jesus Christ, vouchsafe to look upon this thy servant, N., whom thou has vouchsafed to call to the first beginnings (rudimenta) of faith: drive away from him all blindness of heart: break all the snares of Satan with which he has been bound: open to him, Lord, the door of thy religion, and, imbued with the salt of thy wisdom, may he be free from the filth of all evil desires, and, rejoicing in the sweet odour of thy commandments, may he serve thee in thy church and advance from day to day, so that he may be made worthy to come to the grace of thy baptism having received thy medicine, through the same Christ our Lord.[4]

LUTHER, 1523

He who baptizes shall breathe upon the child three times under his eyes, and say:

Come out, thou unclean spirit, and give place to the Holy Spirit.

Then shall he make a cross on his forehead and breast, and say:

Receive the sign of the holy cross both on thy forehead and on thy heart.

(Luther included this prayer in a literal translation, except in two places; see below)

(Luther translated rudimenta by unterricht, "instruction")

(For "church" Luther substituted Christenheit, "Christendom")

[1] A survival from the times when baptism was administered normally at the vigils of Easter and Pentecost, when many candidates could be expected. Luther's rubric expects only one candidate.
[2] Ordo 50.xx.5, Fulda 2631, 2679, R1520; Bamb., Strasb.
[3] Gel. 599 (where it is used not in the normal rite of baptism, but in the order for making an adult pagan a catechumen), R1487, R1520, Bamb.
[4] Gel. 285, Ordo 11.4, Ordo 50.xx.7, Fulda 2632, 2683, R1487, R1520, Sarum, Bamb., Strasb.

Let us pray again.
(Luther retained this prayer, translating
it fairly literally)

O God, the immortal defence of all
who beg, the redeemer of those who
beseech, the peace of those who ask,
the life of those that believe, the resurrection of the dead, I invoke thee upon
this thy servant, N., who, seeking the
gift of thy baptism, desires to obtain
eternal grace by spiritual regeneration.
Receive him, Lord; and because thou
hast vouchsafed to say, Ask and ye
shall receive, seek and ye shall find,
knock and it shall be opened unto you,
grant a reward to him who asks, and
open the door to him who knocks, so
that having obtained the eternal blessing of the heavenly washing, he may
receive the promised kingdom of thy
bounty, who livest and reignest with
God the Father in the unity of the
Holy Spirit, God for ever and ever.
Amen.[1]

The blessing of salt to be given to the catechumens.

I exorcize thee, creature of salt, in the
name of God the Father almighty, and
in the love of our Lord Jesus Christ,
and in the power of the Holy Spirit. I
exorcize thee by the living God, by the
true God, by the holy God, who created thee for a protector of the human
race, and ordered thee to be consecrated by his servants for the people
that come to faith: so that in the name
of the holy Trinity thou mayest be
made a saving sacrament for putting
the enemy to flight. Therefore we ask
thee, O Lord, our God, that this creature of salt thou, Lord, wouldest sanctify and bless, that it may be to all who
receive it a perfect medicine remaining
in their bowels, in the name of our
Lord Jesus Christ, who is to come to
judge the quick and the dead and the
world by fire. Amen.[2]

Then the presbyter shall ask the name of the infant, and shall place some of the salt in the mouth
of the infant, saying:

Now shall he take the child and put salt in his
mouth and say:

---

[1] A prayer of non-Roman origin, found in Alcuin's *Supplement* to the *Hadrianum*,
Fulda 2641, *Sarum*.
[2] *Gel.* 288, *Ordo* 11.5, *Ordo* 50.xx.4, *Fulda* 2635, 2686, *Strasb.*, *Sarum*.

Receive the salt of wisdom for a propitiation for thee unto eternal life.[1]

Peace be unto thee.

After the giving of salt a prayer over both males and females:

God of our fathers, God who dost establish every creature, we humbly beseech thee that thou wouldest vouchsafe to look upon thy servant, that thou wouldest not suffer him who tastes this first morsel of salt to hunger any more that he may be filled with heavenly food: whereby he may be, Lord, ever

fervent in spirit and rejoicing in hope and ever serving thy name, and bring him to the washing of new regeneration, so that with thy faithful people he may be made worthy to obtain the eternal rewards of thy promises: through Christ our Lord. R. Amen.[2]

N., receive the salt of wisdom, which shall preserve thee unto eternal life. Amen.

Have peace.

Let us pray.

Almighty and eternal God, who hast through the flood, according to thy righteous judgment, condemned the unfaithful world, and, according to thy great mercy, hast saved faithful Noah, even eight persons, and hast drowned hard-hearted Pharaoh with all his in the Red Sea, and hast led thy people Israel dry through it, thereby prefiguring this bath of thy holy baptism, and through the baptism of thy dear child, our Lord Jesus Christ, hast sanctified and set apart the Jordan and all water for a saving flood, and an ample washing away of sins: we pray that through thy same infinite mercy thou wilt graciously look upon this N., and bless him with a right faith in the spirit, so that through this saving flood all that was born in him from Adam and all which he himself has added thereto may be drowned and submerged: and that he may be separated from the unfaithful, and preserved in the holy ark of Christendom dry and safe, and ever fervent in spirit and joyful in hope serve thy name, so that he with all the faithful may be worthy to inherit thy promise of eternal life, through Christ our Lord. Amen.[3]

---

[1] Gel. 289, Ordo 11.6, Ordo 50.xx.9, Fulda 2636, 2688, R1487, R1520, Bamb., Strasb., Sarum.

[2] Gel. 290, Fulda 2637, 2689, R1487, R1520, Bamb., Strasb., Sarum.

[3] For the Flood and the passage of the Red Sea as types of baptism see J. Daniélou, Bible et Liturgie (Paris 1958), pp. 104-44.

A prayer over males only, a cross being made on
their foreheads:

God of Abraham, God of Isaac, God of
Jacob, God who didst appear to Moses
thy servant in mount Sinai, and didst
lead the children of Israel out of
Egypt, appointing for them the angel
of thy goodness to guard them by day
and by night, we beseech thee, Lord,
that thou wouldest vouchsafe to send
thy holy angel that he may also surely
guard this thy servant, N., and bring
him to the grace of thy baptism.[1]

(Luther omitted this prayer; but his
previous prayer included a reference to
the passage of the Red Sea)

A prayer over females, making a cross on their
foreheads:

God of heaven, God of earth, God of
angels, God of archangels, God of
prophets, God of all who live good
lives, God whom every tongue confesses of things in heaven and things on
earth and things under the earth, I invoke thee upon this thine handmaid,
N., that thou mightest vouchsafe to
guard her and lead her to the grace of
thy baptism.[2]

(Luther omitted this prayer)

An exorcism for putting to flight the devil from
the baptized:

Therefore, accursed devil, take heed to
thy sentence, and give honour to the
living and true God: give honour to
Jesus Christ his Son and to the Holy
Spirit, that thou come out and depart
from this servant of God, N., because
our God and Lord Jesus Christ has
vouchsafed to call him to himself to his
holy grace and to the fount of baptism.
And this (*here make a cross with your
thumb on the forehead of the infant*) sign
of the holy cross which we put upon
his forehead do thou never dare to
violate. Through our Lord.[3]

(Luther included this prayer)

A prayer over males, making a cross on their
foreheads:

Hearken, accursed Satan, adjured by
the name of the eternal God, with thine
envy conquered, trembling and groan-
ing depart: let there be nothing between thee and this servant of God

(Luther included this prayer)

[1] *Gel.* 291, *Ordo* 11.14, *Ordo* 50.xx.17, *Fulda* 2639, 2690, R1487, *Bamb., Strasb., Sarum.*
[2] *Gel.* 293, *Ordo* 11.16, *Ordo* 50.xx.19, *Fulda* 2640, R1487, *Bamb., Strasb., Sarum.*
[3] *Gel.* 293, R1487, *Bamb., Sarum.*

who now meditates upon heavenly
things, and is about to renounce thee
and thy world and to live in blessed
immortality; therefore give honour to
the Holy Spirit who is coming, that
he, descending from the highest arch
of heaven, having confounded thy deceits, may cleanse a breast, making it a
habitation consecrated for God and a
temple, so that freed from all the stains
of his past sins this servant of God, *N.*,
may ever give thanks to the everlasting
God and bless his name for ever and
ever. Through him who is to come to
judge the living and the dead and the
world by fire. Amen.[1]

Therefore, accursed devil . . .

A prayer over females only, making a cross on
their forehead:

God of Abraham, God of Isaac, God of   (Omitted by Luther)
Jacob, God who didst set free the tribes
of Israel, and didst rescue Susanna
from a false charge, I humbly beseech
thee that thou wouldest free this thine
handmaid, *N.*, and vouchsafe to bring
her to the grace of thy baptism.[2]

Therefore, accursed devil . . .

A prayer over males only, making a cross:

I exorcize thee, unclean spirit, in the   (Luther included this prayer)
name of the Father and of the Son and
of the Holy Spirit, that thou come out
and depart from this servant of God,
N., for he himself commands thee, accursed one, damned and to be damned,
who walked upon thee (*sic*) on foot
and stretched out his right hand to
Peter as he sank.[3]

Therefore, accursed devil . . .

A prayer over females only, making a cross:

I exorcize thee, unclean spirit, in the
name of the Father and of the Son and
of the Holy Spirit that thou come out
and depart from this handmaid of God,
N., for he himself commands thee, accursed and damned one, who opened
the eyes of him that was born blind,

[1] *Gel.* 294, *Ordo* 11.18, *Ordo* 50.xx.21, R1487, *Bamb.*, *Strasb.*, *Sarum.*
[2] *Gel.* 295, *Ordo* 11.19, *Ordo* 50.xx.22, *Fulda* 2642, R1487, *Bamb.*, *Sarum.*
[3] *Gel.* 296, *Ordo* 11.21, *Ordo* 50.xx.24, *Fulda* 2644, R1487, *Bamb.*, *Strasb.*, *Sarum.*

and raised Lazarus on the fourth day from the tomb.[1]

Therefore, accursed devil . . .

I humbly beseech thine eternal and most just goodness, O Lord, Father almighty, eternal God, who art the author of light and truth, for this thy servant, *N.*, that thou wouldest vouchsafe to illuminate him with the light of thy knowledge: cleanse him and sanctify him: give him true knowledge, that he may be made worthy to come to the grace of thy baptism and may keep a firm hope and right counsel and holy doctrine, so that he may be fit to receive the grace of thy baptism. Through Christ our Lord.[2]

The Lord be with you.
And with thy spirit.

The continuation of the holy Gospel according to Mark:

At that time they brought . . .

Then the presbyter holding his hand with his stole upon the head of the infant shall say *Our Father* and *I believe in God.*

Be not deceived, Satan, punishment threatens thee: torments await thee: the day of judgment threatens thee, the day which is to come as a fiery furnace, in which eternal death will come upon thee and all thine angels: And therefore for thy wickedness, damned and to be damned, give honour to the living God and true, give honour to the Holy Spirit, the Comforter, in whose name and power I order thee, whoever thou art, unclean spirit, that thou come out and depart from this servant of God, *N.*, whom today our God and Lord Jesus Christ has vouchsafed to call to his grace and blessing and to the fount of baptism by his gift, so that he may become his temple through the water of regeneration unto the remission of all his sins. In the name of our Lord Jesus Christ, who is to come to judge the living and the dead and the world by fire.[3]

Let us pray.
(Luther included this prayer)

The Lord be with you.
R.   And with thy spirit.

The Gospel of St Mark:

R.   Glory be to thee, O Lord.
At that time they brought . . .

Then shall the priest lay his hand upon the child's head and pray *Our Father*, together with the godparents, kneeling.

(Luther omitted this prayer)

[1] *Gel.* 297, *Ordo* 11.22, *Ordo* 50.xx.25, *Fulda* 2645, R1487, *Bamb., Sarum.*
[2] *Gel.* 298, *Ordo* 11.24, *Ordo* 50.xx.27, *Fulda* 2647, *Bamb., Strasb., Sarum.*
[3] *Gel.* 419, *Ordo* 11.84, *Ordo* 50.xxix.5, *Bamb., Strasb., Sarum.*

Then the presbyter shall dip two of his fingers, that is, his thumb and forefinger, in spittle and anoint the top of the right ear of the infant, saying:

Effeta, that is, be thou opened.

Then on the nose:

Unto an odour of sweetness.

Then he shall touch the top of the left ear, saying:

Be thou put to flight, devil, for the judgment of God is coming nigh.[1]

Then the infant shall be led into church, saying:

The Lord preserve thy going in and thy coming out from this time forth and for ever more.[2]

Next the priest makes the infant renounce the devil through his godfathers, saying:

N., dost thou renounce Satan?
R. I renounce.
Q. And all his works?
R. I renounce.
Q. And all his works (*pomps*?)?
R. I renounce.

Q. Dost thou believe in God the Father almighty, maker of heaven and earth?
R. I believe.
Q. Dost thou believe also in Jesus Christ, his only Son, our Lord, who was born and suffered?
R. I believe.
Q. Dost thou believe also in the Holy Spirit, the holy catholic church, the communion of saints, the remission of sins, the resurrection of the flesh, and eternal life after death?
R. I believe.[3]

Then he shall anoint the infant with the oil of salvation on the breast, saying:

And I anoint thee with the oil of salvation,

Then shall he take spittle in his finger and with it touch the right ear and say:

Ephthah, that is, be opened.

(On the nose and left ear)

But thou, devil, flee away, for the judgment of God comes near.

Then they shall lead the child into the church, and the priest shall say:

The Lord preserve thy going in and thy coming out from henceforth and for evermore.

Then the priest shall make the child through his godparents renounce the devil, saying:

N., dost thou renounce the devil?
R. Yes.
And all his works?
R. Yes.
And all his ways (*wesen*)?
R. Yes.

Then shall he ask:

Q. Dost thou believe in God the Father almighty, maker of heaven and earth?
R. Yes.
Dost thou believe in Jesus Christ, his only Son, our Lord, who was born and suffered?
R. Yes.
Dost thou believe in the Holy Spirit, one holy Christian church, the communion of saints, the forgiveness of sins, the resurrection of the flesh and an eternal life after death?
R. Yes.

Then shall he anoint the child with holy oil on the breast and between the shoulders, and shall say:

And I anoint thee with the oil of salvation

---

[1] *Gel.* 420, *Ordo* 11.85, *Ordo* 50.xxix.6, R1487, R1520, *Bamb.*, *Strasb.*, *Sarum.*
[2] R1487, R1520, *Sarum*, have a different formula.
[3] In *Gel.* 449 and Alcuin's *Supplement* the third question ended at "resurrection of the flesh". *Gel.* also omitted "communion of saints". *Fulda* 2710 and R1520 ended with "eternal life". "Eternal life after death" is found in *Bamb.*, *Strasb.*, and *Sarum.*

then between the shoulders:

in Christ Jesus our Lord.[1]	in Jesus Christ our Lord.
	And he shall ask:
Q. N., dost thou wish to be baptized?	Wilt thou be baptized?
R. I wish it.[2]	R. Yes.

Then by immersing them the priest shall dip first the males and then the females, their head turned to the east, saying: | *Then shall he take the child and dip him in the font, and shall say:*

And I baptize thee in the name of the Father and of the Son and of the Holy Spirit.[3]

And I baptize thee in the name of the Father and of the Son and of the Holy Spirit.

Then the godfathers holding the infant by the feet as he stands in the water, the priest shall say:

Then shall the godparents hold the little child in the font, and the priest shall make on him a cross with the oil on the top of the head, and shall say:

Almighty God, the Father of our Lord Jesus Christ, who has regenerated thee by water and the Holy Spirit, and who has given thee remission of all thy sins, (*then he shall anoint with chrism the infant on the head, saying*) himself anoint thee with the chrism of salvation in Christ Jesus our Lord unto eternal life. Amen.[4]

The almighty God and Father of our Lord Jesus Christ, who has regenerated thee by water and the Holy Spirit, and has forgiven thee all thy sins, anoint thee with the saving oil

unto eternal life.
Amen.

Peace be with thee.
R.   And with thy spirit.

While placing the white band[5] (mitra) on the head of the infant, saying:

And while the godparents still hold the child in the font, the priest shall put on him a cap and say:

Receive a white robe, holy and spotless, which thou shalt bring before the judgment seat of Christ and have eternal life.[6]

Receive the white, holy and pure robe, which thou shalt bring spotless before the judgment seat of Christ, so that thou mayest have eternal life.
Peace be with thee.

In giving a light to the infant, saying:

Then they shall lift him from the font and the priest shall put a candle in his hand:

Receive a lamp burning and without fault: guard thy baptism, that when the Lord comes to the wedding thou mayest be able to meet him together with all the saints in the heavenly hall, that thou mayest have eternal life and live with him for ever and ever. Amen.[7]

Receive this burning torch and guard thy baptism without fault, so that, when the Lord comes to the marriage, thou mayest go to meet him with the saints in the heavenly hall, and have eternal life. Amen.

---

[1] *Gel.* 421 (without the accompanying formula), *Ordo* 50.xxix.58, R1487, R1520, *Bamb., Strasb., Sarum.*

[2] *Ordo* 50.xxix.58, *Fulda* 2710, R1487, R1520, *Bamb., Strasb., Sarum.*

[3] *Ordo* 50.xxix.59, *Fulda* 2711, R1487, R1520, *Bamb., Strasb., Sarum.*

[4] *Gel.* 450, *Ordo* 11.97, *Ordo* 50.xxix.65, *Fulda* 2711f, R1487, R1520, *Bamb., Strasb., Sarum.*

[5] Whereas the formula goes back to a time when a white robe to cover the whole body was given, now there is given a linen band to cover the chrism on the child's forehead.

[6] *Ordo* 50.xxix.66,69, *Fulda* 2713, R1487, R1520, *Bamb., Strasb., Sarum.*

[7] R1487, R1520, *Sarum.*

3. Osiander's Order of Baptism

Andreas Osiander, 1498–1552, a priest in Nuremberg, having come out on the side of the Reformation in 1522, two years later produced an order of baptism in German. His principal source was the Bamberg *Agenda* of 1491, which he followed so closely that it is not necessary to give an English translation of it here. But in some places he was influenced by Luther's first *Taufbüchlein*, published the year before.

In the summer of 1531 Cranmer was sent by Henry VIII to the continent on an embassy to the Emperor and also to make contact with certain Lutheran princes in order to prepare the way for a political alliance. When his business took him to Nuremberg, Cranmer met Osiander, frequently visiting his house, and marrying his niece, Margaret. From this time onwards Cranmer was convinced that the Church needed a radical reformation; and no doubt Osiander's influence did much to lead him to this conviction.

THE ORDER OF BAPTISM
HITHERTO ADMINISTERED IN LATIN
TRANSLATED INTO GERMAN
NÜRNBERG 1524

First a minister of the Christian congregation thereto appointed, when he has to baptize a believer, shall ask his name, and say:

What is thy name?

So shall he do in the case of a believer, but for an infant under age a sponsor thereto appointed shall answer on his behalf: N. Then shall the minister ask again:

N., dost thou renounce the devil?
R. Yes, I renounce.
Q. And all his works?
R. Yes, I renounce.
Q. And all his ways?[1]
R. Yes, I renounce.
Q. Dost thou believe in God the Father almighty, maker of heaven and earth?
R. Yes, I believe.

---

[1] So Luther, instead of "pomps"; see above, p. 15.

Q. Dost thou believe in Jesus Christ, his only Son, our Lord, who was born and suffered?

R. Yes, I believe.

Q. Dost thou believe in the Holy Spirit, one holy Christian[1] church, the communion of saints, the forgiveness of sins, the resurrection of the flesh and after death an eternal life?

R. Yes, I believe.[2]

Then shall the minister breathe on the child three times under the eyes and say:[3]

Begone, thou unclean spirit, and depart from this creature of God who renounces thee. And give honour to the living and true God and to Jesus Christ, his Son, and give place to the Holy Spirit.

Then shall the minister sign the believer with the cross on the forehead and on the breast and shall say:[4]

Receive the sign of the cross of Christ on thy forehead and on thy breast, and accept the faith wherewith thou mayest fulfil the heavenly command. And so walk that thou mayest now be a temple of God. Enter into the church of God, and know with joy that thou hast escaped the snares of death: flee from idols, spurn images, and give honour to God the Father almighty and Jesus Christ, his Son, who with the same Father and the Holy Spirit lives and reigns, one God for ever and ever. Amen.

Then the minister shall say again:

Let us pray.

O Lord God, do thou mercifully hear our prayer, and guard this thy chosen servant by the power of the holy cross with which we have signed him, so that he may keep the first knowledge of thy great holiness and through the observance of thy godly commandments he may come to the grace of the new birth. Through Jesus Christ our Lord. Amen.[5]

---

[1] Like Luther, Osiander avoided the use of the word "catholic".

[2] A renunciation and confession of faith at this early point is unusual. Osiander found it in *Bamb.* It also occurs in *Ordo* 50.xx.3f. *Fulda* 2679 has a renunciation at this point but no confession of faith.

[3] So Luther; above, p. 9.

[4] Osiander has omitted from *Bamb.*, "The sign of the holy cross of our Lord Jesus Christ I place on thy forehead" and "The sign of the Saviour, our Lord Jesus Christ I place upon thy breast". These additional consignations are also found in *Fulda* 2681f, R1487, *Strasb.*, and *Sarum.*

[5] This prayer, not in *Magd.* or the *Taufbüchlein*, is found in *Gel.* 286, *Fulda* 2633, 2684, R1487, R1520, and *Sarum.*

Then shall the minister say again:

Let us pray.

O almighty and eternal God, Father of our Lord Jesus Christ . . .[1]

Then shall the minister say again:

Let us pray.

O God, thou immortal comfort of all . . .[2]

The minister shall now place salt in the mouth of the believer and shall say:

Receive, N., the salt of wisdom which shall preserve thee unto eternal life.

Peace be with thee.

Then shall the minister say again:

Let us pray.

Almighty and eternal God, . . .[3]

Here shall follow three exorcisms which shall be spoken over males only. And then three which shall be spoken over females only. The first exorcism over a male. The minister shall say again:

Let us pray.

God of Abraham, God of Isaac, God of Jacob, . . .
Repetition: Therefore, thou wicked devil, . . .
The second exorcism: Therefore, hearken now, thou wicked devil, . . .
Repetition: Therefore, thou wicked devil, . . .
The third exorcism: I exorcize thee, thou unclean spirit, . . .
Repetition: Therefore, thou wicked devil, . . .

The first exorcism over a girl. The minister shall say:

Let us pray.

God of heaven, God of earth, God of angels, . . .
Repetition: Therefore, thou wicked devil, . . .
The second exorcism: God of Abraham, God of Isaac, God of Jacob, . . .
Repetition: Therefore, thou wicked devil, . . .
The third exorcism: I exorcize thee, thou unclean spirit, . . .
Repetition: Therefore, thou wicked devil, . . .

---

[1] As in *Magd.*; above, p. 9.
[2] Not in *Bamb.* but in the *Taufbüchlein.*
[3] Luther's "Flood Prayer". Osiander has followed Luther in substituting it for the prayer, "God of our fathers . . .".

Then shall the minister say to the boys and girls:

Let us pray.

Lord, holy Father, almighty, eternal God, . . .

The Lord be with you.

R.   And with thy spirit.

The continuation ✠ (*here the minister shall sign the believer with a cross on the forehead*) of the holy ✠ gospel (*on the mouth*) of Saint Mark ✠ (*on the breast*).

R.   Glory be to thee, O Lord.

At that time they brought . . .[1]

Thanks be to God.

Then shall the minister, if he baptizes a child under age, likewise command the sponsors asked for that purpose to instruct him in the following or a similar manner if he is bereft of his parents through death or other accident before he has come to the use of reason and understanding of the Christian faith:

N., I command you that you carefully and faithfully instruct and teach the child in the power of Christian love, if he should be bereft of his parents through death or other mishap before he has come to the use of reason and understanding of the holy Christian faith: first to learn the holy ten commandments, by which he perceives the will of God and his own sins: then the holy Christian faith through which we receive grace, forgiveness of sins, the Holy Spirit and a godly life and become justified in the spirit and devout: and next to exhort him that, because the flesh wars against the spirit, he through original sin which is in the flesh has been delivered to death, so that as Christ has risen again so he may lead a new and godly life: next the holy prayer, Our Father, by which he obtains grace and help from God, so that all things that are now begun in him through faith and baptism may be brought to a blessed fulfilment, and that for all these things almighty God will give and send his grace, word and Spirit. So pray now with reverence and say an Our Father.[2]

Then shall the minister say over the believer, whether a boy or a girl:

Thou shalt know, Satan, . . .

[1] *Bamb.*, Osiander's chief source, used the Matthaean version; but the Marcan version had been used by Luther, who found it in *Magd.*

[2] This exhortation is Osiander's own work. It replaces this rubric in *Bamb.*: "Here the person to be baptized is to be entrusted to the godfather, so that, after the infant himself has come to years of discretion, he may faithfully teach him, if it should be necessary, the Lord's prayer, the angelic salutation, the apostles' creed and the ten commandments, and may likewise encourage him to the observance of the same, and to the leading of a catholic and virtuous life."

Here shall the minister make clay with his spittle and touch the believer on the right ear, and say:

Ephthah, that is, be thou opened (*then under the nose and say*) unto a sweet odour. (*Then on the left ear and say:*) But thou, devil, begone for the judgment of God is nigh thee.

Then the minister shall lead the believer into the church, and say:

God bless thy going in and thy coming out from henceforth and for evermore.

When they come to the font, the minister shall ask as follows:

What is thy name?
R. N.
Q. N., dost thou renounce the devil?
R. Yes, I renounce.
Q. And all his works?
R. Yes, I renounce.
Q. And all his ways?
R. Yes, I renounce.
Q. Dost thou believe in God the Father almighty, maker of heaven and earth?
R. Yes, I believe.
Q. Dost thou believe in Jesus Christ, his only Son, our Lord, who was born and suffered?
R. Yes, I believe.
Q. Dost thou believe in the Holy Spirit, one holy Christian church, the communion of saints, the forgiveness of sins, the resurrection of the flesh, and an eternal life after death?
R. Yes, I believe.

Then the minister shall dip his thumb in the oil of salvation and anoint the believer on the breast and say:

And I anoint thee with the oil of salvation (*then between the shoulders*) *and shall say:* in Christ Jesus our Lord.

Then the minister shall ask again:

What is thy name?
R. N.
Q. N., wilt thou be baptized?
R. Yes, I will.
Q. What is thy name?
R. N.

Q. *N.*, wilt thou be baptized?
R. Yes, I will.
Q. What is thy name?
R. *N.*
Q. *N.*, wilt thou be baptized?
R. Yes, I will.[1]
Q. What is thy name?
R. *N.*

Then the minister shall baptize him and say:

And I baptize thee in the name of the Father and of the Son and of the Holy Spirit. Amen.

Then the minister shall say again:

Let us pray.

The almighty God and Father of our Lord Jesus Christ, who has regenerated thee by water and the Holy Spirit, and who has given thee forgiveness of all thy sins, (*here shall the minister anoint the believer on the top of the head with the chrism of salvation*) anoint thee with the chrism of salvation in Christ Jesus our Lord unto eternal life. Amen.

Then the minister shall put the white robe on him, and shall say:

Receive now the white and spotless robe, and bring it before the judgment seat of Christ, so that thou mayest have eternal life.[2]

Peace be with thee. Amen.

Herein we have not wished to indicate where and how often the words should be changed when a girl is being baptized, and instead of "he" "she" and instead of "servant" "handmaid" should be said, but have trusted to the good sense of everyone.

Osiander altered the Latin rite in the Bamberg *Agenda* very little, the most notable changes being the introduction of the prayer, "O God, thou immortal comfort, . . ." and the "Flood Prayer", both of which he derived from Luther's *Taufbüchlein*. But quite obviously he felt under no obligation at all to make his rite conform in all points with that of Luther. Throughout his rite Osiander consistently substituted "minister" for "priest", and, like Luther, he avoided using the word "catholic".

Osiander's order of baptism had only a short life, being replaced in two years time by Luther's second *Taufbüchlein*, issued in 1526.

[1] Osiander found this unusual triple form of interrogation, probably based upon John 21.15-17, in *Bamb.*
[2] Not having found it in *Bamb.*, Osiander has not included the giving of a burning candle.

4. Luther's Second Taufbüchlein

In the Epilogue to his *Taufbüchlein* of 1523 Luther expressed the view that the numerous external ceremonies in baptism were, except for the act of baptism itself, the least important part of the rite, specifically mentioning in this connection the breathing under the eyes, consignation, putting salt in the child's mouth, the *Effeta* with spittle and clay, the several unctions, the vesting in a white robe, and the giving of the candle. He added that, in order not to offend tender consciences, he had not for the time being made any radical changes in the order of baptism.[1] Hence it was to be expected that, before much time had passed, he would issue a revised baptismal office from which most of the old ceremonies had been removed. In fact it was only three years later, in 1526, that Luther published a *Baptism Booklet translated into German and newly revised*.[2] The almost total elimination of all exorcism and the excision of the many ceremonies which he had declared three years before to be unimportant had the effect of making this new rite extremely brief when compared with that which had gone before.

Luther's second order of baptism opened with a prologue, which is in fact the epilogue of his first rite without the last paragraph, which was no longer apposite.

The minister shall say:

Come out, thou unclean spirit, and give place to the Holy Spirit.

Then he shall make a cross on his forehead and breast and shall say:

Receive the sign of the holy cross both on thy forehead and on thy breast.

Let us pray.

Almighty and eternal God, the Father of our Lord Jesus Christ,[3] I invoke thee upon this thy servant, N., who prays for the gift of thy baptism, and desires thine eternal grace through spiritual regeneration. Accept him, Lord; and because thou hast said, Ask and ye shall receive, seek and ye shall find, knock and it shall be opened unto you, so now grant the reward to him who asks, and open the door to him who knocks, so that he may obtain the eternal blessing of this heavenly

---

[1] Above, p. 8.
[2] The German text may be read in Sehling, op. cit., I.i (1902), pp. 22f.
[3] With the abolition of the giving of salt part of the old prayer ceased to be appropriate.

washing, and receive the promised kingdom of thy bounty, through Christ our Lord. Amen.

Let us pray.

Almighty and eternal God, who hast through the flood ...[1]

I exorcize thee, thou unclean spirit, in the name of the Father ✠, and of the Son ✠, and of the Holy Spirit ✠, that thou come out and depart from this servant of Jesus Christ, N. Amen.

Let us hear the holy Gospel of St Mark.
At that time they brought ...

Then shall the priest lay his hand upon the child's head and pray *Our Father*, together with the godparents, kneeling:

Our Father, ...

Then they shall lead the little child to the font, and the priest shall say:

The Lord preserve thy going in and thy coming out from henceforth and for evermore.

Then the priest shall make the child through his godparents renounce the devil, and say:

N., dost thou renounce the devil?
R. Yes.
And all his works?
R. Yes.
And all his ways?
R. Yes.

Then he shall ask:

Dost thou believe in God the Father almighty, maker of heaven and earth?
R. Yes.
Dost thou believe in Jesus Christ, his only Son, our Lord, who was born and suffered?
R. Yes.
Dost thou believe in the Holy Spirit, one holy Christian church, the communion of saints, the forgiveness of sins, the resurrection of the flesh and an eternal life after death?
R. Yes.
Wilt thou be baptized?
R. Yes.

[1] Luther's own Flood Prayer.

Then he shall take the child and dip him in the font, and shall say:

And I baptize thee in the name of the Father and of the Son and of the Holy Spirit.

Then shall the godparents hold the little child in the font, and the priest shall say while putting the robe on the child:

The almighty God and Father of our Lord Jesus Christ, who has regenerated thee by water and the Holy Spirit, and has forgiven thee all thy sins, strengthen thee with his grace to eternal life. Amen.[1]

Peace be with thee.

R.   Amen.

Luther's second *Taufbüchlein* of 1526 was soon widely used. Osiander, the chief author of the Brandenberg–Nuremberg Church Order of 1533, in that work ordered its use, thereby ending the use of his own order of baptism. It was also authorized for use by the Church Orders of Göttingen (1530) and Northeim (1539), by Herzog Heinrich's *Agenda* (1539), and by the Church Orders of Halle (1541), Schleswig-Holstein (1542), Pomerania (1542), Schweinfurt (1543), Ritzebüttel (1544), and Mecklenburg (1552).[2]

---

[1] This is the old prayer at the presbyteral unction after baptism, altered somewhat since there is now no actual anointing.

[2] See Sehling, op. cit., I.i, p. 21.

5. The Brandenburg–Nuremberg Church Order of 1533

The State of Brandenburg-Anspach had from 1515 been ruled by two brothers, the Margraves Casimir and George, the former of whom was a conservative and the latter a Lutheran. The death of Casimir in 1527 left George in sole command without the restraining influence of his brother. On 1 March 1528 he introduced Lutheran reforms into the churches of his dominion. In 1533 there was issued the *Brandenburg–Nuremberg Church Order*, which contained regulations concerning church government, doctrine, and worship. One of the principal authors of this work was Osiander.

This church order exerted a considerable influence upon later church orders in Germany. Cranmer, who had returned to England before its publication, acquired a copy of it for his library. Bucer used it when he compiled the section on the sacraments in the *Consultation*, which he and Melanchthon drew up for Hermann, Archbishop of Cologne; and although the *Consultation* was rejected in the province for which it was designed, it was one of the sources of the first English Prayer Book of 1549.

There follows here that part of the *Brandenburg–Nuremberg Church Order* which deals with baptism, except for a long section which Bucer incorporated in the *Consultation*, and which we have omitted here to avoid duplication.[1] It may be read in the original German in Sehling, op. cit., XI, pp. 174–80. We have reproduced here an English translation by W. Goode, *The Doctrine of the Church of England as to the Effects of Baptism in the case of Infants* (London 1849), Appendix II.

In all ecclesiastical usages we must diligently mark what God has commanded and instituted, and what men have added thereto, in order that we may hold the divine as the essential part, and diligently practise it, and on the other hand judge the human additions, whether or not they are things indifferent, and if indifferent, whether they are also useful or not, in order that what is contrary to God's word, or otherwise unprofitable, may be done away.

Now God himself has instituted and ordained baptism, that we should baptize with water in the name of the Father and of the Son and of the

---

[1] Below, pp. 60–2.

Holy Ghost. But men have added of their own accord prayer, [recitation of the] gospel, sponsors, chrisom—cloth, blessing of the font, oil, salt, and spittle, etc. Now, whatever of these things tends to profit and improvement should for the present be suffered to remain; but whatever is unprofitable and causes offence should be suffered to fall into disuse.

Now the saying of prayer thereat, and the reading of the holy gospel, is not only allowable but also useful and good; therefore it should be suffered to remain. In like manner also sponsors, especially on account of the Anabaptists, who nowadays pretend that they do not know whether they be baptized or not; in order that the sponsors principally, together with other persons, may give testimony, and in the mouth of two or three witnesses, every matter may be established (Deut. 19). Also in order that some one may answer for the child, and if he should be prematurely deprived of his parents by death, they may remind the children what they have engaged on their behalf at their baptism, and keep a strict watch over them that they may fulfil it, and learn God's commandments, creed and prayer.

But the blessing of the font, oil, salt, and spittle, etc. darken rather than advance the essential parts of baptism, and only serve to superstition. Moreover, the prayer and blessing with which the font, salt, and oil are consecrated, have no foundation in God's word, but are in many respects at variance with it. Moreover, inasmuch as the holy Christian church from the beginning has not considered such things as necessary, but has always acknowledged them to be indifferent, and that if a child be baptized with simple common water, in the name of the Father, and of the Son, and of the Holy Ghost, although all the other additions have been omitted, yet nothing has in this case been done amiss, but the child is rightly baptized, therefore these things ought at this time to be omitted. And since baptism is the sign of the covenant with us Christians under the New Testament, just as circumcision was of that with the Jews under the Old Testament, young children ought, on the request of their parents, to be baptized, at as early a period as possible: for even young children were circumcised, according to God's commands, as early as the eighth day. And Christ says, Except a man be born of water and of the Spirit, he cannot see the kingdom of God; and Paul calls baptism a laver of regeneration. Now young children, however tender their years, have need to be regenerated, if they are to enter the kingdom of God. Moreover, we believe that the apostles baptized children, inasmuch as they baptized whole households, and are sure that no one can prove any other or contrary conclusion from the holy scriptures.

Pastors and ministers, however, must give all diligence, that for such necessary work of Christian baptism, intelligent sponsors be chosen, who know to what end they are there present, in order that the baptism may be conducted with true devotion, sobriety, and propriety. They ought too, themselves to take good heed that they be not light-minded, inconsiderate, in an unsuitable frame of mind, or the worse for wine, in order that they may pronounce the Christian prayers, and above all, the word on which baptism principally depends, distinctly and seriously, that they may not move the audience that stand by to levity, or otherwise offend them, but rather give occasion to devotion and good Christian thoughts. In like manner they shall enjoin the people who are present, especially the children, to avoid all levity, indecency, and scandal, and on the contrary, devoutly to pray for grace, salvation, faith, and everlasting happiness, in behalf of the baptized child; inasmuch as Christ has given us so comfortable a promise, that whatsoever we ask in his name he will give unto us.

And such decency, seriousness, and devotion will doubtless follow, not only in the ministers of the church, but also in the surrounding audience, if we diligently lay to heart the exceeding great benefit which the Father of all compassion, of his mere mercy, bestows upon us through our dear Lord Jesus Christ in the sacrament of holy baptism, and the grace and salutary work which he by the power of his eternal word then and there worketh in us. For thereby we are incited to praise, to invoke, and freely to confess his holy and divine name. For not the ministers, nor any creature, but God himself here worketh eternal life and happiness. Wherefore also our dear Lord Jesus Christ has commanded to baptize, not in our own, nor yet in the name of any saint or angel, but in the name of God the Father, and of the Son, and of the Holy Ghost.

But in order that we may contemplate this work of God with deeper feeling and in a more orderly way, we must first diligently consider in how great misery and wretchedness, according to the testimony of divine scripture, we are all alike involved. Secondly, what great mercy God has shewn towards us through our Lord Jesus Christ, in that he has delivered us from it by baptism. And thirdly, how we should bear in mind such grace of baptism at all times, but especially in trouble, and praise and glorify God for the same.

Next follow three sections which we have omitted here because they reappear in Hermann's *Consultation*; below, pp. 60–2. After regulations concerning private baptism (below, pp. 135f) comes the actual order of baptism, which is that of Luther's second *Taufbüchlein*, with a final exhortation to the godparents from Osiander's own rite of baptism.

6. Strassburg—the First German Rite of Baptism

The Latin rite of baptism used in Strassburg on the eve of the Reformation is found in an *Agenda* of 1513.[1] It is not necessary to reproduce it in full here because we have made numerous references to it in the footnotes when dealing with the Magdeburg *Agenda* which it closely resembles, and because the first German order of baptism used in Strassburg, which we give next, is very similar to it. The noteworthy features of the Latin rite are three. First, there is only one set of exorcisms to be used over children of either sex. Secondly, in those parts of the rite where the sponsors are particularly involved, namely, in the formal request for baptism, in the instructions to the godparents, and in the renunciation of Satan, the use of the vernacular is permitted. Thirdly, there is no giving of a burning candle to the child.

An order of baptism wholly in the vernacular was introduced into Strassburg shortly after the appearance of Luther's first *Taufbüchlein* of 1523. The text of this rite follows here, taken from Hubert's edition,[2] except that to avoid repetition the prayers are not here given in full.

THE ORDER OF BAPTISM
ACCORDING TO THE RIGHT FORM OF
BAPTIZING IN GERMAN

The baptizer shall breathe three times under the eyes[3] (*of the child*] and say:

Depart, thou unclean spirit, and give room to the Holy Spirit.

Then he shall make a cross on the child's forehead and breast, saying:[4]

Receive the sign of the holy cross of our Lord Jesus Christ.

Let us pray.

O almighty, everlasting God, the Father of our Lord Jesus Christ, do

---

[1] *Agenda sive Exequiale Sacramentorum*, ed. G. Kawerau, op. cit., pp. 411ff.
[2] F. Hubert, *Die Strassburger Liturgischen Ordnungen in Zeitalter der Reformation* (Göttingen 1900), pp. 25ff.
[3] This phrase, which is not found in the Latin rubric in the *Agenda*, occurs in Luther's *Taufbüchlein*; above, p. 9.
[4] This is a simplification of the double consignation in the *Agenda*, in accordance with the *Taufbüchlein*.

thou look upon this thy servant (*handmaid*), N., whom thou hast called to the instruction (*unterricht*)[1] in the faith, . . .

Next salt is blessed with the following words:

I exorcize thee, creature of salt, . . .

Here the priest shall take the salt and place it in the mouth of the child, saying:

Receive the salt of wisdom that it may assist thee unto eternal life. Amen.

Peace be with thee. Amen.
O God, . . . the maker of all creatures, . . .

Let us pray.
God of Abraham, God of Isaac, God of Jacob, . . .
Therefore, accursed devil, . . .
Hearken now, accursed devil, . . .
Therefore, accursed devil, . . .
I exorcize thee, unclean spirit, . . .
Therefore, accursed devil, . . .

Then the priest shall lay his hand on the head of the child, saying:

O Lord, . . . we beseech thine eternal and most just goodness . . .
The Lord be with you.
R.   And with thy spirit.

The Gospel of Mark.[2]
R.   Glory be to thee, O Lord.
At that time they brought little children . . . and blessed them.

Through these words of the holy gospel may God forgive all thy sins. Amen.[3]

Then shall the priest lay his hand on the head of the child and order those that stand by to pray an *Our Father, Hail Mary*,[4] and creed on behalf of the child. After the Lord's prayer follows this exorcism:

O Lord, through the glory of thy name hearken and be gracious to us.[5]

Be not deceived, thou loathsome devil, . . .

---

[1] The word which Luther used to translate *rudimenta*.
[2] The Marcan version is used, as in the *Taufbüchlein* and Magdeburg *Agenda*.
[3] As in the *Agenda* of 1513.
[4] In the 1513 *Agenda*, but omitted by Luther.
[5] Unusual, but in the 1513 *Agenda*.

Then he shall spit in his left hand, and dip a finger in the spittle, and touch with it the right ear of the child and say:

Effeta, that is, be thou opened.

Here they go to the font. Then the priest asks:

Do you desire that this child be baptized?
R. Yes.

Then they shall instruct the godparents that the child learn the *Our Father, Hail Mary* and creed.

R. Yes, we will.

Then they shall raise their hands[1] in the stead of the child, speaking and promising the following things:

Raise your finger and say after me:
    N., dost thou renounce the devil?
R. Yes.
    And all his works?
R. Yes.
    And all his ways (*wesen*)?[2]
R. Yes.
    Dost thou believe in God the Father almighty, maker of heaven and Earth?
R. Yes.
    Dost thou believe in Jesus Christ, his only Son, our Lord, who was born and suffered?
R. Yes.
    Dost thou believe in the Holy Spirit, one holy Christian[3] church, the communion of saints, the forgiveness of sins, the resurrection of the flesh, and after death an eternal life?
R. Yes.

Then shall the priest take the child in his left hand and anoint him with holy oil on the breast and between the shoulders, and say:

    N., I anoint thee with the oil of salvation in Christ Jesus our Lord. Amen.
Q. Do you wish that this child be baptized?
R. Yes.

---

[1] Another unusual feature retained from the *Agenda* of 1513.
[2] In Latin rites the word used was *pompis*, translated in the 1513 *Agenda* by *gezienden*. *Wesen* was the word used by Luther at this point.
[3] As in the *Taufbüchlein*, the use of the word "catholic" is avoided.

Ask or say:

Name this child.

Then shall the priest take the child, and cast water three times crosswise over the child and say:

N., I baptize thee in the name of the Father and of the Son and of the Holy Spirit.

Then shall the priest make a cross with chrism on the child's head, saying:

Almighty God, ... who has regenerated thee by water and the Holy Spirit ... Amen.

Peace be with thee.

R.   And with thy spirit.

Then he shall place on the child a white caul, saying:

Receive this white robe ...

Peace be with thee. Amen.

7. A Rite of Baptism, Used at Strassburg, 1525–30

Such was the rite of baptism used in Strassburg when Martin Bucer (Butzer) arrived there in 1523, although allowance must be made for the possibility that those clergy who were most zealous for reform had already begun to omit some of the ceremonies. Bucer was not slow in carrying the work of reform a stage further. In a work dated 26 December 1524, and written under the heading, "Ground and reason from holy scripture for the reforms . . . introduced in Strassburg in accordance with the word of God", Bucer wrote, "Therefore our principal reform with regard to baptism is that, following the teaching of scripture, we hold the external rite of baptism for a sign of the true baptism of Christ, that is, of the inner purification, rebirth and renewal, on account of which you should consider and think of yourselves and others as those who are committed to Christ and will obtain this inner new birth; and the washing away of sins and renewal of the mind will be attributed to Christ alone, who cleanses his elect by his Spirit, granting them faith and salvation, which is called his baptism for the reason that he has won and obtained this Holy Spirit for us by his passion.

"The other reform or innovation in regard to baptism is that we pay no heed to the teaching about chrism, oil, salt, clay and candles, nor do we use them. The reason for this is that they are human inventions without warrant in God's word, which have been the cause of much superstition. Hence it has come to pass that this chrism and oil can be consecrated only by a bishop and only on Maundy Thursday. So also many people have not been allowed to bathe their children until the priest has been paid a penny (*pfennig*) or a groat (*kreuzer*) to wipe off the chrism and oil. Such magic tricks ill become intelligent and rational Christians, who ought to pay heed to the word of their Lord and follow it alone. Therefore our practice is to baptize children without all this pomp after a short exposition of the nature and significance of baptism and common prayer that Christ will baptize the child with his Spirit and cleanse him from all his sins, and to commend them to their godparents and the other brethren, that they may love them as their fellow members in Christ and lead them to Christ as soon as possible by wholesome doctrine" (quoted by Hubert, op. cit., p. lvii).

Hubert (pp. 37–43) includes three versions of the order of baptism used in Strassburg between 1525 and 1530. In them the earlier rite has been drastically revised in accordance with Bucer's ideas, all ceremonial acts except the baptism itself being omitted. The three versions, D, F, and G, differ only in the wording of the exhortations and prayers. From F and D respectively come the following introduction and order of baptism.

ON BAPTISM

You shall no longer use oil, chrism and enchanted water at baptism: for they have caused a false trust in such things on the part of the people when they ought to trust in Christ alone. Instead you shall explain and present the whole of baptism as an initial sign of faith and an entry into the Christian life, whereby the parents testify before the church that they will bring up their child to the glory of God and will teach and explain to him what happened at his baptism, so that he may remember to order his life in a Christian manner and not to live like the heathen. And you should lay much greater stress on living a Christian life by means of a true faith than on excessive consideration of the signs themselves, which derive all their power from the mystery and the secret alone. Therefore the more a man attains to the great mystery, Christ Jesus, the more nearly and the more truly may he use the signs. He who has little inevitably uses the signs according to the little which he has.

You shall explain to the curious and warn them not to rush with their ailing infants to baptism in disorder and anxiety, as if the whole of salvation depended on an outward washing alone, for God has not confined his grace to any external element, but gives it freely to those whom he has chosen as and when it pleases him. On the other hand you shall say that baptism is not to be neglected, since instead of circumcision and like circumcision in Judaism it is given to the little child as a sign of his initiation into Christianity, whereby we testify for our part that the infant must be of God's people (until he shows himself otherwise by a wicked life afterwards) because he is born of Christian parents. In order that this may take place with greater solemnity and decency, you shall admonish the people only to bring their children to be baptized on Sundays, so that people may not hasten to the font from lack of faith and so that the baptism of the child, the presentation and entrusting of him to the church with the prayers for him may take place with due solemnity and reverence in the presence of God's people. And this is the order of baptism:

The minister asks:

Are you willing that this child be baptized?
Answer: Yes.
Name this child.
Answer: N.

The minister says:

Remember then that our Saviour Jesus Christ has said that all that we ask in our prayer, if only we believe that we shall receive it, so will it be done to us: so let us pray with comfortable assurance that this infant may be given faith, which is a gift of grace, and does not increase by nature, reason or long experience over the years and cannot otherwise be obtained but comes only by the operation of the invisible power of God, which is bound neither by time nor place, youth nor age. Let us pray, therefore, that the Lord will baptize him with water and the Holy Spirit, so that the outward washing which he will perform through me may inwardly be fulfilled in deed and in truth by the Holy Spirit; for that second birth which is signified by baptism takes place in water and in the Holy Spirit, as the Lord says in John 3.

And so let us say in true faith and confidence an *Our Father* . . .

And let us affirm our faith: *I believe in God* . . .

Almighty, eternal God, merciful Father, since the righteous lives only by faith alone and without faith it is impossible for anything to please thee, we beseech thee that thou wilt grant to this child, who is thy creature, the gift of faith, and that thou wilt seal and confirm his heart in the same with the Holy Spirit according to thy Son's promise, so that thy inward renewal and the regeneration of the Spirit may truly be signified by this our baptism, and so that, as he is baptized into the death of Christ Jesus, he may be buried with him and raised by him from the dead to walk in newness of life to the praise of God's majesty and to the edification of his neighbours. Amen.

Now hear the gospel:

At that time they brought little children to Jesus that he might touch them . . .

Believe these words and pray that this infant also shall be one of these and that the kingdom of heaven shall be his, and that he may truly have from God the gift of faith, through which he may be a child of God and a fellow heir of Christ.

Seeing that we have now prayed to God, our Father, as we are taught by his Spirit to pray for all men, that he would make this infant a fellow heir, fellow member and fellow partaker of the promises in Christ, therefore let us now impart to him the sign of faith and through baptism recognize him as a member of the body and of the congregation of Christ for a confirmation of his faith, as Abraham received circumcision for a seal of the righteousness which was already his by faith; and let us on his behalf call upon the name of the Lord, in which he is to be baptized, as the apostle Paul after the vision and wonderful enlightenment and reception of grace arose and was baptized by the prophet Ananias, and suffered him to wash away all his sins.

Then they proceed to the baptism and the minister says:

You godparents and you brothers and sisters shall each of you teach this child Christian order, discipline and fear of God, each of you, as God gives him grace.
Answer: We will.

The minister takes the child and says:

Name the child.
Answer: N.

The minister says while pouring the water:

I baptize thee in the name of the Father and of the Son and of the Holy Spirit. Amen.

And he gives the child to the godparents and says to the people:

God give you all his grace and lead you on in the knowledge of him. Amen.

The peace of God be with you all. Amen.

This is the common order of baptism among us, but according to the circumstances of the people the address may be longer or shorter: sometimes there may be no introduction, but baptism may be administered as shortly as possible. For you should set no bounds to Christian freedom, but shun any usage as soon as it becomes a fixed custom, for the minds of the simple immediately descend to that level and they will put their trust in them, which is contrary to a pure faith in Christ.   End of baptism.

8. The Strassburg Order of Baptism after 1537

ON HOLY BAPTISM

So that this holy sacrament of regeneration may be treated with rather more reverence and devotion, there shall be special times on Sunday and in the week appointed for baptism in the cathedral: on Sunday after the midday sermon and in the week on Wednesday after the morning sermon, in other parishes on Sunday at evening prayer. If, however, anybody has occasion to ask for baptism at another time, the ministry of the church will not be refused him in this.

When then there are children to be baptized, the minister first explains what baptism is, namely a washing of regeneration, a sacrament in which the fellowship of our Lord Jesus and the sonship of God are for the first time imparted through the ministration of the church. Then will be cited and expounded the passages where baptism is clearly set forth, such as John 3, Acts 22, Rom. 6, 1 Cor. 12, Gal. 3, Eph. 5, Tit. 3, 1 Pet. 3.

Secondly, the minister exhorts the adults who are present to have a right trust in this great grace of God which was bestowed upon them long ago, and to live accordingly putting away whatever in their lives is contrary to this grace and to their adoption as God's children, so that they may be truly born again, cleansed from their sins, buried in the death of Christ, incorporated into Christ, clothed with him, purified and sanctified by him, and renewed and saved by the Holy Spirit.

Thirdly, that they reckon that our children are born in death on our account, but God has graciously adopted us, that he also desires to be the God of our seed and to adopt and sanctify our children, even as our Lord Jesus commanded children to be brought to him, with a brief exposition of the passages Genesis 17, "I will be the God of thy seed", 1 Cor. 7, "Your children are holy", and Matt. 19, "Suffer the little children to come unto me".

Fourthly, he exhorts them to have a firm faith in this gracious and favourable promise of God on behalf of our children, and in this faith to pray that the Lord will not recompense them for our sins and unrighteousness but through his Son, our Lord Jesus, will graciously receive them for his own children in his covenant of grace, and will commit and incorporate them in Christ, his Son, our Lord to sanctify them. Then he allows the people time for silent prayer by themselves, and after this prayer he leads them in common prayer in the following words:

Almighty, eternal God, merciful Father, seeing that only those who are born again may see thy kingdom, and nothing pleases thee that lives not by thy Spirit, we beseech thee that thou wilt bestow thy Holy Spirit upon this child (*these children*), created in thine image, and wilt confirm and seal his heart (*their hearts*) with the same according to thy Son's promise, and grant that by thy operation we, as thy ministers and ministers of the new covenant, may by this thy holy baptism truly impart to and bestow upon this child (*these children*) in thy name and

38

according to thy command and promise the inner renewing of the Spirit and a true rebirth as thy child, so that he (*they*), baptized into the death of thy dear Son, Jesus Christ, may be buried with him to die to all sin, and be raised by him to the life and service of righteousness and every good thing, to the end that thy holy name ever may be more hallowed and magnified by him (*them*), thy kingdom may come to us and be extended, and that both here and everywhere he (*they*) may delight to live according to thy will, which alone is good, as in heaven.[1] We also pray thee to keep him (*them*) in health of body, to provide for him (*them*) in every necessity and of thy fatherly love to deliver him (*them*) from all evil; through our Lord Jesus Christ. Amen.

A second prayer.

Almighty and merciful God and Father, who hast promised to us in Abraham, our father and the father of all believers, that thou wilt be our God and the God of our seed, who didst will that thy covenant of grace should be conferred upon the children of the ancients by circumcision, and thy Son, our Lord Jesus, graciously received the little children who were brought to him and most lovingly gave them his blessing, saying, "Of such is the kingdom of heaven"; O bountiful God and Father, made confident by this thy gracious promise and deed, we appear before the eyes of thy divine majesty in the name of thy Son, our Lord Jesus, beseeching thee that thou wilt forgive us that we have never been truly thankful for thy grace and the redemption of thy Son, which thou hast imparted to us in holy baptism (and in so many other ways), and have never truly striven to die to self and to live to thee alone, our heavenly Father. Wherefore we pray and beseech thee, O merciful God and Father, give and increase in us thy Holy Spirit, that we may daily perceive more and more that thine unspeakable grace which thou hast shown us in holy baptism, whereby thou hast adopted us as thy children, and may show ourselves thankful for the same in our whole life and so may truly be thy people and thy children. Graciously accept from us this infant (*these infants*), the offspring of thy servants, which thou hast given them and hast created in thine own image: deal not with him (*them*) after our sins and unrighteousness, in which he is (*they are*) unfortunately born of us, but grant that he (*they*) may partake in the death and resurrection of thy Son, our Lord Jesus, through whom he (*they*) will be born again in thine image; and as he,

---

[1] A similar use of the Lord's prayer is made in a prayer in the *Cassel Church Order*; see Sehling, op. cit., VIII, p. 117.

4—C.I.

our Lord and only Saviour, wills to be in the midst of us and bids us bring our children to him, grant, O heavenly Father, that we may truly and with our whole heart desire to lay hold on this thy grace and the redemption of thy Son for this child (*these children*) with true faith, and may not doubt that, as we baptize him (*them*) in thy name, as we now by thy grace purpose to do, thou wilt entirely forgive him (*them*) his (*their*) inborn sin through our Lord Jesus and never more impute it to him (*them*), and wilt make him (*them*) thy true child(*ren*) and heir(*s*), and fellow heir(*s*) of our Lord Jesus Christ in all things. In this faith, O heavenly Father, grant that we may baptize this infant (*these infants*), that we may accordingly all be moved and ever led to regard him (*them*) henceforth as our fellow member(*s*) in Christ in all things, that we may faithfully pray for him (*them*), carefully bring him (*them*) up and assist him (*them*) in every way, so that by him (*them*) thy name may be hallowed and thy kingdom extended, and that both here and everywhere he (*they*) may delight to live in accordance with thy will, which alone is good, as in heaven. We also pray thee to keep him (*them*) in health of body, to provide for him (*them*) in every necessity, and of thy fatherly love to deliver him (*them*) from all evil; through Jesus Christ our Lord. Amen.

After this prayer the minister says:

Seeing that we have now prayed to the Lord in accordance with his own gracious promise, wherefore we should not doubt that he of his fatherly goodness hears us, let us baptize this child (*these infants*), but in order that our faith may with greater consolation see, recognize and perceive the work of the Lord in this holy sacrament, let us also hear the words of our Lord Jesus himself concerning the little children who are brought to him, how he promises and himself bestows upon them his blessing to eternal life and true fellowship in the kingdom of God.

So let us read Matt. 19, Mark 10, Luke 18:

At that time they brought little children to Jesus . . .

After the reading of the gospel the minister says again:

The Lord grant us all to remember well that no one may enter into the kingdom of God and appear before him, unless he accept it as a little child, that is, unless he receive it as a free gift and present of the Lord, to which he contributes in no way by his own strength, and that our Lord Jesus, who now deigns to be present in our midst and to accomplish everything, may confer his blessing upon our children also. It is his baptism, we are only his ministers and instruments, through whom he will dispense the mystery.

So now confess with me our holy Christian faith and thus arouse yourselves that you may grow valiant in the same and faithfully bring this infant (*these children*) up to share this faith.

I believe in God, . . . (the apostles' creed with "Christian" for "catholic").

Now let us baptize this child (*these children*) into the fellowship of this faith. Know and recognize him (*them*), all of you, as (*a*) member(*s*) of Christ, our Lord, and your own fellow member(*s*), and let each one of you see, so far as he may ever be enabled thereto by the Lord, that this infant (*these infants*) may be brought up in the Lord, that we all through my ministry which I shall perform here on behalf of the whole community of the church may incorporate him (*them*) now in the Lord by holy baptism. You, however, who have been specially invited and named as godparents, must show particular diligence and, so far as your other godly obligations allow you, prove yourselves spiritual fathers and mothers to him (*them*). May our dear Lord Jesus grant that you and we may all faithfully perform this. Amen.

Next the minister asks them to hand him the child as appointed: he takes him into his hands, undresses him, and when he has asked what he is to be called, he names him with his name, pours water upon him three times and says:

N., I baptize thee in the name of the Father and of the Son and of the Holy Spirit. Amen.

Then he calls the congregation to pray with him and give thanks.

The Lord be with you.

Let us pray.

Almighty God, heavenly Father, we give thee everlasting praise and thanks for that thou hast given this child (*these children*) to thy church, and hast granted him (*them*) a new birth through thy holy baptism, and hast incorporated him (*them*) in the body of thy dear Son, our eternal Saviour, and hast now made him thy child and heir. Grant, O loving and faithful Father, that we all may show ourselves thankful all our lives for this thy great mercy, and may faithfully bring up this child (*these infants*) who is (*are*) now thine to please thee in all things, and also that together with this child (*these infants*) we may evermore die to ourselves and daily increase in the life of thy Son, our Lord

Jesus, so that thou mayest always be praised by us and our neighbour be edified; through our Lord Jesus Christ. Amen.

Go forth in peace. The Lord grant that a holy angel who beholds his face in heaven may preserve this child (*these children*) from all evil and make him (*them*) to advance in all goodness. Amen.

9. The Council of Cologne of 1536

After becoming Elector and Archbishop of Cologne in 1515, Hermann von Wied (1477–1552) grew ever more appalled at the many abuses in the Church which cried out for redress. He hoped at first that reform would come from within the Church, and that its price would not be the disruption of ecclesiastical unity. At length in 1536 he summoned a council to institute a number of reforms in his own province of Cologne. So far the Archbishop had shown no desire to go over to the Lutherans, neither did the canons of this council put him in a state of schism with the Roman hierarchy.

We include here only the canons on baptism. In their original Latin they may be read in *Canones Concilii Provincialis Coloniensis* (Cologne 1538), fol. 25, and in Mansi 32, cols. 1256–8.

Part 7; *Cap.* III And to begin with holy baptism, the people is to be taught that therein the old man is abolished, and there is remission for all sin; and a new man arises, purged from all stain through faith in Christ; that therein he who is baptized is washed with the washing of regeneration and renewal of the Holy Spirit in the blood of Christ shed for us: that therein we put off the old Adam, being buried with him by baptism into death, so that as Christ rose from the dead through the glory of the Father, so also we should walk in newness of life: as the *Enchiridion* will teach at greater length.

Cap. IV Those who raise an infant from the font (who are called godparents) are suitably admonished that it is they who in the name of the church and in the faith of the church offer little children to Christ through baptism, and make themselves as it were guarantors for the little children, replying in the name of the little child: whom even after he has grown up they shall not fail to teach the creed together with the Lord's prayer, and always to lead a life in Christ and worthy of the profession made in baptism, and especially when need seems to demand it to exhort him, and therefore we prefer those to be chosen of a mature age rather than those who have not reached puberty, so that an infant should not be seen to present an infant, and to appoint himself a sponsor for another before God, since he does not understand what he promises; and therefore much less can he teach what he does not understand.

Cap. V In addition they shall teach the people what is done, that the

43

person to be baptized is catechized: what the other ceremonies which
the church has wished to be added signify, namely: Why there is an in-
sufflation upon the face of the person to be baptized, why the sign of
the cross is made on the breast and the forehead, why salt is put into the
mouth, why the ears and nose are touched with spittle and anointed,
why there is an anointing of the breast and shoulders, and why after
the dipping of baptism there is an anointing on the head. Finally what
the white clothing means, in which the infant or other baptized person
is vested:[1] all which things are full of mysteries, as the *Enchiridion* will
declare.

Cap. VI Since the most blessed apostle orders all things in church to be
done decently and in order, baptism must be given and received with
the strictest attending of the mind to God and to the most holy mysteries which are being performed. Wherefore whatever diverts the
sponsors or others who stand by from this is to be removed far away.
So the sacrament should be approached after laying aside all pride, in a
humble spirit, and with a right faith in God, even as they approached
who offered their little children to Jesus that he might lay his hands on
them. For here Satan is renounced, and all his works and all his pomps.
And agreement should be reached beforehand among the godparents
about the name of the infant, so that in the actual baptism the attention
is on the winning of a soul for Christ rather than on the remembering
of a name.

Cap. VII Again, certainly with great cause it seemed good to the fathers
of the church that baptism should be received in the sight of the church
and in a holy place, unless however pressing need advised something
else to be done. Wherefore we are displeased that certain arrogant
persons despising the temple of the Lord are ambitious rather to have
their infants baptized privately at home. Henceforth unless need require and knowledge of the cause is received in advance, we refuse to
allow this.

---

[1] It would seem that the Cologne order of baptism, like the orders in *Bamb.* and *Strasb.*,
did not include the giving of the candle.

10. The Enchiridion of Cologne

The canons of the Council of Cologne were largely the result of the work of John Gropper (1503–59), the most influential member of the Cologne Chapter, and later the leader of the opposition to Archbishop Hermann when he began to embrace Lutheranism. In several places the canons promised that certain points would be dealt with at greater length in a handbook for the guidance of the clergy. This promise was fulfilled when in 1538 there appeared the *Enchiridion Christianae Institutionis*, also the work of Gropper. The *Enchiridion* is of interest because amongst other things it shows the point of view of conservatives who opposed the theological and liturgical reforms of Luther, and who in Cologne succeeded in bringing about Hermann's eventual downfall. The section on baptism illustrates what the medieval rite meant to those who did not wish to discontinue its use or see it shorn of the many ceremonies which in the course of the centuries had been added to baptism. If the Reformers demanded that these additions should be abolished on the ground that they led to superstition, there were others, such as the authors of the *Enchiridion*, who believed that the answer to the charge of superstition lay not in abolishing the ceremonies but in teaching and explaining their meaning to the people.

We give here an English translation of the Latin original, published in Cologne in 1538, the section on baptism being found on folios lxxviii to lxxxiii.

BAPTISM

... it [*sc.* baptism] is received for the washing of regeneration, which is the first of all the sacraments, and the gateway by which entry is made into the church and the other sacraments.

In baptism there are two things, the word and the element. The word is the actual invocation of the Trinity resting upon this divine promise, Who believes and is baptized will be saved: which is accomplished by these words handed down from Christ, namely, I baptize thee in the name of the Father and of the Son and of the Holy Spirit. Moreover in regard to this first of all the word is to be observed. For in the water the word cleanses, take away the word and what is the water but water: the word is added to the element and it becomes a sacrament. Whence comes that great power of the water to bathe the body and wash the heart, unless from the action of the word? Not because it is said or pronounced but because it is believed. For even in the word itself the passing sound is one thing and the abiding power

45

another. . . . Cleansing therefore would never have been attributed at
all to a fluid and moving element, unless the word were added, by the
addition of which it becomes a sacrament, which becomes as it were a
visible word. . . . For what else is baptism but a covenant of God with
man and of man with God? For inasmuch as man renounces Satan and
the glory of the world and its pomps, and binds himself to the true
God, so as to mortify his sinful members all his life, it is a covenant of
man with God.[1] . . .

[after quoting John 3.5] And even from this very passage the impious Anabaptists are refuted, who impiously reject and refuse the
baptism of infants. For in the Old Law God ordered infants to be
circumcised, so that they might join the synagogue, and added the
word of promise: I will be their God. So too through baptism, which
has superseded circumcision, children are to be brought into the church,
outside which there is no salvation, lest they should be excluded from
the kingdom of God, which Christ clearly declared to belong to them:
Suffer (he says) the little children to come to me, for of such is the
kingdom of heaven. Also: It is not the will of your Father who is in
heaven that one of these little ones should perish. And again: See that
you despise not one of these little ones, for I say to you that their angels
always see the face of my Father who is in heaven, by which words he
testifies that little children please God, and are guarded by God. And
just as the covenant of circumcision did not the less apply to infants for
the reason that they did not understand what was done, so neither does
baptism avail less in the case of infants for this reason that they do not
yet understand the covenant of divine grace, by which original sin is
remitted to them. For in the faith of the church believing through the
word, offering, blessing, dipping, even such little infants are cleansed,
although not yet able to believe with the heart to righteousness and to
confess with the mouth to salvation. But what need is there to refute at
greater length an error always condemned by the catholic church from
the time of the apostles. So much about the word of baptism.

Now the element or outward material of this sacrament is water.
Now to this end it is performed by means of water that as water
washes away the filth of the body, so we believe that we too are
spiritually cleansed from all sin through baptism, renewed and regenerated, so that which is incorporeal washes invisibly. Whence it is
also called the washing of regeneration. For by nature we are born sons

---

[1] Gropper is here using a well-known passage in Augustine, *In Joan. Evang. Tract.* 80,
P.L. 35, col. 1840.

of wrath, but baptism regenerates us as sons of grace. By nature we are born of bloods of the will of the flesh, of the will of man, that is, in sins, but by baptism we are reborn as sons of God indeed grafted by baptism into Christ, the Son of God, as Paul says, All you who have been baptized into Christ have put on Christ.

Gropper then considers certain Old Testament types of baptism, notably the Flood and the passage of the Red Sea, from which he concludes that water is a suitable material for baptism.

Now we will say a few words about the mystical rites which the church uses in baptism. She uses them . . . not lightly but as certain lively incitements to faith and piety necessary to the creation of religion, by which indeed the ordinary people are led by the hand to the understanding and the keeping in mind of the mysteries of Christ. For in education there is need also of milk in the beginning, so that they may grow accustomed to the discipline of Christ. And there is no doubt that the great majority of the ceremonies which are used in the administration of baptism have come down to us from the primitive and apostolic church, so that it is impious to reject what has been held sacrosanct for so many centuries and by so many most holy men.

First of all the font of baptism is consecrated and signed with the oil of unction on two solemn days in the year, when in the primitive church baptism was usually received, namely Easter and Pentecost, which rite coming down to us from the womb of the church the divine Augustine attests in many places, although in time of need it is permissible to baptize even with unconsecrated water, as Victor the Roman pontiff who lived about the year 190 decreed, from which decree the practice of the primitive church is clearly proved.

But when baptism is administered, at the beginning an exorcism is used, which is performed by word and exsufflation, that the unclean spirit may be driven away from the person to be baptized, and so that by means of the pure ministration of a priest the evil spirit as he flees away may yield to the Holy Spirit. For, as Augustine says, it is not nature that is exorcized or breathed upon but he under whom they are born in sin.[1] They are adjured in order that the adverse power which has deceived mankind, so that it might possess mankind, may be driven away from them, so that hereafter he may not try to subvert them, nor ever dare to violate this holy sign. That this rite is most ancient we

[1] *Serm. de Symbolo ad Catechumenos, P.L.* 40, col. 628.

learn from Tertullian, Jerome, Ambrose and Augustine, whom we have cited, Chrysostom, Pope Coelestine, and other fathers.

Next the sign of the cross is made first on the forehead to show that he who is to be baptized gives his name to Christ crucified, in whom he is to trust, and whom he is never to be ashamed publicly to confess.[1] Then over the eyes, so that we may understand that he who is to be baptized is being prepared to see the glory of God. Over the ears also, that we may understand that he is being consecrated to hear the word of the truth of God. Over the nose also, so that he may perceive the sweetness of the odour of God. The breast also is signed, so that he may believe in him, because with the heart man believes to righteousness. The shoulders also, that he may take on him the yoke of the service of God, in accordance with Christ's command: Take my yoke upon you. Last of all the mouth, so that he may confess to him because with the mouth confession is made to salvation.

During the exorcizing consecrated salt is put into the mouth of the person to be baptized, so that seasoned with the symbol of salt he may be rid of, and be shewn to be rid of, the filth of wickedness, and so that he may no longer waste away with the worms of sins, but rather may be preserved unhurt to receive greater grace, and for the tasting of wisdom.

Next is read the gospel, Little children were brought to Jesus, by which we show that we offer our little children to Christ, because he himself has said, Suffer the little children to come unto me. And when he adds, For of such is the kingdom of heaven, we also offer them to Christ to be baptized. For if theirs is the kingdom of heaven, Christ will not deny them baptism, which is (as we said) the door by which we enter into the church and therefore into the kingdom of heaven.

Afterwards, the godparents lay a hand on the infant, and recite the creed and Lord's prayer which belong to the church, who offers children to the Lord to be baptized, and receives them into her faith. Little children in fact are offered for receiving spiritual grace not so much by those in whose arms they are carried, although they are offered by them too if they are good and faithful members, as by the whole company of saints and faithful.[2] For they are truly offered by all who are pleased that they are offered, and by whose holy and personal charity they are assisted to the conferring of the Holy Spirit. So the whole church,

---

[1] Compare this with the prayer at the consignation before baptism in the Prayer Book of 1549; below, p. 90.

[2] Here Gropper is quoting from Augustine's letter to Boniface, Ep. 98.5, P.L. 33, col. 302.

which is in the saints, as a mother does this, because the whole church brings all and each to birth. Therefore it is not that particular faith which is found in the will of believing godparents, but the sacrament of faith which makes a person faithful. So in the church of Christ little children believe through others, just as from others they inherited the sins which are remitted in baptism. Then the godparents appoint themselves as it were guarantors for the baptized. And therefore they must always admonish them that they guard their chastity, love justice, hold fast to charity, but above all learn the creed and the Lord's prayer.

Then spittle is smeared on their noses and ears after the example of Christ, who smeared the eyes of the man born blind with clay made from spittle, and thus sent him to the waters of Siloam. The smearing symbolises the call to the grace of baptism, the anointed person does not yet see but is sent to wash in the waters of Siloam so that he may be baptized in Sent, that is in Christ, for Siloam means that. And there is spoken to him the word of the gospel which Jesus, when he healed the dumb and deaf man, touching his tongue with spittle, and putting his fingers in his ear-lap, said: Ephphatha, which is, Be opened, the word being evidently appropriate to the sacrament. For those to be baptized are advised by the symbol of saliva and by the deed of the Saviour that their noses be opened to the odour of the knowledge of God and the acquiring of eternal life, so that the baptized may say: We are the good odour of Christ, and so that his ears may be opened to the hearing of the word and commandments of God. Saliva is a type of wisdom and the grace of God and discernment of faith, whose reception is signified in the hearing and discernment in the nose.

After the exorcism is finished there follow the mysteries which are celebrated at the font itself. First of all the name of the infant is asked. For by a most ancient custom of the church before baptism those to be baptized give in their name, by which it is shown that they by the renunciation of their former owner are giving their name to Christ, so that they may pass over into his dominion. For they come from the name which was received from Adam in being called sons of Adam, to the new name by which they are called sons of God: furthermore then only do they acquire the name, for before we are baptized we have been without faith and the name. But after the name of God is invoked upon us, we have been called after his name. The name being given, he who is to be baptized renounces three times. For when he has been asked, Dost thou renounce Satan? he replies: I renounce. And all his works? he replies, I renounce. And all his pomps, all the vainglory of the world, pride, luxury and pleasures, in short all vices? he replies, I renounce. That this was the custom of the primitive church Tertullian teaches in *On the Soldier's Crown*.[1] The baptized therefore must all his life be mindful of his oath and never do anything to make him fail in the keeping of his bond. . . .

After this he who is to be baptized is anointed with the oil of the catechumens on the breast and between the shoulders, but after baptism with chrism on the head. About chrism we shall speak at greater length later. Now as for the unction which takes place in baptism, blessed Augustine says that it is part of the apostolic tradition, that it has come down to us from the times of the apostles,[2] and the canons of Clement and Fabian,[3] the popes, and several councils declare this. The mystery of the former unction which takes place before baptism Augustine explains: We are anointed (he says) on the breast and shoulders since faith is conceived in the mind and completed by work. The breast is anointed so that this breast may be shown to be dedicated to Christ, and this mind to be strengthened in the faith of the holy Trinity, and in it there should remain no more any traces of the lurking foe. He is anointed between the shoulders that it may be shown that he who is to be baptized is fortified on all sides by grace for the performing of good works, and receives fortitude to bear the burden of the Lord, as the divine Ambrose says: Thou wast anointed as an athlete of Christ, as one about to wrestle in the contest of this world.[4]

The unction was followed by catechizing, that is, the enquiry about faith in the Trinity, and that in accordance with the command of our Lord Jesus Christ and Saviour, who when he ascended to the Father in heaven gave commandment to the apostles: Go, he said, teach all nations, baptizing them in the name of the Father and of the Son and of the Holy Spirit. But in asking, Dost thou believe in the holy church, the remission of sins, the resurrection of the flesh and eternal life after death, we do not ask that one should believe in the holy church in the same way as one believes in God, but that continuing in the holy church we believe in God. For the church is holy and catholic for the reason that in it there is a right faith in God. And then the question is asked, Dost thou wish to be baptized? And the reply is, I wish it. For nobody is saved against his will, but willingly, so that the form of

[1] *de Corona* 3, P.L. 2, cols. 98f.
[2] *de Gen. ad Litt.* 39, P.L. 34, col. 426.
[3] Below, p. 163.
[4] *de Sacramentis* I.2.4; H. Chadwick, *Saint Ambrose On the Sacraments* (London 1960), p. 10.

righteousness may be complete. For just as man by his own free will was obedient to the serpent and perished, so, the grace of God calling him, he is saved by his own change of mind.

After this, the infant is finally baptized with these words of the Lord: And I baptize thee in the name of the Father and of the Son and of the Holy Spirit. But what those words mean and what covenant is made between God and man by these words, we have said above.

The infant is immersed or dipped three times in the water of baptism. For we are baptized into the Father and the Son and the Holy Spirit, at each of the names, at each of the persons we are dipped, so that the equality and same power and majesty of the persons may be made manifest, so that the single mystery of the Trinity may be seen. The three times repeated immersing or dipping provides a type of the three days burial of the Lord, by which we are buried together with Christ in baptism and have risen with Christ in faith, so that washed from sins we may live in the holiness of virtues, imitating Christ.

After baptism the baptized is anointed with chrism, but on the head; the mystery of this the divine Ambrose explains, saying: Remember what he said to you, that is, the baptizing priest: God, he says, the Father almighty who has regenerated you by water and the Holy Spirit, and has forgiven you all your sins, himself anoint you to eternal life.[1] Do not, therefore, prefer this life to that eternal life. For example, if any enemy arise, if he wishes to take away from you your faith, if he threatens you with death that you may transgress, see what you choose: do not choose him in whom you have not been anointed, but choose him in whom you have been anointed and prefer eternal life to temporal life through Jesus Christ our Lord. The baptized is also anointed on the head that he may perceive that he has been joined to Christ the head, that he may know that he has received now from Christ a name, and that he has given his name to Christ, that is, that he is engaged in the warfare of Christ. For from chrism the Christian has his name, just as also the chrism has its name from Christ, by the invocation of whose name chrism is prepared for that purpose of anointing which we have described.

Finally the baptized is vested in a white robe, which is the sign of manumission and liberty, as Tertullian testifies. It indicates also the Christian innocence and purity which after the washing away of the old stains of his sins he must preserve spotless by the zeal of his holy

[1] de Sacramentis II.7.24, ed. cit., p. 22.

conversation, so that he may bring it before the judgment seat of Christ. Formerly in the primitive church baptized adults for a whole week wore their white robes, wherefore that Sunday next after Easter is known as the Sunday *in albis*, in which ceremony the church endeavoured to impress on our minds both faith and innocence of life and purity of religion. . . .

Now if any one were to ask, If it is true that in baptism is abolished the sin which we inherited from our parents, why does the tinder of evil desire still remain, and is a kind of incentive to sin? For there is no doubt that from our first parents was transmitted to us that law of sin or law of our members, that is, concupiscence, which Paul opposes to the law of the mind or the law of God, saying: For I delight in the law of God according to the inner man. But I see another law in my members, fighting against the law of my mind, and imprisoning me in the law of sin, which is in my members. Since we are all born in sinful pleasure, albeit unwillingly, even after baptism we feel lawless and almost bestial impulses which cause a continual warfare within us, as Paul testifies: For the flesh lusts against the spirit and the spirit against the flesh, etc. So to this question the reply must be given that in baptism the imputation and guilt of all sin is taken away, because the handwriting of our condemnation is deleted, and the answer of death which remained[1] in us as a result of the old wound. For guilt or properly imputation for sin is sin. For blessed is the man to whom the Lord does not impute sin. But there remains concupiscence which even by Paul is sometimes called sin, as when he says, But if what I would not that I do, now it is not I who do it but sin which dwells within me. But after baptism the tinder is not imputed for sin, unless the mind or will assents to it. And this is the excellent virtue of baptism, which not only takes away sin, but also confers grace against this tinder, that now concupiscence may not hurt us, provided that we abstain from consent, to make which possible for us God imparts to us in baptism the Spirit, following whose lead not in our own power but in his we triumph over concupiscence and the devil: and in this way Paul resolved the question: O wretched man that I am, he says, who will deliver me from the body of this death? By the grace of God through Jesus Christ our Lord . . .

The minister of the sacrament is a priest, in whom (as far as concerns the efficaciousness of the sacrament) we do not look for worthiness of

---

[1] Reading *manebat* for *manabat*.

life. For in fact it is not man but Christ who baptizes, but the priest performs only a delegated task on behalf of Christ, and through him Christ baptizes. And although the priest says, I baptize thee, yet in order that you may understand that he does this only as a minister not in his own name, he says that he baptizes in the name of the Father and of the Son and of the Holy Spirit, as Paul says: Was Paul crucified for you, or were you baptized in the name of Paul?

11. Hermann's Consultation

Gropper's attitude to the contemporary rite of baptism is quite clear. The rite as such did not stand in need of reform. The many ceremonies in the rite required not abolition but explanation, so that the people might understand the inner meaning of each outward act; if many of them were not explicitly commanded in Scripture, it was sufficient that they had commended themselves to the primitive Church and the ancient Fathers. Since the Chapter of Cologne supported Gropper, it is evident that Archbishop Hermann would encounter serious trouble if he tried to secure a drastic revision of the rites and ceremonies used in his province.

But when the Recess of the Diet of Regensburg (Ratisbon) on 29 July 1541 ordered a Christian reformation of the Church, Hermann felt encouraged to carry the reform of the Church in Cologne a stage further; and by the end of 1542 his sympathies lay more and more with the Lutherans. Accordingly, to the disgust of Gropper and the Cologne Chapter a number of leading Lutheran theologians were invited to come to Cologne to assist the Archbishop in his programme of reform. The most notable of those who accepted the invitation were Melanchthon and Bucer.

On 24 July 1543 Melanchthon wrote about a conference in Bonn, at which the subject for discussion was a proposed form for the restoration of the Churches.[1] The work laid before this conference was a Church Order, compiled mainly by Melanchthon and Bucer, the latter being responsible for the section dealing with the sacraments.

It was published in German in the autumn of that year under the formidable heading, "A simple and religious consultation of us Hermann by the grace of God Archbishop of Cologne, and Prince Elector, etc., by what means a Christian reformation, and founded in God's word, of doctrine, administration of divine sacraments, of ceremonies, and the whole cure of souls, and other ecclesiastical ministries, may be begun among men committed to our pastoral charge, until the Lord grant a better to be appointed, either by a free and Christian council, general or national, or else by the states of the Empire of the nation of Germany, gathered together in the Holy Ghost."[2] For convenience it is known in short as the *Einfaltigs Bedencken* or *Pia Deliberatio*; and we shall refer to it simply as the *Consultation*. In 1545 it was translated into Latin,[3] and

---

[1] *Epp.* IX, n. 2730 in *C.R.* V, p. 449; quoted by B. J. Kidd, *Documents Illustrative of the Continental Reformation* (Oxford 1911), p. 353.
[2] Tr. John Daye. London 1548.
[3] A copy of the Latin translation soon found its way into the library of Archbishop Cranmer at Lambeth, and is now preserved in the cathedral library at Chichester. For the contents of Cranmer's library see E. Burbidge, *Thomas Cranmer, An Account of his Library* (1892).

two years later into English by John Daye, who issued a second English translation in 1548. Daye's two English translations, differing only in a few small points, follow the Latin translation closely. The Latin translation, however, is in some places a rather free rendering of the original German, words or phrases being omitted or inserted for the sake of clarity. But, so far as baptism is concerned, none of the translations has altered the general sense, nor has it been able noticeably to reduce the verbosity of Bucer's German. We give here the section on baptism in Daye's translation of 1548.

OF BAPTISM
(folios cliv–clxxi)

Baptism is a sacrament of regeneration, whereby we be planted and incorporated into Christ the Lord, and be buried into his death, and put on the same, and be made through him the sons and heirs of God. Wherefore we must handle and receive this sacrament with great reverence and religion. And therefore we must use that manner of administering this sacrament, and such time must be appointed for the administration of the same, that all things may serve to stir up and increase reverence and religion, that this holy sacrament may be godly and wholesomely administered and received.

Among the ancient fathers baptism was openly ministered only at two times in the year, at Easter and Whitsuntide,[1] which constitution because it should be hard perchance to renew, we will that baptism be ministered only upon the Sundays and holy days, when the whole congregation is wont to come together, if the weakness of the infants let not the same, so that it is to be feared that they will not live till the next holy day, for our mind is that the handling of the sacrament of Christ's body and blood called Eucharistia may be joined with baptism, and that they which bring the infants to baptism may use the body and blood of our Lord Jesus Christ after the manner and institution of the primitive church.

But that all things may be ministered and received religiously and reverently, the parents of the infants shall signify the matter betimes to the pastors, and with the godfathers shall humbly require baptism for their infants, that if the parents or the godfathers or both be subject to manifest crimes, they may be corrected of the pastors if they will admit correction, or if they be incorrigible, that they may be kept from the communion of baptism, lest they be present at so divine a ministration unto damnation, and with danger of offending the church. For they as

[1] See *Hall Church Order* (1526); A. L. Richter, *Die Evangelischen Kirchenordnungen* (Weimar 1846), I, p. 40.

5—C.I.

well make themselves guilty of the body and death of Christ which unworthy[1] be present at this sacrament of baptism, and require the same
for their infants without true faith in Christ, as they which take the
body and blood of the Lord unworthily, that is to say, not after the
institution of Christ, namely without true repentance and faith in
Christ. Wherefore if such come unto the pastors to ask holy baptism,
whether they be the parents of the children, or their godfathers, as be
defiled with manifest crimes and abominations, the preachers shall exhort them unto repentance, and warn them that they be not present at
the administration of the sacrament for that time lest they pull damnation upon themselves and offend the church. For such by reason of their
wicked acts have no part in the kingdom of God, neither be they to be
admitted to the participation of the sacraments, except they repent
openly. But if the parents be found in such crimes they shall desire
their kinsfolk or other friends which be as yet the true and lively members of the church that in their stead they will ask baptism for their infants. If the godfathers shall be judged unworthy of the church, other
shall be desired, which have good testimony. In the request of baptism
the pastors shall ask them whether the infants have not received baptism
already, which thing is wont to chance, when the child is in peril of
death. For if they be baptized, then the pastors shall do those things,
that we will declare hereafter concerning such infants. But if they be
not baptized, or not certainly baptized, or not as it behoved, and if the
parents and godfathers be not subject to those crimes, for which they
should be kept off from baptism, they shall be diligently warned by the
pastors of the exceeding benefit of regeneration in Christ which they
desire to their children, item of the horrible fall and guilt from which
the infants are delivered in baptism through Christ. Then he shall exhort[2] them that they be present religiously at the exorcism and catechism and so afterward at the ministration of baptism, last of all that
they use together the sacrament of the body and blood of the Lord.
For it becometh this thing to be done, not only for this cause that they
be the members of Christ, and it behoveth not to be present at the
Lord's board without partaking, but also because it is an unworthy
thing, to ask the communion of Christ for infants, and to receive it in
baptism, and not to receive the same in the sacrament for themselves,
wherein it is offered to them also. For if they ask and receive the communion of Christ in baptism with true faith, they cannot but ask the

[1] 1547: "unworthily".   [2] Latin: *hortabuntur*.

same for themselves and receive it desirously being offered in the sacrament of Christ's body and blood.

The old fathers administered this sacrament of the supper of the Lord even to infants with baptism. But seeing that that custom is worn away not without a cause, it is convenient and it pertaineth to godliness that the parents with the godfathers and the kinsfolk who obtain the most holy sacrament of generation[1] for their infants should use the Lord's supper with singular desire of the Spirit that they may receive the communion of Christ to themselves which they obtain in baptism for their infants. Which thing helpeth to the edification of other also, yea of the whole congregation, and it commendeth the holy communion of Christ to other.

Therefore that all things may be done more diligently and with greater religion in the administration of holy baptism, we will that, whensoever it may be conveniently done, the catechism or instruction of the parents and godfathers and the exorcism of the infants be used[2] the day before the holy day or Sunday that baptism shall be ministered. For seeing that baptism must be ministered in an high administration when all the church is gathered together it is convenient that in these holy actions such moderation of both the sacraments be used that may help to stir up the devotion of the people, and that through long tarrying it give not some occasion of negligence or of diminishing the godly ferventness of the mind. Wherefore, when it may so be, it shall be profitable to separate in time the handling of the catechism and exorcism from the ministration of baptism after the custom of the old fathers. But when the people cannot be commodiously present, because that many of them dwell far from the temple, or for some other just cause, then the exorcism and catechism may be handled together with baptism.

Howbeit the pastors shall labour as much as is possible that this most holy sacrament of baptism, which is the first adoption, receiving and entering into the kingdom of Christ be not administered and received but before the whole congregation with great gravity and reverence.

When the catechism then and exorcism shall be handled the day before baptism, let the infants be brought forth at the evening assembly at the which the people, because of the holy day following or Sunday, is wont to be present. The parents and the kinsfolk after the example of the old saints must also be present, and bring their infants to the

---

[1] 1547: "regeneration".   [2] 1547: "exhibited"; Latin: *exhibeatur*.

temple. Which parents and other being come together, the pastors and ministers must first plainly declare the mystery of holy baptism, and the exceeding benefits of God exhibited therein, to them which brought the children and to the rest of the people, with singular gravity and religion. Secondly they shall exhort them to a godly and faithful receiving of so great a sacrament and so inestimable benefits of Christ. Then they shall require of the parents and godfather to renounce Satan, and the world, and to confess the principal articles of our faith and religion, which confession and renunciation they must make plainly and gravely before the whole congregation.

A FORM OF CATECHISM
THAT IS TO SAY OF INSTITUTION
EXHORTATION AND DEMANDS MADE TO
THE GODFATHERS AND ALL THEM THAT
BRING INFANTS TO HOLY BAPTISM

First the pastor, other ministers standing by him, shall thus exhort them that bring the infants to baptism.

Beloved[1] in Christ Jesus, we hear daily out of the word of God, and learn by our own experience[2] that all we from the fall of Adam are conceived and born in sins, that we are guilty of the wrath of God, and damned through the sin of Adam, except we be delivered by the death and merits of the Son of God, Christ Jesu, our only Saviour. Seeing then that these present infants be born in the same estate and condition that we were, it is plain that they also be spotted with original sin and disease, and that they be subject to eternal death and damnation. But God the Father according to his unspeakable gentleness and mercy towards mankind sent his Son to save the world. Wherefore he will also that these infants be saved. He bare the sins of all the world, and delivered and saved as well the infants as us which be of greater age from sins, death, the devil and everlasting damnation, who would have the infants to be offered unto him that he might give them his blessing.[3]

Wherefore according to your Christian godliness take this child, bring him unto Christ and offer him with your godly prayers, that he may obtain of him remission of his sins, and be removed into the king-

[1] Here begins a passage borrowed from the *Saxon Church Order* of 1539 (see Sehling, op. cit., I, p. 266).
[2] Omitted here from the Latin: *tam in vita quam in morte.*
[3] Here ends the excerpt from the *Saxon Church Order.*

dom of grace, being delivered from the tyranny of Satan, and that he may be made heir of eternal salvation. And be ye most certain hereof, that our Lord Jesus Christ will mercifully regard this work of your charity towards this infant, and that he will hear your prayers, for he himself thus commanded with his word: "Suffer the little ones to come unto me, for unto such pertaineth the kingdom of God." Wherefore,[1] beloved, I exhort you, and beseech you, as many as be present, that you will religiously consider with yourselves the greatness of this ministration and work, that we go about. For ye see how the church humbly but constantly bringeth hither these miserable weak infants, and destitute of all strength, with which deed they confess plainly that they be children of the wrath of God, of sin and everlasting death. They pray for them with godly and fervent wishes desiring to obtain for them the grace and help of God, that through baptism being born again of God, they may be the children of God. Think not then that any trifling or childish thing is handled in this holy administration, wherein war is taken in hand against Satan, wherein he is not only driven out of the infant but the infant is bound with an oath that he ever war against him, as the enemy of his king Christ unto his last breath with all his power. Wherefore God must be called upon with great confidence and most fervent prayers, that he will not only deliver this child from the power of Satan, but also strengthen and defend him that throughout all his life, and chiefly in the point of death, he may stand and fight against Satan valiantly.

Wherefore lift ye up your minds also, and think that you must in this place hear the word of God with singular devotion, that you must call upon God with lively faith, and that you are provoked to prayer for a most weighty cause.

Therefore behave yourselves so that God may see your religion, and allow it, neither suffer ye that this most holy sacrament of baptism be unworthily handled through you, and be made a mock unto Satan, and so shame be done to God, who here poureth forth so great riches of his grace. For he himself calleth this sacrament the laver of regeneration, whereby he maketh us his own sons, heirs of everlasting life, and partakers of all his benefits, because we be the co-heirs of his Christ, being delivered from the tyranny of the devil, sin, death and hell. Wherefore I beseech you for God's sake and your salvation, that ye will worthily esteem and thankfully embrace so wonderful abundant

---

[1] The following section is based upon the Epilogue to Luther's first *Taufbüchlein*; above, pp. 6f.

grace of God which is exhibited in this sacrament. For baptism is a
great comfort unto us in our dangers and afflictions, and it is the first
entrance unto all the benefits of God, and to the blessed fellowship of
all saints.

Therefore that we may consider this unspeakable benefit of God
with a presenter mind and greater religion we must first remember
into how great evils the fall of Adam threw us. And contrariwise how
unmeasurable grace God exhibited to mankind through his Son in that
he hath redeemed us from the same evils by baptism. Thirdly, how this
so great mercy of God ought to be ever before our eyes in all perils,
and with how great praises we should magnify the grace of God which
we have received through baptism.

First,[1] then, we must consider with all diligence, that all we through
the sin of Adam and envy of Satan be subject to the wrath of God, and
moreover damned, and be holden prisoners under the power and kingdom of the devil, under death, sin and hell, so that we being by nature
the children of wrath could appease God by no strength of man, no
virtues or works. For all that is in us and all our works be cursed of
God and subject to the tyranny of Satan, by reason of our corrupted
nature.

For seeing that through the inobedience of our first father Adam (of
whom we are all born into this natural and earthly life) we come into
the world guilty and cursed of God, so that we must all die in him and
bear his earthly image in this mortal body, it followeth that all our life
and all the deeds of our nature so corrupted be condemned of God,
though they appear never so godly and holy before men. For whatsoever is born of the flesh is flesh, that is to say, strange from God, re-
pugning to the spirit, and judged to death and hell. Wherefore flesh
and blood shall not attain to the kingdom of God. For whatsoever is
flesh it savoureth fleshly things, and so liveth, it is adversary to God, for
it is not subject to the law of God. Wherefore they that be fleshly cannot please God, the wisdom of the flesh is death. And therefore our
Lord Christ disputing with Nicodemus concludeth thus, Verily, verily,
I say unto thee, except a man be born of water and of the Spirit, he
cannot enter into the kingdom of God.

Secondly we must consider how plentiful the grace of God given to
us in baptism is, wherein his bounteousness and love towards men
truly appeareth, inasmuch as he hath saved us, not through the works

---

[1] Here begins a long extract from the *Brandenburg–Nuremberg Church Order* of 1533;
above, p. 29.

of righteousness which we had done, but according to his mercy by the laver of regeneration and renovation of the Holy Ghost. For he, through the virtue of his word washeth away and abolisheth whatsoever maketh us guilty and condemneth us, as in the old time he drowned in the Red Sea the enemies of his people, and destroyed all mankind with the flood, eight souls reserved which were saved in the ark. So this laver of water saveth us through the word not in washing away the filth of the flesh as it chanceth in all other washings, but through the certification of a good conscience towards God, by the resurrection of Jesus Christ. For by the virtue of God's covenant we are cleansed in our consciences, and we are certified both through the word and outward sign that all the sins that defiled and condemned us be plainly abolished, because they be forgiven and be dead.

Therefore through baptism we determine certainly that we are acceptable unto God and joined unto him with an everlasting covenant of grace so that nothing can separate us from him, or condemn us. Wherefore henceforth we must not only eschew sins, but also fear them, and abhor from them none otherwise than from hell, as men dead unto sins. For all we, as St Paul witnesseth, which be baptized into Christ Jesus, be baptized into his death, for we are buried with him[1] into death. Therefore we be dead to sin, and to the whole old man and brought forth in Christ so far that nothing can condemn us, or separate us from the grace of God. For he that is dead is justified from sin, he is no more subject to the tyranny of sin, death and hell; though he feel the remnants of sin in the flesh, yet those be not imputed unto condemnation by reason of the justification of the spirit in Christ.

Furthermore baptism worketh a new life in us and acceptable to God. For as Christ was raised from the dead by the glory of the Father, so he worketh in us with his spirit, that we also may walk in newness of life. For if we be grafted in him by the likeness of his death, surely we shall also be partakers of his resurrection unto everlasting life, knowing this that our old man is crucified with him, that the body of sin should be abolished, that hereafter we serve not unto sin.

Wherefore let us recount that we be dead to sins indeed and live to God in Christ our Lord in whom also we be circumcised with a circumcision made without hands, while we put off the body of sins, through the circumcision of Christ. We are buried with him through baptism wherein we have also risen again with him, by the faith of the

---

[1] Latin: *per baptismum*, omitted here.

working of God. For God who raised Christ from the dead hath quick-
ened us with him even when we were dead through sins, by the uncir-
cumcision of the flesh, or fleshly life. For though our life be hidden in
God with Christ, yet when Christ our life shall appear, then shall we
also in him be manifested in glory as men whom God of his exceeding
mercy hath begotten again into a lively hope through the resurrection
of Jesus Christ from the dead, unto (I say) an incorruptible inheritance,
undefiled, and that fadeth not away, not of corruptible seed but incorruptible, namely the lively word of God, by which word baptism
consisteth, and worketh all the foresaid things in us truly and effectually.

Thirdly we shall comfort ourselves with so great excellency[1] of the
grace of God and benefits bestowed upon us through baptism, and we
shall ever thank God, and that so much the more studiously as we shall
be oppressed with more grievous calamities, confirming our faith by
this, that God worketh in us, mortifieth the old man and repaireth the
new, though not after a visible sort, yet by virtue of baptism through
the word and the Spirit. Wherefore let us confirm our consciences and
think that God careth for us, and that for the merit of his Son we be
acceptable and dear to him. And when we be exercised with adversity
and sundry miseries, we must remember that we are baptized, and that
in baptism all our sins and evils be overcome and dead, and that they
be daily wasted and abolished more and more through the cross and
sundry afflictions which God sendeth unto us, and that the new man is
continually renewed and repaired through the virtue of the resurrection of Christ. Therefore of right we ought to thank God for his so unspeakable mercy, and we must also pray therewith that he will vouchsafe even to further, and at the last to finish his work which he hath
begun in us and in all them whom he hath called to baptism.[2]

The preachers shall use such exhortations longer or shorter according to the time
out of the foresaid places of the scripture and other like and then they shall add the
the questions following:

Interrogations or demands which shall be pronounced to the godfathers and to the
parents of infants:

Do ye believe that those things be true which I shewed you out of the
word of God concerning the corruption of nature through original sin,
and concerning regeneration in Christ our Lord, and everlasting

---

[1] Latin: *amplitudine.*
[2] End of excerpt from the *Brandenburg–Nuremberg Church Order.*

communion with God, which is exhibited through holy baptism?
Answer: We believe.
Do you require then with all your hearts and with true faith that this your infant whom you have brought and offered to Christ be delivered from this corruption of nature through the merit and virtue of Christ in baptism, and be reconciled to God, and born again into a new and perpetual life?
Answer: We require it.
Do ye then renounce in your name, and in the name of the child, the devil and all his works?
Answer: We renounce.
And the world also and all his concupiscences?
Answer: We renounce.
Do ye believe in God the Father almighty, maker of heaven and earth?
Answer: We believe.
And do ye believe that God will be a father to you and to this infant, when it is baptized, and that he will keep you from all evil through his almighty power, wisdom and mercy, and heap benefits upon you, and that therefore you ought to fear him and love him above all things?
Answer: We believe.
Do ye believe in our Lord Jesus Christ, his only Son, who to redeem us became man, suffered and died, and was raised from death, ascended into heaven, and sitteth on the right hand of the Father, and from thence governeth his church, through his almighty power, and shall come in the end of the world, and appear to all men, a judge of the dead and the quick?
Answer: We believe.
Do ye confess out of this faith that our Lord Jesus Christ is also your Saviour and Saviour of this child, who by his death hath purged your sins also, and hath reconciled you to God and justified you through his resurrection, and will at length fully finish up the image and life of God in you, being cleansed from all sin?
Answer: We confess.
Do ye believe also in the Holy Ghost, the holy and universal[1] church, the communion of saints, the remission of sins, the resurrection of the flesh, and life everlasting?
Answer: We believe.
Out of this confession do you believe that the Holy Ghost will be your

[1] Latin: *catholicam ecclesiam.* The word "catholic" is rejected here as in the *Taufbüchlein*; above, p. 15.

teacher and comforter, and the teacher and comforter of this child, and
that you be the true members of the body of Christ our Lord, and of
his church, and that this child by baptism shall be a true[1] member of
Christ and his church, wherein he shall have remission of sins, a sure
hope of resurrection, and life everlasting?

Answer: We believe.

Will ye then be godfathers to this infant,[2] and count him for a very
son of God, a brother and member of Christ, and as soon as he cometh
to the use of reason, if peradventure he shall lose his parents, or, if they
shall be negligent in this behalf, will ye take the charge of him, that he
may learn the ten commandments, the articles of our faith, the Lord's
prayer, the sacraments, both at home and in the congregation, that
from his childhood he may begin to understand the mystery of baptism
and the benefits of Christ given to him therein, and afterwards when
he is well instructed in the religion of Christ, that he confess his faith in
the congregation with his own mouth, and through the participation
of Christ that he give himself to obedience towards God and the
congregation?

Answer: We will.

Here the pastor shall exhort again the parents and the multitude standing by.

Remember, then, beloved, that ye must with all faithfulness and diligence perform the thing that ye have promised here in the sight of God
and Christ our Saviour, who is among us, and before his holy congregation. And all you parents, godfathers, and others that stand by,
acknowledge this child after that he hath received baptism as the son
of God, and member of Jesus Christ to whom the angels be present as
ministers, and serve him, neither doubt ye but that whatsoever good or
evil ye do to this seely[3] infant, you do the same to God and to Christ
the Lord. Let it not be any pain to you then, that every one of you
according to his state, kindred and vocation procure this child to be
godly and religiously brought up and instructed, that at length he may
keep all those things that Christ our Saviour commanded to us. It pertaineth then unto you, which are given of God to this child to be
parents, kinsfolk or godfathers, to procure as soon as he is grown up,
to bring him to schools, to the congregation, that he may be instructed
more fully in the mysteries of Christ and in other things, that he may

---

[1] "true" was omitted in 1547.
[2] 1547: "take the infant from baptism". Latin: *infantem e baptismo suscipere.*
[3] Latin: *infirmo.*

perceive the grace and exceeding benefits of God given in baptism, that he give account of his faith before the congregation, that he renounce in deed the devil and the world with all concupiscences, that he wholly give himself to Christ our Lord and to his congregation to be obedient in all points according to his gospel, and so continue in Christ our Lord unto the end, and so[1] go forward in newness of life as a lively member of Christ, and that being a fruitful branch in this vineyard he bring forth the plentiful fruit of all good works to the praise of God and edification of the church.

Here followeth the exorcism or adjuration:

Here the pastor shall command the child to be brought near him and shall demand his name which known he shall say:

I command all evil spirits in the name of our Lord Jesu Christ to depart from this infant, and to do him no hurt any manner of ways.

After this making the figure of the cross with his thumb upon his forehead and upon his breast, let him say:

Take the figure of the holy cross in thy forehead,[2] that thou never be ashamed of God and Christ thy Saviour or of his gospel: take it also on thy breast, that the power of Christ crucified may be ever thy succour and sure protection in all things.

Then let him say to the people:

The Lord be with you.

Let the people answer:

And with thy spirit.

The pastor:

Let us pray.

Almighty and everlasting God, the Father of our Lord Jesus Christ, I call thee upon this N., thy servant, for whom the church requireth the sacrament of baptism, and therein thy grace and spiritual regeneration, and as thou saidst, Ask and ye shall receive, etc, so give thy grace and mercy to this child, as thy church prayeth thee that he may obtain the redemption of thy Son and inheritance of everlasting and blessed life, which thy congregation seeketh for him through baptism. Open to him the door of thy kingdom, at which thy church knocketh for him: through Christ our Lord. Amen.

[1] 1547: "ever".
[2] An expansion of a formula found in Luther's *Taufbüchlein* and in medieval Latin rites; above, pp. 9, 18.

Let us pray.

Furthermore,[1] almighty God, who in old time didst destroy the wicked
world with the flood, according to thy terrible judgment, and didst
preserve only the family of godly Noah, eight souls, of thy unspeakable mercy, and who also didst drown in the Red Sea obstinate
Pharaoh, the king of the Egyptians, with all his army and warlike
power, and causedst thy people of Israel to pass over with dry feet, and
wouldest shadow in them holy baptism, the laver of regeneration,
furthermore who didst consecrate Jordan with the baptism of thy Son,
Christ Jesu, and other waters to holy dipping and washing of sins, we
pray thee for thy exceeding mercy look favourably upon this infant,
give him true faith and thy Holy Spirit, that whatsoever filth he hath
taken of Adam, it may be drowned and be put away by this holy flood
that being separated from the number of the ungodly he may be kept
safe in the holy ark of the church, and may confess and sanctify thy
name with a lusty and fervent spirit, and serve thy kingdom with constant and sure hope, that at length he may attain to the promise of
eternal life with all the godly. Amen.

The pastor: The Lord be with you.
The people: And with thy spirit.

Hear the gospel of our Lord Jesus Christ. Mark 10.
In that time they brought children to Jesus that he might touch them.
But the disciples rebuked them that brought them. When Jesus saw
that, he took indignation and said unto them, Suffer the little ones to
come unto me, etc.

Believe these words and this deed of our Lord Jesu Christ upon them,
and doubt not but that he will so receive your children also, and embrace them with the arms of his mercy, and give them the blessing of
eternal life and the everlasting communion of the kingdom of God.
The same Lord and our Saviour Jesus Christ confirm and increase your
faith. Amen.

After this the pastor shall lay his hands upon the child's head, and the godfathers
touching the child shall pray with him: *Our Father which art, etc.* Then they shall
also rehearse the creed: *I believe in God the Father, etc.*

Let us pray.

After this the church shall sing the Psalm ciiii, item cxv and cxxxvi.

When Israel went forth, etc. Not to us, Lord, etc. *Item,* Praise the name
of the Lord, etc. Ye servants, praise the Lord.

[1] "Furthermore" is not in the Latin version. This prayer is a fairly close translation of
the Flood Prayer in Luther's *Taufbüchlein*; above, p. 11.

The pastor: The Lord be with you.
The people: And with thy spirit.

Let us pray.

Almighty and everlasting God, heavenly Father, we give thee eternal thanks that thou hast vouchsafed to call us to this knowledge of thy grace and faith towards thee. Increase and confirm this faith in us evermore. Give thy Holy Spirit to this infant, that he may be born again and be made heir of everlasting salvation, which of thy grace and mercy thou hast promised to thy holy church, to old men and to children, through our Lord Jesus Christ, which liveth and reigneth with thee now and for ever. Amen.

Thus giving his blessing let him dismiss the congregation.

OF ADMINISTRATION OF BAPTISM

The day following let the infants being exorcized the day before be brought again to the congregation, a little before the supper of the Lord, whom there the pastor after that the gospel is read and declared and the creed sung, shall bid to be brought to the font-stone,[1] and shall exhort the parents, the godfathers and kinsfolk after the manner following:

Beloved in Christ, yesterday by the grace of God we heard how exceeding and unspeakable mercy is exhibited in baptism. Ye have renounced Satan and the world, ye have confessed the faith of Christ, and ye have promised obedience to Christ and the congregation, and ye have required of God the Father that for his Son's sake our Lord Jesus Christ he will deliver these infants from the kingdom of darkness and settle them in the kingdom of his beloved Son. You must remember these things, and doubt nothing but that we shall receive all these things that we require if we believe. Therefore lifting up your minds unto the Lord, appear ye here with all religion, as in the sight of almighty God the Father, the Son and the Holy Ghost, and receive ye with[2] sure faith and thanksgiving the benefit of regeneration and adoption into everlasting life, of the one God himself, the Father, the Son, and the Holy Ghost. And because the Lord himself commanded us to baptize in the name of the Father, the Son and the Holy Ghost, undoubtedly God himself baptizeth our infants, cleanseth them from sins, delivereth them from everlasting death, putteth upon them his own righteousness, and giveth them life eternal. We must acknowledge with true faith and ever magnify these exceeding benefits of God.

---

[1] Latin: *baptisterium.*　　　[2] "with" was omitted in 1547.

Wherefore that we may stir up our faith and minds, let us hear the words of St Paul following concerning this matter:

To Titus, Chapter 3.

But after that the goodness and love of our Saviour God towards men appeared, not of the works of righteousness which we did, but after his mercy he saved us by the laver of regeneration and renewing of the Holy Ghost, etc.

The pastor: The Lord be with you.
The people: And with thy spirit.

Out of the Gospel of Matthew, the last chapter.

The Lord Jesus said unto his disciples, All power in heaven and in earth is given unto me. Go ye therefore into all the world and preach the gospel to all creatures, and teach all the heathen, baptizing them in the name of the Father and the Son and the Holy Ghost, etc.

The pastor: The Lord be with you.
The people: And with thy spirit.

Let us pray.

Almighty[1] and merciful God and Father, thou didst promise to Abraham our father, and the father of all that believe, and in him thou didst promise to us also his children, that thou wouldest be a God to us and our seed. Wherefore as thou didst receive the infants of the old people into grace and into thine own people by circumcision, and thy Son Christ Jesus our Lord and Saviour admitted children offered unto him right gently, and blessed them testifying that the kingdom of God pertaineth to such,[2] so let it be thy pleasure to beget our infants again, and to adopt them into sons unto the fellowship of everlasting life by the sacrament of baptism. Grant then, heavenly Father, that we may earnestly require so great riches of grace set forth in baptism for these infants, and that we may acknowledge and receive them with true faith being offered both in the word and in the sacrament, finally that we may ever thank thee and magnify thee for them. And impute not to these infants the sin of Adam issued into them, and engendered by their parents, and regard not the merits of their parents and of all this people, but let the death and merit of thy Son our Lord Jesus Christ prevail in them, and impute unto them his righteousness and obedience.

[1] The opening of this prayer is taken from the Strassburg rite of 1537; above, p. 39.
[2] End of the quotation from the Strassburg rite.

Plant them into his death and resurrection, make them members of his body, put him upon them, that they may be thy sons and heirs, and continue for ever. Grant us also that after baptism we may acknowledge them for thy children, and members of the body of thy Son that we may godly bring them up in the fear of thee unto thy glory, that we may help them in all corporal and spiritual things, that[1] also by them thy holy name may be more magnified, the kingdom of thy Son enlarged, thy will be done in this earth as in heaven. Furthermore keep them safe, give them bounteously the necessaries of life, and preserve them from all evil. Amen.

This prayer ended, let the pastor require the infants to be given him, let him ask the names that they shall have, and let him baptize them, saying:

I baptize thee N. in the name of the Father, the Son and the Holy Ghost.

Let the godfathers forthwith receive the infant from baptism, the priest saying as it followeth:

The almighty everlasting God and Father of our Lord Jesus Christ, who hath begotten thee again with water and the Holy Ghost, and hath forgiven thee all thy sins, confirm thee with his grace unto everlasting life. Amen.[2]

The pastor: The peace of the Lord be with you.
Answer: Amen.

Here let the whole congregation sing in German, *Now all thanks,* etc. or the psalm, *God be merciful unto us.* Then let the pastor go forth in the ministration of the Lord's Supper.

---

[1] The rest of this prayer resembles the conclusion of the above-mentioned prayer in *Strassburg* 1537.
[2] This prayer is taken from Luther's *Taufbüchlein;* but the unction has been abolished. See above, p. 25.

12. The Downfall of Hermann and the Antididagma

From the first there was strong opposition in Cologne to the reforms ordered in the *Consultation*. In a letter dated 10 August 1543, Melanchthon related that he and Bucer at a diet in Bonn produced a book which contained the order for reforming the Churches, and that the old Archbishop, Hermann, asking for it to be read from beginning to end, listened most attentively: but while many approved its contents, the evil ones were in the majority.[1] In another letter written a week later Melanchthon complained that, although there were present many men of sound views, Gropper and a few others stirred up a lively opposition.[2] On 1 October of the same year the Chapter of Cologne petitioned the Archbishop to suppress publication of the book; but their request came too late. So early the next year the Chapter published first in German and then in Latin a full-scale reply to the *Consultation*, this counterblast being mainly the work of Gropper, and being known in short as the *Antididagma*.

The *Antididagma* replied to the *Consultation* chapter by chapter. In the section on baptism (folios 54–63) the claim was made that exorcism and catechizing had their origin in apostolic times. Passages from Dionysius Areopagiticus, Chrysostom, and Augustine were quoted to prove that exsufflation was of a like antiquity. The adjuration and blessing of created things—such as the water in the font—were neither a recent invention nor repugnant to Scripture. The sign of the cross was used in blessing things in the primitive Church. The giving of salt and the Effeta were ancient customs. The exorcism and renunciation of Satan could be traced back to the apostolic age. The water for baptism ought to be consecrated except in cases of emergency, seeing that Basil had included the blessing of the font among a number of practices resting upon unwritten but primitive tradition.[3] From the time of the apostles sponsors had replied not in their own names but in the name of the child being baptized. Dionysius Areopagiticus, Tertullian, and others attested the use of chrism after baptism.[4]

The case against the *Consultation* as regards baptism was summarized thus:

That book almost entirely abolishes the Christian, apostolic and catholic forms, ordinances and customs of the church together with all the above mentioned ceremonies. It omits the exorcism in which the devil is adjured, the manifold markings with the sign of the saving cross, the

---

[1] *Letters*, Lib. IX, no. 2736; C.R. V, p. 154.   [2] Ibid., no. 2740; ed. cit., p. 159.
[3] *de Spiritu Sancto*, 66; P.G. 32, col. 188.   [4] Paris edition, 1549, folios 54–60.

imposition of hands and finally all the prayers which the church has observed from the time of the apostles. Here there is neither exsufflation of the devil, nor the giving of consecrated salt, here there is no opening of the ears, no intinction with saliva, and no unction at all, neither before nor after baptism, here there is no consecration or blessing of the font of baptism, and mention is very far from being made of the lighted candle. Here the godparents renounce not on behalf of their godchild, but rather and principally on behalf of themselves. Here there is kept a catechizing not of the infants but of the parents and the sponsors. Moreover it is prescribed that the presbyter directs his address to the latter. And so the godparents reply for themselves and in their own name to all the articles of the apostles' creed as if they themselves were to be rebaptized. And finally there is no mention of the white robe. In short the catholic form and ordinance is here almost entirely rejected, and a new invention is substituted in its place. Nor is it required that in the same place the same form of words be adhered to, but many and various forms are appointed, and power is given to every pastor according to his own judgment to prolong or abbreviate those forms.[1]

Thus the ceremonies abolished in the *Consultation* were defended in the *Antididagma* by an appeal to primitive and apostolic tradition, but not to the letter of Scripture itself. The defence was not as strong as Gropper thought, because it was not then generally known that Dionysius Areopagiticus whom he quoted more than once was not the contemporary of St Paul but a pseudonymous Syrian writer of the fifth century.

We may note in passing that Gropper did not try to defend the use of oil in baptism by advancing the argument put forward in modern times by Chase,[2] Thornton,[3] and others,[4] that the anointing referred to in 1 John 2.20 and 27 implies an actual unction during the rite of baptism.

Gropper's arguments, therefore, were not likely to convince those who were satisfied in their own minds that Scripture itself alone could supply an adequate justification for each and all of the liturgical customs of the Church.

The opposition of Gropper and the Chapter of Cologne, coinciding with the victory of the Emperor, Charles V, over William, Duke of Cleves, in 1543, led to the downfall of Hermann, who, after being summoned before emperor and pope was excommunicated and deposed in 1546. So ended the attempt to introduce Lutheran reforms into the Church of Cologne.

But this was not the end of Hermann's *Consultation*, because, although it was rejected in the province for which it was designed, a copy of it found its way

---

[1] Ibid., p. 61.
[2] F. H. Chase, *Confirmation in the Apostolic Age* (London 1909), pp. 58f.
[3] L. S. Thornton, *Confirmation: Its Place in the Baptismal Mystery* (London 1953), pp. 22f.
[4] E.g., J. Ysebaert, *Greek Baptismal Terminology* (Nijmegen 1962), p. 263.

6—C.I.

into Archbishop Cranmer's library at Lambeth, with the result that it was able to exert a considerable influence upon the compilation of the first English Prayer Book of 1549. But in fairness to Cranmer it should be noted that he tried to see both sides to the question, because he also had a copy of the *Antididagma* in his library.

13. England—The Bishops' Book

In England during the first half of the sixteenth century the rite of baptism most widely used was that in the *Sarum Manual*,[1] a rite which was in Latin and contained all the ceremonies which Luther abolished in 1526. As late as the year 1537 opinion in England concerning the sacrament of baptism could be described as conservative. In the latter part of that year a committee of bishops produced *The Institution of a Christian Man*, commonly known as the *Bishops' Book*. It dealt with the creed, the seven sacraments, the ten commandments, the Lord's prayer, the Hail Mary, and the articles on justification and on purgatory. We include here the section on baptism, to be found in C. Lloyd, *Formularies of Faith* (Oxford 1856), pp. 92f.

As touching the holy sacrament of baptism, we think it convenient that all bishops and preachers shall instruct and teach the people committed unto their spiritual charge, that they ought and must of necessity believe certainly all those things which have been always by the whole consent of the church approved, received and used in the sacrament of baptism. And first that the sacrament of baptism was instituted and ordained by God in the New Testament as a thing necessary for the attaining of everlasting life according to the saying of our Saviour Jesu Christ, where he saith that no man can enter into the kingdom of heaven, except he be born again of water and the Holy Ghost.

Item That it is offered unto all men, as well infants as such as have the use of reason, that by baptism they shall have remission of all their sins, the grace and favour of God, and everlasting life, according to the saying of Christ, Whosoever believeth and is baptized shall be saved.

Item That the promise of grace and everlasting life (which promise is adjoined unto this sacrament of baptism) pertaineth not only unto such as have the use of reason, but also to infants, innocents and children; and that they ought therefore and must needs be baptized: and that by the sacrament of baptism they do also obtain remission of their sins, the grace and favour of God, and be made thereby the very sons

[1] See Fisher, *Christian Initiation: Baptism in the Medieval West* (London 1965), pp. 158–79.

73

and children of God. Inasmuch as infants and children dying in their infancy shall undoubtedly be saved thereby, and else not.

Item That infants must needs be christened, because they be born in original sin, which sin must needs be remitted, which cannot be done but by the sacrament of baptism, whereby they receive the Holy Ghost, which exerciseth his grace and efficacy in them, and cleanseth and purifieth them from sin by his most secret virtue and operation.

Item That children or men once baptized ought never to be baptized again.

Item That all good Christian men ought and must repute and take all the Anabaptists' and the Pelagians' opinions, which be contrary to the premises, and every other man's opinion, agreeable unto the said Anabaptists' or the Pelagians' opinions in that behalf, for detestable heresies and utterly to be condemned.

Item That men or children, which, having the use of reason, and being not christened already, desire to be baptized, shall, by virtue of that holy sacrament, obtain the grace and remission of all their sins, if they shall come thereunto not only perfectly and truly repentant and contrite of all their sins before committed, but also perfectly and constantly confessing and believing all the articles of our faith according as is mentioned in the creed called the apostles' creed. And finally, if they shall also have firm credence and trust in the promise of God, adjoined to the said sacrament, that is to say, that in and by this said sacrament, which they shall receive, God the Father giveth unto them, for his Son Jesu Christ's sake, remission of all their sins, and the grace of the Holy Ghost, whereby they be newly regenerated, and made the very children of God, according to the saying of St John, and the apostle St Peter, where they say, Do you penance for your sins, and be each of you baptized in the name of Jesu Christ, and you shall obtain remission of your sins, and shall receive the gift of the Holy Ghost. And according to the saying also of St Paul, where he saith, God hath not saved us for the works of justice which we have done, but of his mercy by baptism and renovation of the Holy Ghost, whom he hath poured out upon us most plentifully, for the love of Jesus Christ our Saviour, to the intent that we being justified by his grace, should be made the inheritors of everlasting life, according to our hope.

The authors of this book clearly had the intention, amongst other things, of refuting the teaching of the Anabaptists; in stressing the need for infants to be baptized soon after birth they repeated the view widely held in the Middle Ages in the West[1] that infants dying unbaptized were deprived of eternal salvation. The words, ". . . infants and children dying in their infancy shall undoubtedly be saved thereby, and else not", were to be modified six years later.[2]

[1] See Fisher, op. cit., pp. 112f.   [2] Below, p. 77.

14. The King's Book

A revision of the *Bishops' Book* was published on 29 May 1543, under the title *A Necessary Doctrine and Erudition for any Christian Man*, known in short as the *King's Book*, since it was "set forth by the King's majesty". It contained twelve articles on the clauses of the apostles' creed, after which it dealt with the seven sacraments, the ten commandments, the Lord's prayer, the Hail Mary, and the articles on free will, on justification, on good works, on prayer for souls departed. Like the *Bishops' Book* before it, it took a conservative position in regard to sacramental doctrine, maintaining, for instance, that there were seven sacraments, when the Lutherans had for twenty years been asserting that there were only three. But it had more to say than the earlier book on the subject of baptism. This can be read in Lloyd, op. cit., pp. 253–7, or in T. A. Lacey, *The King's Book* (London 1932), pp. 41–4.

As touching the holy sacrament of baptism, it is to be noted first, that this sacrament was instituted and ordained by our Saviour Jesu Christ in the New Testament, as it doth appear by Christ's own words unto his apostles, where he saith . . . (Matt. 28.19).

Furthermore, that the effect and virtue of this sacrament is forgiveness of sin, and grace of the Holy Ghost, as is manifestly declared in the second chapter of the Acts of the Apostles, where it is said, Do penance, and be baptized every one of you, and ye shall have forgiveness of sin, and shall receive the gift of the Holy Ghost. Which effect of grace and forgiveness of sin this sacrament hath by virtue and force of the working of almighty God, according to his promise annexed and conjoined unto this sacrament, as is manifestly declared by the word of Christ, saying (Mark 16), Whosoever believeth and is baptized shall be saved. Which saying of our Saviour Christ is to be understand of all such persons which die in the grace conferred and given to them in baptism, and do not finally fall from the same by sin.

Moreover, because all men be born sinners, through the transgression of our father Adam, in whom (as the apostle saith) all have sinned,[1] and cannot be saved without remission of their sin, which is given in baptism by the working of the Holy Ghost, therefore the sacrament of

---

[1] Rom. 5.12, as mistranslated by Augustine, following Ambrosiaster, *Comm. in Rom.* ad loc., *P.L.* 17, col. 92. See N. P. Williams, *The Ideas of the Fall and of Original Sin* (London 1927), p. 379.

baptism is necessary for the attaining of salvation and everlasting life, according to the words of Christ, saying, No man can enter into the kingdom of God, except he be born again of water and the Holy Ghost. For which causes also it is offered and pertaineth to all men, not only such as have the use of reason, in whom the same, duly received, taketh away and purgeth all kind of sin, both original and actual, committed and done before their baptism; but also it appertaineth and is offered unto infants, which, because they be born in original sin, have need and ought to be christened: whereby they being offered in the faith of the church, receive forgiveness of their sin, and such grace of the Holy Ghost, that if they die in the state of their infancy they shall thereby undoubtedly be saved.[1]

And here we must know, that as touching original sin in infants, like as they take of their parents their original and natural qualities, even so they receive from them original sin, by which they are made the children of the ire of God, and by the same have a natural inclination to sin, by lusts and desires, which, in further age and time, sensibly move and stir them to wickedness. For although the parents be never so clean purged, and pardoned of their original sin by baptism, and grace given in the same, yet nevertheless the children of them begotten be conceived and born in original sin. Example we may take of corn, which, though it be never so clean winnowed and purged from the chaff, yet if it be cast into the ground and sown, the new which springeth of it is full of chaff again, until it be also winnowed and cleansed: so likewise the children of Christian men be full of the chaff and corruption of original sin, until that by baptism they be washed, cleansed, and purged from the same, as their parents were.

And whereas we have before shewed that original sin is remitted and taken away by baptism, both in infants and all others which having the use of reason duly receive the same, yet further we think good to note a special virtue and efficacy of this sacrament of baptism; which is, that albeit there remain in us that be christened a certain infirmity or inclination of sin, called concupiscence, which by lusts and desires moveth us many times to sin and wickedness, yet almighty God of his great mercy and goodness hath given us such grace in this his holy sacrament of baptism, that such carnal and fleshly lusts and desires shall or can in no wise hurt us, if we do not consent unto them. And by the same grace also conferred unto us in baptism, we be made more

---

[1] It is significant that the phrase, "and else not" in the *Bishops' Book* (above, p. 75) has been deliberately omitted here.

strong and able to resist and withstand the said concupiscence and carnal desires than is another man that never was christened.

Furthermore, forasmuch as in these days certain heresies have risen and sprung up against the christening of infants, it is to be noted, that (as the holy doctors of the church do testify) the universal consent of the churches in all places and of all times, using and frequenting the christening of infants, is a sufficient witness and proof that this custom of the church in baptizing of infants was used by Christ's apostles themselves, and by them given unto the church, and in the same hath been always continued e en unto these days. And this custom and perpetual usage of the church, even from the beginning, is agreeable with the saying of St Paul, Christ loved his church, and hath given himself to the death for his church's sake, to sanctify her, and make her holy, in cleansing her by the fountain of water in the word, etc. So that no man is nor can be of this church but he which is cleansed by the sacrament of baptism: like as the text before alleged sheweth, where Christ saith, Whosoever is not born again of water and the Holy Ghost shall not enter into the kingdom of heaven. Wherefore seeing that out of the church neither infants nor no man else can be saved, they must needs be christened and cleansed by baptism, and so incorporated into the church. And as the infancy of the children of the Hebrews, in the Old Testament, did not let, but that they were made participant of the grace and benefit given in circumcision; even so, in the New Testament, the infancy of the children doth not let, but that they may and ought to be baptized, and so receive the graces and virtues of the same.

In this part also it is to be noted that children or men once baptized ought never to be baptized again. And all good Christian men ought and must repute and take all the Anabaptists' and the Pelagians' opinions, which be contrary to the premises, and every other man's opinion agreeable unto the said Anabaptists or the Pelagians in that behalf, for detestable heresies, and utterly to be condemned.

Moreover, for because as well this sacrament of baptism as all other sacraments instituted by Christ, have all their virtue, efficacy and strength by the word of God, which by his Holy Spirit worketh all the graces and virtues which be given by the sacraments to all those that worthily receive the same; we must understand and know, that although he which doth minister the sacrament be of a sinful and evil conversation, yet the virtue and effect of the sacrament is thereby nothing diminished or hurted, neither in infants, nor yet in them which being endued with the use of reason come thereunto truly contrite and

penitent of all their sins done before, believing and confessing all the
articles of the creed, and having a sure faith and trust in the promises of
God, of remission of their sins, and purposing ever after to live a
Christian life.

Finally, this sacrament of baptism may well be called a covenant between God and us, whereby God testifieth, that he for his Son Christ's
sake justifieth us, that is to say, forgiveth us our sins, and endueth us
with his Holy Spirit, and giveth us such graces that thereby we be
made able to walk in the works of justice ordained by God to be exercised of us in this present life, to the glory and praise of God: and so
persevering, to enjoy the fruit of the life everlasting. And we again,
upon our part, ought most diligently to remember and keep the
promise that we in baptism have made to almighty God, that is, to believe only in him, only to serve and obey him, to forsake all sin and the
works of Satan, to mortify our affections of the flesh, and to live after
the Spirit in a new life. Of which promise and covenant by us made to
God, St Paul putteth us in remembrance, saying, Know ye not that all
we which are baptized in Jesu Christ are baptized to die with him? For
we be buried with him by baptism to die, that likewise as Christ was
raised up from death by the glory of his Father, even so we should walk
in a new life. By the which words St Paul giveth us to understand that
all we which be baptized in Christ, that is to say, which by baptism are
incorporated into the mystical body of Christ, have professed and
bound ourselves in baptism to die from sin, and utterly to abstain from
the corruption of our old sinful life, and to walk and proceed in a new
life of grace and the Spirit, into the which we are called by the word of
God, and by faith and due receiving of this holy sacrament are brought
and set into the same.

15. The Rationale of Ceremonial

To this same period belongs another book, the nature of which is evident from its title, the *Rationale of Ceremonial*. It has been edited by C. S. Cobb,[1] who shows that it cannot have been written before October 1538, or after January 1546, and that it is not likely to have been in existence before April 1540, when Parliament confirmed the action of Henry VIII in appointing a committee for the express purpose of drawing up a rationale of ceremonies.[2]

Having never been officially approved by Church or by State,[3] it had only the authority of the scholars who produced it.[4] They designed it not as "an attempt to formulate a system of ceremonies to suit the times, but as an explanation of those existing ceremonies which were to be observed "for a decent order".[5] As regards baptism, it gives an explanation of the ceremonies in the Latin order of baptism in the *Sarum Manual*, and presents a conservative point of view as held in England at a time when more radical ideas from Germany had not yet made their influence felt.

4. *Now followeth the Rites and Ceremonies*
   observed about the Sacrament of Baptism

First is the catechism, which goeth before the same, and it is as much to say as a teaching or an instruction for in the primitive church, when that many came to the Christian faith at the years and age of discretion, it was used that such before they were admitted to baptism should be taught the articles of the faith and the sum of Christian religion, and should promptly and readily render the same to their pastor or curate, which were yet to be used, if that any such would desire to receive baptism, but for so much as the old ancient church even from the apostles' time hath used and yet useth to baptize infants and children, which for lack of age cannot be instructed, therefore the priest shortly expresseth there such instruction, and then chargeth the godfathers and godmothers furthermore to teach to the child or children when they come to lawful age, and then beginneth to make a cross upon the forehead of the child, that is offered to be baptized, in tokening that he is

---

[1] C. S. Cobb, *The Rationale of Ceremonial 1540–1543*. Alcuin Club Collections *XVIII*. London 1910.
[2] Ibid., p. liv.
[3] Ibid., p. lxiv.
[4] For their identity, see p. xlix.
[5] Ibid., p. lxiv.

come to be professed and totally to be dedicated to Christ crucified, whom he will never be ashamed openly before men to confess and knowledge.[1]

Then he maketh another cross upon the breast, from whence cometh the belief, signifying that it is not enough to confess Christ with mouth openly unless he doth steadfastly believe in heart inwardly, and therefore the minister prayeth almighty God to take away the blindness of his heart and to make him apt to receive the grace given in baptism.

And then he putteth hallowed salt into his mouth to signify the spiritual salt, which is the word of God, wherewith he should be seasoned and powdered that thereby the filthy savour of stinking sin should be taken away preserving him from corruption and making him a more apt vessel to continue in the moisture of wholesome and godly wisdom, and therefore the minister prayeth that he may be replenished with his heaven food, and that he receiving this grace of baptism may obtain everlasting reward.

Then the minister maketh a sign of the cross in the child's forehead, adjuring the devil to depart, and no more to approach to him, but to knowledge his sentence of damnation and to give glory unto God, and to Jesus Christ which triumphed upon the cross over him in his own person, praying that this child now purged from the wicked spirit may be the sanctified temple of the Holy Ghost. After this is read the gospel taken out of Matthew, the xix chapter, beginning "Oblati sunt Jesu pueri", wherein is showed that the oblation of young children is acceptable unto Christ, of whose church without baptism they cannot be made members, wherefore the people according to this example offereth their children to the minister to be baptized.

Then the minister wetteth with spittle the nose thurles and ears of him that shall be baptized, putting us in remembrance of the miracle of the deaf and dumb wrought by Christ who looking up in to heaven put his spittle with his fingers into the ears and touching his tongue said Epthatha, that is to say, be opened and so he healed him signifying thereby the grace and godly influence descending from heaven which by the operation of the Holy Ghost openeth our nose to take the sweet odour and savour of the knowledge of Christ and our ears to hear his words and commandments. Then the minister exhorteth the godfathers and godmothers with all other that are present to pray to God

---

[1] The words in this relative clause are similar to some words in the exorcism in Hermann's *Consultation* (above, p. 65). But the words used in the consignation in the order of baptism in the Prayer Book of 1549 (below, p. 90) resemble more closely those in the *Rationale* than those in the *Consultation*.

that that child may worthily receive that blessed sacrament of baptism to the honour of God and to the salvation of the soul and to the confusion of our ghostly enemy the devil, and so the minister and all they together say the Pater noster, etc. Then immediately the minister maketh the sign of the cross in the right hand of the infant, which cross should in all our life time admonish us valiantly to defend, resist and withstand the crafty assaults of our enemy the devil with all our corrupt and perverse affections and desires, and so blessing the child in the name of the Father, the Son and the Holy Ghost, taketh it by the right hand and biddeth it enter into the church, there to be admitted as one of Christ's flock and congregation, and so proceedeth to the font.

And there entering into the baptism, first inquisition is made of the name of him that should be baptized to the intent that by giving in his name he may now profess himself to a new master Christ for of a custom such professions were made by such inscriptions and giving in of their names.

Then there followeth a stipulation made under prescript words, the minister demanding certain questions, and he that is baptized or his surety making answer to every question or demand particularly (which demands, questions and answers to the intent the godfather and godmother with others there present may know what is a Christian man's profession at his baptism we think it very convenient and meet to be uttered hereafter in the English tongue),[1] and first to this interrogation of the minister.

The minister saith, Forsakest thou the devil? He or his sureties for him answereth, I forsake him.

The minister saith, And all his works? It is answered, I forsake them.

The minister saith, And all his pomps and vanities? The answer is, I forsake them.

After this the minister with the holy oil anointeth the child before upon the breast and behind between the shoulders, which unction upon the breast signifieth that our heart and affections should be wholly dedicated to Christ and established in a perfect faith in his mercy which the oil commonly doth signify in scripture. And the anointing between the shoulders with the sign of the cross signifieth that we should be steadfast, stout and strong to bear the yoke of our Lord and patiently to sustain such cross of persecution, trouble and affliction as our most merciful Lord shall lay upon us.

---

[1] The words in brackets are a marginal note in one of the Mss.

Then further the minister maketh inquisition of his belief that is to be christened saying, Believest thou in God the almighty Father, maker of heaven and earth? It is answered, I believe.

The minister saith, Believest thou in Jesus Christ, his only Son our Lord? The answer is made, I believe.

The minister saith, Believest thou in the Holy Ghost, the holy catholic church, the communion of saints, the remission of sins, the resurrection of the body and after death to have life everlasting? It is answered, I believe.

All which promises and professions of renouncing the old error and believing and embracing the truth made in baptism every Christian man ought to have in his often remembrance, and after this the minister saith to him that is to be baptized these words.

What askest thou? It is answered, Baptism. The minister demandeth further saying, Wilt thou be baptized? It is answered, I will. For there is no man saved against his will but willingly. For as a man by his own free will obeying the serpent did perish, so when God calleth by grace by the conversion of his own mind every man truly believing and intending to work accordingly is saved.

Then the minister calleth the child by the name and baptizeth it in the name of the Father and of the Son and of the Holy Ghost, putting it into the water of the font and taking it out again, or else pouring water upon the infant, whereby the person christened hath not only remission of all his sins by the operation of the Holy Ghost, but also by the same is signified not only the death and resurrection of Christ, the only cause of our health and salvation, but also that we should daily mortify our evil desires and corrupt affections, and so washed from sin walk in a new, pure and godly life and conversation.[1]

Then after his baptism he is anointed with holy chrism, on the head as the supreme and principal part of man, signifying thereby that he is made a Christian man by Christ the head of his congregation; and that he is anointed with the spiritual unction of the Holy Ghost, that by his assistance and grace he may attain everlasting life.

Then he that is baptized is clothed in a white vesture, in token of his manumission[2] and freedom from the former captivity of the devil, and it signifieth also a Christian purity and innocency, which after the washing away of the spots of his old sin, he ought studiously to

---

[1] See the final exhortation in the 1549 baptism service; below, p. 95.
[2] See the *Enchiridion*; above, p. 51.

conserve and keep, and so to come to the presence of Christ at the day of judgment and reign with him in glory everlasting.

Finally the minister putteth a candle light in the right hand of him that is baptized, in token that he should through all his life time show before all men a light of good example and godly works, that he may be always in a readiness with the saints to meet our Lord and receive the fruition of everlasting joy.

7. Oleum Chrismatis

The use of holy oil and chrism is convenient and laudable to be observed, for it signifieth principally the imperial and priestly dignity of Christ and his anointing with the spiritual unction of the Holy Ghost above all creatures, and secondarily the defacing and abolishing of all the consecrations of the old law which were dedicate in oil, and therefore in Cena Domini[1] the old oil is burnt and destroyed and new consecrated, signifying thereby the new regeneration of Christ and the holy inunction which we have by his Spirit, and it admonisheth us of our state and condition which we have by Christ, for as of chrisma Christ is named, so of Christ we be called Christians. In figure whereof kings, priests and prophets were anointed to put them in remembrance also of brightness of conscience and sweet odour of fame to God's glory and edifying of their neighbour.

20. The Hallowing of the Font upon Saturday in the Easter-Even

Upon Saturday Easter-Even is hallowed the font which is as it were vestigium or a remembrance of the baptism that was used in the primitive church, at which time and Pentecost there was used in the church two solemn baptizings and much concourse of people came unto the same. The first was at Easter time because that the mystery of baptism agreeth well to the time, for like as Christ died and was buried and rose again the third day, so, by putting into the water, it signified our death to sin, and the immersions betokeneth our burying and mortifying to the same; and the rising again out of the water declareth us to be risen unto a new life according to the doctrine of Saint Paul, Rom. 6. And the second solemn baptizing, that is to say, at Pentecost, was because that then is celebrate the feast of the Holy Ghost, which is the worker of the spiritual regeneration, which we have in baptism; and therefore the church useth yet to hallow the font also at that time.

[1] I.e., Maundy Thursday.

25. A General Doctrine to what intent ceremonies be Ordained and of what Value they be of

Finally these rites and ceremonies here before expressed and mentioned, with other good and laudable now used in the ministration of sacraments for their godly signification, are very commendable and to be observed, and in no wise to be omitted without a reasonable cause, except it shall be seen to the rulers and governors upon good considerations to take away, alter or change them or any of them; so that the people use the same without superstition, taking them for good tokens and signs to put them in remembrance of things of higher perfection, and for a decent and a convenient order to be had in the church, and none otherwise, and not to repose any trust of salvation in them, or that they have power to remit sin, but to stir and lift up their minds to God by whom with the Holy Ghost, be laud, honour and praise for ever. Amen.

We have omitted the notes and signs by which Cobb in his edition indicated the variations between the Mss. of this work.

16. Tyndale

While the Latin rite of baptism in use in England at this time received no adverse criticism in the *Bishops' Book* or the *King's Book* or the *Rationale of Ceremonial*, it came under heavy fire from William Tyndale, who, although he left England in 1524 for the continent, where he remained till he was put to death in 1536, continued to exert a considerable influence on English thought through his writings. We give here passages from *The Obedience of a Christian Man*, published in 1527, to be found in *Works* (Parker Society), I, pp. 253, 276f, 283.

Baptism hath also his word and promise, which the priest ought to teach the people, and christen them in the English tongue; and not to play popinjay with "*Credo* say ye", and "*Volo* say ye", and "*Baptismum* say ye"; for there ought to be no mumming in such a matter. . . .

Baptism is called volowing in many places of England, because the priest saith, "*Volo* say ye". "The child was well volowed", say they; "yea, and our vicar is as fair a volower as ever a priest within this twenty miles!"

Behold how narrowly the people look on the ceremony. If aught be left out, or if the child be not altogether dipt in the water, or if, because the child is sick, the priest dare not plunge him into the water, but pour water on his head, how tremble they! How quake they! "How say ye, Sir John, say they, is this child christened enough? Hath it his full christendom?" They believe verily that the child is not christened . . .

Dumb ceremonies are no sacraments, but superstitiousness. Christ's sacraments preach the faith of Christ, as his apostles did, and thereby justify. Antichrist's dumb ceremonies preach not the faith that is in Christ; as his apostles, our bishops and cardinals, do not. . . . Hereby seest thou what is to be thought of all other ceremonies; as hallowed water, bread, salt, boughs, bells, wax, ashes, and so forth; and all other disguisings and apes' play; and of all manner conjurations, as the conjuring of church and church yards, and of altar-stones, and such like. Where no promise of God is, there can be no faith, nor justifying, nor forgiveness of sins; for it is more than madness to look for anything of God, save that he hath promised. . . .

17. Cranmer

Although he wrote no treatise on baptism as such, Thomas Cranmer made many references to baptism when he was dealing with other subjects, and in particular with the Eucharist. From these numerous and scattered references Bromiley has at considerable length shown what was the doctrine of baptism which the Archbishop held.[1] In the following passage in the *Confutation of Unwritten Verities* Cranmer expressed his attitude to those ceremonies in the Sarum rite of baptism which rested only on the authority of primitive tradition, and further proved, at least to his own satisfaction, that infant baptism, which he had no intention of rejecting, was derived not merely from ancient custom but from Scripture itself.

He [*sc.* Tertullian] reciting many traditions, as to renounce the devil, his pomp and his angels, afore baptism, to dip the children thrice in the font, to give it pap of honey and milk first thing after baptism, and not to wash it in a whole week after, to offer both at the day of the burial and birth, on the Sunday neither to fast, nor to pray kneeling, nor also from Easter to Whitsuntide, crossing our foreheads, with divers such like, saith: "If thou require a law of these and other such disciplines, there can be no pretence of a law for them out of the scriptures. But thou shalt either perceive by thyself, or learn of some other that perceiveth it, that custom, being author, confirmer, conserver, and observer of faith, shall maintain and defend the cause of this tradition and custom of faith."[2]

By the scriptures before alleged it is evidently proved, that all things requisite for our salvation be set forth in the holy books of the bible, and that it is not lawful to put any thing thereto under pain of everlasting damnation. . . .

Tertullian speaketh here not of doctrines of faith, hope and charity, but of traditions, outward gestures, rites and ceremonies, which be not necessary for our salvation, but be ordained for a decent order and conformity in the church. . . .

Yet they bring forth, to maintain their error, the baptism of infants, which, they say, is not contained in the scriptures: and yet this is to be

---

[1] G. W. Bromiley, *Thomas Cranmer Theologian* (London 1956), pp. 57–68.
[2] *de Corona*, 3f.

observed upon pain of damnation of the said children. Ergo, there is something to be done, of necessity to our salvation, that is not contained in the scriptures.

O what a gap these men open both to the Donatists and to the Anabaptists, that deny the baptizing of infants! For, if it were not written in the word of God, no man ought to believe it, or use it: and so the Donatists' and Anabaptists' doctrine were true, and ours false. But in deed the baptism of infants is proved by the plain scriptures. First, by the figure of the old law, which was circumcision. Infants in the old law were circumcised: *ergo*, in the new law they ought to be baptized. Again: infants pertain to God, as it is said to Abraham, "I will be thy God, and the God of thy seed after thee." Christ saith also: "Suffer children to come unto me; for of such is the kingdom of heaven." And again: "See that ye despise not one of these little ones: for their angels in heaven always behold the face of my Father which is in heaven: for the Son of Man is come to save that which is lost." And again, Paul saith, that "your children are holy now". By these and many other plain words of scripture it is evident that the baptism of infants is grounded upon the holy scripture.[1]

Cranmer's views on the medieval ceremonies were expounded at some length in the article printed at the end of the Prayer Book of 1549 under the title, Of Ceremonies, why some be abolished and some retained, and included in the introductory matter in the Prayer Book of 1662. He also showed his preference for a most simple ceremonial in baptism when he once referred for purposes of argument to private baptism: "Children in danger of life are christened by the midwife, or some other woman, without any of these ceremonies."[2]

[1] Ch. X, in *Works* (Parker Society), II, pp. 56f, 60.
[2] Ibid., II, p. 58.

18. Baptism in the Prayer Book of 1549

OF THE ADMINISTRATION OF PUBLIC BAPTISM
TO BE USED IN THE CHURCH

It appeareth by ancient writers that the sacrament of baptism in the old time was not commonly *ministered but at two times in the year, at Easter and Whitsuntide,* at which times it was openly ministered in the presence of all the congregation: *which custom* (now being grown out of use) *although it cannot for many considerations be well restored again,* yet it is thought good to follow the same as near as conveniently may be. Wherefore the people are to be admonished, that it is most convenient that *baptism should not be ministered but upon Sundays and other holy days, when the most number of people may come together.* As well for that the congregation there present may testify the receiving of them, that be newly baptized into the number of Christ's church, as also because in the baptism of infants every man present may be put in remembrance of his own profession made to God in his baptism. For which cause also it is expedient that baptism be ministered in the English tongue. Nevertheless (if necessity so require) children ought at all times to be baptized, either at the church or else at home.[1]

When there are children to be baptized upon the Sunday or holy day, the parents shall give knowledge over night or in the morning afore the beginning of Mattins to the curate. And then the godfathers, godmothers and people with the children must be ready at the church door, either immediately afore the last canticle at Mattins or else immediately afore the last canticle at Evensong, as the curate by his discretion shall appoint. And then, standing there, the priest shall ask whether the children be baptized or no. If they answer No, then shall the priest say thus.[2]

Dear beloved, forasmuch as all men be *conceived and born in sin,* and that no man born in sin can enter into the kingdom of God (except he be regenerate and born anew of water and the Holy Ghost) I beseech you to call upon God the Father through our Lord Jesus Christ, that of his bounteous mercy he will grant to these children that thing, which by nature they cannot have,[3] that is to say, they may be baptized with the Holy Ghost, and received into Christ's holy church, and be made lively members of the same.[4]

Then the priest shall say:

Let us pray.

Almighty and everlasting God, which of thy justice didst destroy by

---

[1] The main source of this rubric is Hermann's *Consultation;* above, p. 55. The words in italics are actual quotations from it.

[2] In the *Consultation,* as in all early rites, baptism was set in the context not of the Offices but of the Eucharist.

[3] This relative clause occurred also in the third prayer in the *Sarum* rite.

[4] This preface is a drastic abbreviation of the preface in the *Consultation.*

floods of water the whole world for sin, except viii persons, whom of
thy mercy (the same time) thou didst save in the ark: and when thou
didst drown in the Red Sea wicked king Pharaoh with all his army, yet
(at the same time) thou didst lead thy people the children of Israel safely
through the midst thereof, whereby thou didst figure the washing of
thy holy baptism: and by the baptism of thy well beloved son Jesus
Christ thou didst sanctify the flood Jordan and all other waters to this
mystical washing away of sin: We beseech thee (for thy infinite mercies) that thou wilt mercifully look upon these children, and sanctify
them with thy Holy Ghost, that by this wholesome laver of regeneration whatsoever sin is in them may be washed clean away, that they,
being delivered from thy wrath, may be received into the ark of
Christ's church, and so saved from perishing; and being fervent in
spirit, stedfast in faith, joyful through hope, rooted in charity, may
ever serve thee, and finally attain to everlasting life with all thy holy
and chosen people. This grant us, we beseech thee, for Jesus Christ's
sake our Lord. Amen.[1]

Here shall the priest ask what shall be the name of the child, and when the godfathers and godmothers have told the name, then shall he make a cross upon the
child's forehead and breast, saying:

N., receive the sign of the holy cross, both in thy forehead, and in thy
breast,[2] in token that thou shalt not be ashamed to confess thy faith in
Christ crucified, and manfully to fight under his banner against sin, the
world and the devil, and to continue his faithful soldier and servant
unto thy life's end. Amen.

And this he shall do and say to as many children as be present to be baptized, one
after another:

Let us pray.

Almighty and immortal God, the aid of all that need, the helper of all
that flee to thee for succour, the life of them that believe, and the resurrection of the dead, we call upon thee for these infants, that they coming to thy holy baptism may receive remission of their sins by spiritual
regeneration. Receive them, O Lord, as thou hast promised by thy
well beloved Son, saying, Ask and you shall have: seek and you shall
find: knock and it shall be opened unto you. So give now unto us that

[1] This is a fairly free translation of Luther's Flood Prayer, which Bucer had included in
the *Consultation*. The latter part of it Luther had taken from the Latin Magdeburg *Agenda*.
[2] A similar signing of forehead and breast was found in *Sarum*, but with a different
formula. The words used here are similar to those in the *Consultation*: but there is a somewhat closer resemblance with those in the *Rationale*; above, pp. 65, 80f.

ask: let us that seek find: open thy gate unto us that knock, that these infants may enjoy the everlasting benediction of thy heavenly washing, and may come to the eternal kingdom which thou has promised by Christ our Lord. Amen.[1]

Then let the priest, looking upon the children, say:

I command thee, unclean spirit, in the name of the Father, of the Son, and of the Holy Ghost, that thou come out and depart from these infants, whom our Lord Jesus Christ hath vouchsafed to call to his holy baptism to be made members of his body and of his holy congregation. Therefore, thou cursed spirit, remember thy sentence, remember thy judgment, remember the day to be at hand, wherein thou shalt burn in fire everlasting, prepared for thee and thy angels. And presume not hereafter to exercise any tyranny toward these infants, whom Christ hath bought with his precious blood, and by this his holy baptism calleth to be of his flock.[2]

Then shall the priest say:

The Lord be with you.
The people: And with thy spirit.
The minister: Hear now the Gospel written by St Mark.

At a certain time they brought children to Christ that he should touch them, and his disciples rebuked those that brought them. But when Jesus saw it, he was displeased, and said unto them: Suffer little children to come unto me, and forbid them not: for to such belongeth the kingdom of God. Verily I say unto you: whosoever doth not receive the kingdom of God as a little child, he shall not enter therein. And when he had taken them up in his arms, he put his hands upon them, and blessed them.[3]

After the gospel is ended, the minister shall make this brief exhortation upon the words of the gospel:

Friends, you hear in this gospel the words of our Saviour Christ, that he commanded the children to be brought unto him, how he blamed those that would have kept them from him, how he exhorteth all men

---

[1] The opening invocation and the last clause are from *Sarum*. The middle portion is mostly found in the *Taufbüchlein*; above, pp. 23f. The corresponding prayer in the *Consultation* is rather different; above, p. 65.

[2] Except for the last sentence this is taken from various parts of the exorcisms in *Sarum*. The opening words were also in the *Taufbüchlein*; above, p. 24. "Tyranny" in the last sentence occurs four times in the *Consultation*, and also in the Epilogue to the *Taufbüchlein*; above, p. 7.

[3] The Matthaean version of this event was used in *Sarum*, the Marcan in the *Consultation*, the *Taufbüchlein*, and the Magdeburg *Agenda*.

to follow their innocency. Ye perceive how by his outward gesture and deed he declared his good will toward them. For he embraced them in his arms, he laid his hands upon them, and blessed them: *Doubt ye not, therefore, but earnestly believe, that he will likewise favourably receive these present infants, that he will embrace them with the arms of his mercy, that he will give unto them the blessing of eternal life: and make them partakers of his everlasting kingdom.* Wherefore we being thus persuaded of the good will of our heavenly Father toward these infants, declared by his Son Jesus Christ, and nothing doubting but that he favourably alloweth *this charitable work of ours*, in bringing these children to his holy baptism, let us faithfully and devoutly give thanks unto him, and say the prayer which the Lord himself taught. And in declaration of our faith, let us also recite the articles contained in our creed.

Here the minister with the godfathers, godmothers and people present shall say:

Our Father, which art in heaven, hallowed be thy name, etc.

And then shall say openly:

I believe in God the Father almighty, etc.

The priest shall add also this prayer:

Almighty and everlasting God, Heavenly Father, we give thee humble thanks that thou hast vouchsafed to call us to knowledge of thy grace and faith in thee: Increase and confirm this faith in us evermore: Give thy Holy Spirit to these infants, that they may be born again, and be made heirs of everlasting salvation, through our Lord Jesus Christ: who liveth and reigneth with thee and the Holy Spirit, now and for ever. Amen.

Then let the priest take one of the children by the right hand, the others being brought after him. And coming into the church toward the font, say:[1]

The Lord vouchsafe to receive you into his holy household, and to keep and govern you alway in the same, that you may have everlasting life. Amen.

Well beloved friends, ye have brought these children here to be baptized, ye have prayed for them that our Lord Jesus Christ would vouchsafe to receive them, to lay his hands upon them, to bless them, to release them of their sins, to give them the kingdom of heaven, and everlasting life. Ye have heard also that our Lord Jesus Christ hath promised in his gospel to grant all these things that ye have prayed for:

[1] No interval of time is intended between the service at the church door and the baptism, whereas in the *Consultation* the catechism and exorcism could take place on the day before baptism; above, p. 67.

which promise he for his part will most surely keep and perform. Wherefore, after this promise made by Christ, these infants must also faithfully for their part promise by you that be their sureties, that they will forsake the devil and all his works, and constantly believe God's holy word and obediently keep his commandments.

Then shall the priest demand of the child (which shall be first baptized) these questions following: first naming the child, and saying:

N., dost thou forsake the devil and all his works?

Answer: I forsake them.

Minister: Dost thou forsake the vain pomp and glory of the world with all covetous desires of the same?

Answer: I forsake them.

Minister: Dost thou forsake the carnal desires of the flesh, so that thou wilt not follow nor be led by them?

Answer: I forsake them.

Minister: Dost thou believe in God the Father almighty, maker of heaven and earth?

Answer: I believe.

Minister: Dost thou believe in Jesus Christ his only begotten Son our Lord, and that he was conceived by the Holy Ghost, born of the Virgin Mary, that he suffered under Pontius Pilate, was crucified, dead and buried, that he went down into hell, and also did rise again the third day, that he ascended into heaven, and sitteth on the right hand of God the Father almighty, and from thence shall come again at the end of the world to judge the quick and the dead: dost thou believe this?[1]

Answer: I believe.

Minister: Dost thou believe in the Holy Ghost, the holy catholic[2] church, the communion of saints, remission of sins, resurrection of the flesh and everlasting life after death?

Answer: I believe.

Minister: What dost thou desire?

Answer: Baptism.

---

[1] Luther and Osiander retained the shorter Latin form of this second baptismal interrogation: "... Our Lord, who was born and suffered". Above, pp. 15, 18, 21. Bucer in the *Consultation* considerably expanded the question, but without adhering closely to the words of the creed. Here the question is based upon the apostles' creed.

[2] There is not here the antipathy to the word "catholic" that is found in the Lutheran rites.

Minister: Wilt thou be baptized?
Answer: I will.[1]

Then the priest shall take the child in his hands, and ask the name, and naming the child shall dip it in the water thrice, first dipping the right side, second the left side, the third time dipping the face toward the font,[2] so it be discreetly and warily done, saying:

N., I baptize thee in the name of the Father and of the Son and of the Holy Ghost. Amen.

And if the child be weak, it shall suffice to pour water upon it,[3] saying the foresaid words,

N., I baptize thee, etc.

Then the godfathers and godmothers shall take and lay their hands upon the child, and the minister shall put upon him his white vesture, commonly called the crisom,[4] and say:

Take this white vesture for a token of the innocency which by God's grace in this holy sacrament of baptism is given unto thee, and for a sign whereby thou art admonished, so long as thou livest, to give thyself to innocency of living, that after this transitory life thou mayest be partaker of the life everlasting. Amen.

Then the priest shall anoint the infant upon the head, saying:

Almighty God, the Father of our Lord Jesus Christ, who hath regenerated thee by water and the Holy Ghost, and hath given unto thee remission of all thy sins, he vouchsafe to anoint thee with the unction of his Holy Spirit, and bring thee to the inheritance of everlasting life. Amen.[5]

When there are many to be baptized, this order of demanding, baptizing, putting on the crisom and anointing shall be used severally with every child, those that be first baptized departing from the font, and remaining in some convenient place within the church until all be baptized. At the last end the priest calling the godfathers and godmothers together shall say this short exhortation following:

Forasmuch as these children have promised by you to forsake the devil

[1] These questions are from *Sarum*. It was to these questions in their Latin form in *Sarum* that Tyndale objected; above, p. 86.

[2] Apart from securing a threefold dipping in accordance with ancient custom, this regulation caused the whole of the child's body to be touched by the water.

[3] Baptism by affusion was permitted in the *Rationale*; above, p. 83.

[4] While Luther and Osiander retained the giving of the white robe, Bucer omitted it in the *Consultation*; above, p. 69.

[5] This is a modified form of the prayer at the presbyteral unction immediately after baptism in the old Latin rites. Luther, Osiander, and the *Brandenburg Church Order* of 1540 (Sehling, op. cit., III, p. 54) kept the unction. But in the *Consultation* the unction itself was omitted, and the accompanying prayer adapted accordingly. The mention of "the unction of his Holy Spirit" in the rite of 1549 could be interpreted as giving this unction the force of a presbyteral confirmation.

and all his works, to believe in God and to serve him, you must remember that it is your parts and duty to see that these infants be taught, so soon as they shall be able to learn, what a solemn vow, promise and profession they have made by you. And that they may know these things the better, ye shall call upon them to hear sermons, and chiefly you shall provide that they may learn the creed, the Lord's prayer and the ten commandments in the English tongue, and all other things which a Christian ought to know and believe to his soul's health, and that these children may be virtuously brought up to lead a godly and Christian life, remembering always that baptism doth represent unto us our profession which is to follow the example of our Saviour Christ, and to be made like unto him, that as he died and rose again for us, so should we which are baptized die from sin, and rise again unto righteousness, continually mortifying all our evil and corrupt affections, and daily proceeding in all virtue and godliness of living.[1]

The minister shall command that the crisoms be brought to the church, and delivered to the priests after the accustomed manner, at the purification of the mother of every child, and that the children be brought to the bishop[2] to be confirmed of him, so soon as they can say in their vulgar tongue the articles of the faith, the Lord's prayer and the ten commandments, and be further instructed in the catechism, set forth for that purpose, accordingly as it is there expressed.[3]

And so let the congregation depart in the name of the Lord.

Note that if the number of children to be baptized and multitude of people present be so great that they cannot conveniently stand at the church door, then let them stand within the church in some convenient place nigh unto the church door, and there all things be said and done, appointed to be said and done at the church door.

[1] See *Rationale*, above, p. 83.

[2] In the *Consultation* visitors were allowed to confirm; below, p. 195.

[3] For a similar expression of the need for post-baptismal instruction in the pre-Reformation Church see the Council of Lambeth (1281), cap. 9: ". . . we enact that every priest in charge of a congregation four times in the year, that is, once in each quarter, on one solemn day or more, shall himself or through some other expound to the people simply and without any subtle and fanciful embroidery the fourteen articles of the faith, the ten commandments of the Decalogue, the two evangelical precepts regarding the twofold love, also the seven works of mercy, the seven capital sins with their progeny, the seven principal virtues and the seven sacraments of grace." (See F. M. Powicke and C. R. Cheney, *Councils and Synods, with other Documents relating to the English Church*, II (Oxford 1964), p. 900.)

19. Bucer's Censura

The victory of the Emperor, Charles V, over the German Protestants at Mühlberg in April 1547 brought nearly all Germany under a government opposed to the Lutheran reformation. The Interim of Augsburg, proclaimed the following May, amongst other things required assent to the doctrines of transubstantiation and the seven sacraments, and to the use of the medieval ceremonies. Finding his position there too dangerous, Bucer fled from Strassburg to find safety in England, whither he had been invited by Cranmer. He was at once appointed Regius Professor of Divinity in Cambridge, occupying this position until his death in 1551.

When Bucer first set foot in England in April 1549, the Prayer Book, due to come into use on Whitsunday that year, was already in process of publication. Hence Bucer arrived too late to assist personally in the compilation of that book, although indirectly he exerted a strong influence upon it by means of the *Consultation*.

Very soon Bucer was asked to give his views about the Prayer Book; but as he could not read English, it first had to be translated into Latin for him. His considered opinion was expressed in a Latin work, known in short as the *Censura*, the twenty-eight chapters of which were finished in January 1551. In the prologue Bucer recorded his satisfaction with the book in general, although he added that there were not lacking a few small points where it could be thought insufficiently congruous with the word of God. The section on baptism is in Bucer's *Scripta Anglicana* (Basle 1577), pp. 477–81. The text, however, is not always to be trusted.

THE JUDGMENT OF MARTIN BUCER
UPON THE BOOK OF SACRED RITES OR OF THE
ORDERING OF THE CHURCH
AND ECCLESIASTICAL MINISTRATION IN
THE KINGDOM OF ENGLAND
WRITTEN AT THE REQUEST OF THE
REVEREND ARCHBISHOP THOMAS CRANMER

ix. *On the ceremonies prescribed for
the administration of Holy Baptism*

First of all before the description of the manner in which baptism is to be administered, there is placed in front this rubric, salutary enough, to the effect that baptism should be administered on feast days and in the

96

presence of the whole church, so that thereby both the church may the more easily keep in mind who have been baptized, and also that every-one from the baptism of infants should be reminded of his own baptism and of the covenant of salvation into which he entered at his baptism. But the more congruous this rubric is with the Lord's institution and with that great benefit of his which he confers on his people through baptism, the less is it said to be observed—especially as regards the point that baptism should be celebrated in the presence of the whole church and also on feast days.

Now who could have any appreciation of Christian fellowship and fail to recognize how appropriate it is that those who are members of one another in Christ should all be present in person when somebody born of their number into eternal death has to be reborn in the church to eternal life, and be received among the children of God, so that they may pray together for that benefit and may both pray for it from God and as the church of Christ confer it together through the minister, so that just as he becomes a member of every one of them by this sacra-ment, so also he may be received by every one of them as a member, and each may bind himself to him in the presence of the Lord in regard to the mutual obligations of Christian fellowship, both bodily and spiritual?

So the greatest care must be taken by bishops and archdeacons to en-sure both that the ministers faithfully teach this rubric to their people, and also that they themselves religiously observe it, giving no occasion for superstition or licence. For not a few of those whose infants are baptized are more concerned about those things which have to do with the worldly pomp with which Satan has invested these holy things, than those which concern baptism and regeneration: whose perversity is not to be encouraged but abolished.

And since neither at Morning Prayers nor at Evening Prayers is the church in the habit of assembling, it would surely have been better for baptism to be administered immediately after the sacred assembly, when the congregation is still present in the greatest numbers, before the administration of the Holy Supper is begun, as both the ancient churches used to do and today some maintain the custom.[1] This would be readily agreed by all who recognize the power of regeneration and

---

[1] In the *Consultation* Bucer had combined baptism with the Eucharist, as was customary in the primitive Church; above, p. 55. Only on those occasions when Morning Prayer was immediately followed by the Holy Communion was any close link between baptism and the Eucharist preserved in England when the Prayer Book of 1549 was in use.

the fulness of the divine gift which is conferred in baptism. For naturally men are accustomed in regard to those whom they have decided to admit into a college of repute and into its society, as in the case of academies and many other societies of men of much lesser importance, to do so when the colleges assemble in greater numbers, so that they may as it were be received by all into the college, and each may confer upon them the duties of the college, and they themselves in their turn may publicly bind themselves to those duties.

So also the second rubric in this book is to be strongly recommended, namely, that those who have infants to be baptized should signify the fact in time to the pastors and devoutly request baptism from the church at their hands. For unless men set the highest value upon these mysteries of Christ, they receive them to themselves to condemnation.

Those who were the authors of that practice, concerning which the third rubric is issued, namely, that a number of prayers should be offered for the infants who are to be baptized in front of the church door, seem to have followed that usage, so that by that very sign men may admit that their children themselves are conceived and born of them in sins.

But since a multitude of signs does not become a new people, and men sufficiently recognize and confess this very fact that all are conceived and born in sin both in clear words and in the request for and receiving of baptism, I rather think that this rite in itself is possessed of enough decency, order and edification, the things with which all ceremonies must be instituted and ordered. For the infants of the faithful are holy, so that they are to be brought into church and sanctified by baptism. Therefore would any absurdity be introduced if infants were brought once into the church itself and into the solemn place of prayer, and in the same place and near the baptistery there should be made over them all the prayers and readings, where all the people could hear them? For in all these things, and, as I have said, in baptism itself, a sufficiently clear admission is made of the fact that all ours are born in sins, as we ourselves were.

Now we observe that the common people is delighted by dramatic actions and uses many signs, of which, however, the majority do not understand the meaning, and very few think about it. Moreover it is proper for Christians to worship the Lord in spirit and in truth, and, most especially in the so sacred mysteries of our redemption and regeneration to eternal life, to do nothing at all with insufficient prudence and lightly, as when in these holy rites too many signs are introduced by the ordinary people. For Satan continually deceives us, and tries to convert the serious and salutary things of the Lord into his own obnoxious sports. But in every way we have to resist these pernicious efforts of Satan and the superstitions of men as well as their irreligious deceits.

So in these matters, as it now seems to me, and as we all see how reluctantly the people will allow itself to be taken away from useless bondage or even from the profane sport of external signs to the worship and adoration of Christ in spirit and in truth, I for my part would prefer that infants to be baptized were brought straight into the churches and into the midst of the people of God in a place from which all the people could properly hear all that is said there, so that true understanding and reverence for this first and great sacrament may be restored, and true religion may be conserved and increased.[1]

x. On the White Robe and Chrism

Each of these is a very ancient sign, but it cannot be proved from this that the use of them is suitable for us also, and is now too for the edification of the people. To use many signs rightly and [without?] vain pretence in things both human and divine is only for those who have a most fervent affection for these things to which the many signs apply; for instance we see that it is right for mothers who most passionately love their children to employ as many signs as possible of their love towards their children. But we see that those people behave unbecomingly and coldly who overwhelm those whom they wish to appear to love and respect with many signs of love and reverence, when it is clear, however, that they are not actuated by any true affection and reverence for them, or not as much as they show by their signs. The old saints were ablaze with the utmost reverence for God and gratitude for his benefits: the people used to be present at baptism with great devotion: so for them those signs were able to promote reverence towards God and to arouse and sustain more devotion towards so great a mystery.

But for some time we have seen the effect produced by the Romish Antichrists and by the impiety innate in all men, by which they continually turn sacred ceremonies for the worship of God into various wicked shows, so that today those signs among the great majority of people serve more for the maintenance and increase of superstition and show than of piety and religion. Now the occasions for these abuses

[1] For the result of this suggestion see below, p. 106.

are to be cut out, not retained. And if we were to say that the use of these signs be rendered salutary again by teaching, we see that among some the teaching is lacking, and among others it does not profit. So I would prefer these signs to be abolished rather than retained. But if it were in any event to happen that they are retained, I wish that the wholesome use of them be taught and urged as carefully as possible.

xi. *On the actual description of Baptism*

In the first prayer over the infant I would wish these words to be omitted, "and by the baptism of thy well beloved Son" as far as "we beseech thee, etc.". In these words it is said that God through the baptism of his blessed Son, Jesus Christ, has sanctified the flood of Jordan and all other waters for this mystical washing away of sins. For scripture does not proclaim this: and this manner of speaking encourages the superstitious belief that a kind of power of sanctifying in the waters is imposed upon the baptism of Christ; for men always have a predilection for teaching magical changes in things, as is shown by the fiction of transubstantiation and the opinion held about almost all the things which the Papists publicly consecrate, such as water, salt, herbs, candles, bells and other things which they are accustomed to bless and preserve with some kind of religious consecration.[1]

In this connection, in order that baptism may be for us the sacrament of the washing away of sins, the Lord accomplished it for us not only by his own baptism in the Jordan but also and much more fully by the baptism of the cross; finally, although water is used to confer it in baptism, yet the washing away of sins is not the function of the water but of Christ the Lord.

Much deference and respect is to be paid to the early churches and the most holy fathers; but how much more must God be regarded and followed by every man; and the more faithfully must we take care not to attribute anything to either the grace or authority of any men, whereby the benefits of God can be obscured and the worship in spirit and in truth which we owe him. Especially must we always see what becomes us as children of God, treating it also in the light of the New Testament, and what adorns the already revealed glory of Christ, and what truly establishes faith in the cross of Christ.

---

[1] The words to which Bucer took exception here did not apparently seem objectionable to him when he compiled the order of baptism in the *Consultation*; above, p. 64. Either Hermann had insisted on their inclusion, or Bucer had changed his mind in the meantime.

xii. *On the sign of the cross and the prayer with which it is fashioned upon the forehead and breast of those to be baptized*

I think it neither inappropriate nor useless that this sign should be used, both because it is of most ancient use in the church and because it is also simple and serves for a present reminder of the cross of Christ, provided that its use is properly understood, and it is devoutly accepted without the intrusion of any superstition or bondage to an element and not as a vulgar custom.

But the words which the book prescribes to be said when they fashion this sign on the forehead and breast of the infants I cannot approve, not on the ground that they do not contain in themselves a holy prayer, but because they are ordered to be said to the infant, who does not understand them. For scripture teaches no such thing; and all spectacular and theatrical things ought to be far removed from these mysteries together with every superstition and every semblance of magic. So I should wish those words to be changed into the form of a prayer of this kind: "O God, grant to this infant, thy creature, so to receive the merit and power of the cross of the Son of God that he may never be ashamed of it, and may ever be crucified to the world, and the world to him, and he may fight strenuously under this sign against sin, the world and Satan, and may persevere faithful in thy righteousness and obedience even to the end of his life. Amen."

In the following prayer, where it has "that they coming to holy baptism", I should prefer it to have, "who are brought to thy holy baptism"; for this is true, and the utmost simplicity and truth are appropriate in these mysteries.[1]

xiii. *On the Exorcism*

This practice of exorcizing those who are to be baptized is also very ancient: but nothing is to be preferred to that which is taught by scripture, the word of God, than which nothing is older. For there only those to whom has been given the gift of power are ordered to adjure demons, and these are ordered to expel demons not from any men but only from demoniacs: and, thanks be to God, such are not all men, nor indeed many of those who are brought or who come to baptism. For if you wished to treat as a demoniac every man that is not living in Christ the Lord, and is therefore still subject to the power of

---

[1] For the notice taken of Bucer's comments in the Prayer Book of 1552 see below, p. 107.

evil spirits, you will thereby reduce to nothing the miracles of the Lord
and of the apostles, which they performed in the expulsion of evil spirits
from men.

So these words of exorcism and adjuration against evil spirits require to be changed to words of prayer, perhaps after some such
fashion as this: Eternal Son of God, who hast conquered all the power
of evil spirits by thy death, drive away from this infant whom thou
hast vouchsafed to call to thy holy baptism, so that he may become a
member of thy body, all the deceit and violence of Satan and of his
angels, and bring him, freed from the power of darkness, into the
kingdom of thy beloved Son, so that no unclean spirits can ever harm
him either in body or in soul, for the glory of thy name. Amen.[1]

xiv. *On the Catechizing of those to be baptized.*

Here the godfathers and godmothers are ordered to renounce Satan,
and profess the faith on behalf of the infants, so that while they ask the
infants whether they renounce the devil and his works, etc., and
whether they believe in God the Father, and the Son and the Holy
Spirit, they themselves reply in the place of the infants. But however
ancient this observance is, scripture does not teach it; and there is no
inherent reason why you should question him who does not understand what you say, and why another in his stead should answer what
he perceives thereof, and why you should do this in the most important matters, and in matters which especially depend upon the personal
faith of everyone, as for instance the renunciation of Satan and his en-
deavours and the profession of faith in God.

A matter not altogether dissimilar and rightly to be abominated is
narrated by St Chrysostom about the Marcionites in his commentary
on the 15th chapter of the First Epistle to the Corinthians, on that verse,
Else what do they do who are baptized for the dead, etc.? For he writes
that these heretics, when one of their catechumens died, were accustomed to hide somebody under the bed of the dead person, and then to
ask the dead person whether he wished to be baptized: when the latter
said nothing seeing that he was dead, the person who lay hid under the
bed replied in his stead that he wished it: then they baptized this person
on behalf of the dead one. And Chrysostom writes that they had
as it were taken part in a play.

---

[1] A brief exorcism had been retained in the *Consultation*; above, p. 65. Either Hermann
had ordered Bucer not to abolish exorcism altogether from the *Consultation*, and Bucer
had reluctantly obeyed, or Bucer had changed his mind on this subject.

How much does this catechizing of our infants, in which the infants are questioned and the sponsors reply in their stead, differ from this madness of the Marcionites? True, the infants are alive; but they hardly understand either about the questions which are put to them by the ministers, or about the responses which are given on their behalf by the godfathers and godmothers. And this preposterous way of going on has given no little occasion to very many people to turn all the more quickly to the sect of the Anabaptists, so far as the baptism of infants is concerned.

It was a practice rightly observed among the ancients and to be observed today, that no adult be baptized, unless when thus questioned he replied in person about his faith. But what has this to do with infants who cannot even understand anything, nor speak?

I would wish, therefore, that all those questions in this catechism—I don't know why it is so called—should be addressed to the godfathers and godmothers themselves, in some such manner as this: Will you for your part faithfully undertake that this infant, when he is of an age, shall learn the catechism of our religion, and, having learnt that, shall renounce Satan and profess his belief in God the Father and the Son, etc.? If this alteration of this passage found favour, it should thus be altered: and the following exhortation to the godfathers and godmothers, as it is most godly and vitally necessary, ought therefore not to be read as it were in passing by the ministers, but be commended with the utmost seriousness to the sponsors and enjoined upon them.

But it ought to be thought sufficient if they from their heart promise all possible diligence in this matter. For these things are done in the sight of God, and these promises are made to God. So the greatest care must be taken that nothing be said or done here thoughtlessly, and in the manner of the vulgar people, and not straight and altogether from the heart, as in the presence of God. Always it must be seen that we only undertake and do those things which the law of God teaches us, which are true, which are serious, and which build up faith in Christ.

xv. *On the conferring of baptism on ailing infants in private*

In this ordinance everything is well arranged: would that it may be kept so, and especially that rule that the baptism of infants be not deferred. For when that happens, a way is opened to the devil to introduce contempt for the church and as a result for all Christ's redemption and fellowship, which through the sect of the Anabaptists has in a too undesirable manner gained currency among very many people.

8—C.I.

But on the point that the godfathers and godmothers are questioned and reply concerning the infants' faith in the place of the infants, I have already explained a little way back why and how I wish a change to be made.

xvi. *On the Consecration of Baptism*

What evil Satan has introduced into the churches of Christ through these blessings and consecrations of inanimate objects I have touched upon in a certain passage where I dealt above with that prayer in the Communion for the blessing and sanctifying of the bread and wine. For it is agreed how magical a change in things these blessings have been distorted to make men believe. Since, therefore, no scripture teaches them, and the actual words of these prayers altogether suggest that God must impart some power immanent in these things, I do not see on what ground in this great light of the gospel, and in the great liberty which the Lord has given this kingdom of establishing everything in accordance with its doctrine, blessings of this kind can be retained. Our sacraments exist in the use: they are actions in which the Lord imparts remission of sins and fellowship with himself to his people, not to water, not to bread and wine: and that too when these signs with his word conjoined with them are exhibited in accordance with his commands, and apart from this usage they are taken as bread and wine and water. Granted that these kinds of consecrations of things are exceedingly ancient, yet how much more ancient than them is the word of God? Always we must observe what truly profits for edification.

For there are ever so many decisions and practices of the holy fathers concerning the discipline of the church, which have been derived from the word of God itself. These, alas, are most recklessly, not to say wantonly, trampled under foot, when they seem to conflict with our wishes. How preposterous, therefore, would it be for religion to abolish those rites which were accepted by the ancients but which are not agreeable with the word of God, and also in the case of too many people assist Satan to establish the most evident superstitions and clearly magical opinions? To this tends that blessing of the water of baptism in so far as, when people are baptized in some ordinary water, they are not believed to have received such a good and holy baptism as those who are baptized in consecrated water, and not without reason. For either that special consecration of the water adds something to baptism which is not in the water, or it adds nothing. If nothing, it is not suitable in the churches of Christ because it is useless. If something, how shall we make good this omission in the case of those who are baptized in common water? For it is not right that they should be rebaptized.[1]

---

[1] The first prayer in the 1549 blessing of the font had included an invocation of the Holy Spirit and the petition, "Sanctify ✠ this fountain of baptism . . ."; below, p. 154. For the treatment of the blessing of the font in 1552 see below, p. 109.

20. *Baptism in the Prayer Book of 1552*

THE MINISTRATION OF BAPTISM
TO BE USED IN THE CHURCH

It appeareth by ancient writers that the sacrament of baptism in the old time was not commonly ministered but at two times in the year, at Easter and Whitsuntide. At which times it was openly ministered in the presence of all the congregation: which custom now being grown out of use, although it cannot for many considerations be well restored again, yet it is thought good to follow the same as near as conveniently may be: wherefore the people are to be admonished that it is most convenient that baptism should not be ministered but upon Sundays, and other holy days, when the most number of people may come together, as well for that the congregation there present may testify the receiving of them that be newly baptized into the number of Christ's church, as also because in the baptism of infants every man present may be put in remembrance of his own profession made to God in his baptism. For which cause also it is expedient that baptism be ministered in the English tongue. Nevertheless, if necessity so require, children may at all times be baptized at home.[1]

When there are children to be baptized upon the Sunday or holy day the parents shall give knowledge over night or in the morning, afore the beginning of Morning prayer to the curate. And then the godfathers, godmothers and people with the children must be ready at the font,[2] either immediately after the last lesson at Morning prayer,[3] or else immediately after the last lesson at Evening prayer,[4] as the curate by his discretion shall appoint. And then standing there, the priest shall ask whether the children be baptized or no. If they answer, No, then shall the priest say thus:

Dearly beloved, forasmuch as all men be conceived and born in sin, and that our Saviour Christ saith none can enter into the kingdom of God, except he be regenerate and born anew of water and the Holy Ghost, I beseech you to call upon God the Father through our Lord Jesus Christ, that of his bounteous mercy he will grant to these children that thing which by nature they cannot have, that they may be baptized with water and[5] the Holy Ghost, and received into Christ's holy church, and be made lively members of the same.

Then the priest shall say:

Let us pray.

Almighty[6] and everlasting God, which of thy great mercy didst save Noah and his family in the ark from perishing by water, and also didst

---

[1] This last sentence is an abbreviated version of that in the 1549 Book; above, p. 89.
[2] 1549: "at the church door". At Bucer's suggestion (above, p. 99) the service at the church door was abolished, and therefore the revised rite of baptism began at the font.
[3] 1549: "Mattins".   [4] 1549: "Evensong".   [5] "water and" inserted in 1552.
[6] This is a revised form of the prayer in 1549; above, pp. 89f.

safely lead the children of Israel, thy people, through the Red Sea, figuring thereby thy holy baptism, and by the baptism of thy well beloved Son, Jesus Christ, didst sanctify the flood Jordan and all other waters to the mystical washing away of sin:[1] we beseech thee for thy infinite mercies that thou wilt mercifully look upon these children, sanctify them and wash them with thy Holy Ghost, that they, being delivered from thy wrath, may be received into the ark of Christ's church, and being stedfast in faith, joyful through hope, and rooted in charity, may so pass the waves of this troublesome world, that finally they may come to the land of everlasting life, there to reign with thee, world without end: through Jesus Christ our Lord. Amen.

Almighty and immortal God, the aid of all that need, the helper of all that flee[2] to thee for succour, the life of them that believe, and the resurrection of the dead: we call upon thee for these infants, that they coming to thy holy baptism,[3] may receive remission of their sins by spiritual regeneration. Receive them, O Lord, as thou hast promised by thy well beloved Son, saying, Ask and you shall have, seek and you shall find, knock and it shall be opened unto you. So give now unto us that ask: let us that seek find: open the gate unto us that knock, that these infants may enjoy the everlasting benediction of thy heavenly washing, and may come to the eternal kingdom, which thou hast promised by Christ our Lord. Amen.[4]

Then shall the priest say:

Hear the words of the gospel, written by Saint Mark in the tenth chapter.

At a certain time they brought children to Christ that he should touch them, and his disciples rebuked those that brought them. But when Jesus saw it, he was displeased, and said unto them: Suffer little children to come unto me, and forbid them not; for to such belongeth the kingdom of God. Verily I say unto you: whosoever doth not receive the kingdom of God as a little child, he shall not enter therein. And when he had taken them up in his arms, he put his hands upon them, and blessed them.

After the gospel is read, the minister shall make this brief exhortation upon the words of the gospel:

Friends, you hear in this gospel the words of our Saviour Christ, that he commanded the children to be brought unto him, how he blamed

[1] *Pace* Bucer; above, p. 100.   [2] 1559: "fly".   [3] *Pace* Bucer; above, p. 101.
[4] At this point in 1549 there followed the exorcism of the child. This was abandoned in 1552 in accordance with Bucer's recommendation; above, pp. 101f.

those that would have kept them from him, how he exhorteth all men to follow their innocency. You perceive how by his outward gesture and deed he declared his good will toward them. For he embraced them in his arms, he laid his hands upon them, and blessed them. Doubt not ye, therefore, but earnestly believe, that he will likewise favourably receive these present infants, that he will embrace them with the arms of his mercy, that he will give unto them the blessing of eternal life, and make them partakers of his everlasting kingdom. Wherefore we being thus persuaded of the good will of our heavenly Father towards these infants, declared by his Son, Jesus Christ, and nothing doubting but that he favourably alloweth this charitable work of ours in bringing these children to his holy baptism, let us faithfully and devoutly give thanks unto him, and say:[1]

Almighty and everlasting God, heavenly Father, we give thee humble thanks that thou hast vouchsafed to call us to the knowledge of thy grace and faith in thee: increase this knowledge,[2] and confirm this faith in us evermore: give thy Holy Spirit to these infants that they may be born again, and be made heirs of everlasting salvation: through our Lord Jesus Christ who liveth and reigneth with thee and the Holy Spirit now and for ever. Amen.

Then the priest shall speak unto the godfathers and godmothers on this wise:

Well beloved friends, ye have brought these children here to be baptized; ye have prayed that our Lord Jesus Christ would vouchsafe to receive them, to lay his hands upon them, to bless them, to release them of their sins, to give them the kingdom of heaven and everlasting life. Ye have heard also that our Lord Jesus Christ hath promised in his gospel to grant all these things that ye have prayed for: which promise he for his part will most surely keep and perform. Wherefore after this promise made by Christ these infants must also faithfully for their part promise by you that be their sureties that they will forsake the devil and all his works, and constantly believe God's holy word, and obediently keep his commandments.

Then shall the priest demand of the godfathers and godmothers[3] these questions following:

Dost thou forsake the devil and all his works, the vain pomp and glory of the world with all covetous desires of the same, the carnal desires of the flesh, so that thou wilt not follow nor be led by them?

---

[1] In 1549 the recitation of the Lord's prayer and creed followed here.

[2] "this knowledge" was inserted here in 1552.

[3] In response to Bucer's criticism (above, pp. 102f) the questions which in 1549 were addressed to the child (above, p. 93) are here addressed to the godparents.

Answer: I forsake them all.

Minister: Dost thou believe in God the Father almighty, maker of
heaven and earth? And in Jesus Christ, his only begotten Son, our
Lord, and that he was conceived by the Holy Ghost, born of the
Virgin Mary, that he suffered under Pontius Pilate, was crucified,
dead and buried, that he went down into hell, and also did rise again
the third day; that he ascended into heaven, and sitteth at the right
hand of God the Father almighty, and from thence shall come again
at the end of the world to judge the quick and the dead;

And dost thou believe in the Holy Ghost, the holy catholic church,
the communion of saints, the remission of sins, the resurrection of
the flesh and everlasting life after death?

Answer: All this I stedfastly believe.

Minister: Wilt thou be baptized in this faith?

Answer: That is my desire.

Then the priest shall say:

O merciful God, grant that the old Adam in these children may be so
buried, that the new man may be raised up in them. Amen.[1]

Grant that all carnal affections may die in them, and that all things
belonging to the Spirit may live and grow in them. Amen.

Grant that they may have power and strength to have victory and to
triumph against the devil, the world and the flesh. Amen.

Grant that whosoever is here dedicated to thee by our office and
ministry may also be endued with heavenly virtues and everlastingly rewarded through thy mercy, O blessed Lord God, who dost live and
govern all things world without end. Amen.

Almighty everliving God, whose most dearly beloved Son, Jesus
Christ, for the forgiveness of our sins did shed out of his most precious
side both water and blood, and gave commandment to his disciples
that they should go teach all nations, and baptize them in the name of
the Father, the Son and the Holy Ghost; regard, we beseech thee, the
supplications of thy congregation; and grant that all thy servants which
shall be baptized in this water may receive the fulness of thy grace, and
ever remain in the number of thy faithful and elect children; through
Jesus Christ our Lord. Amen.[2]

---

[1] There were more of these short prayers in 1549; below, p. 155.

[2] This is the final prayer from the 1549 blessing of the font, but without the words
"prepared for the ministration of thy holy sacrament" after "water". Thus in 1552, as
Bucer wished (above, p. 104), all suggestion that the water is consecrated has been removed.

Then the priest shall take the child in his hands, and ask the name, and naming the child shall dip it in the water, so it be discreetly and warily done, saying:[1]

N., I baptize thee in the name of the Father and of the Son and of the Holy Ghost. Amen.

And if the child be weak, it shall suffice to pour water upon it, saying the foresaid words:

N., I baptize thee in the name of the Father and of the Son and of the Holy Ghost. Amen.

Then the priest shall make a cross upon the child's forehead, saying:

We receive this child into the congregation of Christ's flock, and do sign him with the sign of the cross, in token that hereafter he shall not be ashamed to confess the faith of Christ crucified, and manfully to fight under his banner against sin, the world and the devil, and to continue Christ's faithful soldier and servant unto his life's end. Amen.[2]

Then shall the priest say:

Seeing now, dearly beloved brethren, that these children be regenerate and grafted into the body of Christ's congregation, let us give thanks unto God for these benefits, and with one accord make our prayers unto almighty God, that they may lead the rest of their life according to this beginning.

Then shall be said:

Our Father, which art in heaven, etc. . . .[3]

Then shall the priest say:

We[4] yield thee hearty thanks, most merciful Father, that it hath pleased thee to regenerate this infant with thy Holy Spirit, to receive him for thy own child by adoption, and to incorporate him into thy

[1] In this rite this is the first time that the child is called by his name, whereas in 1549 the name was used during the service at the church door. Hence the 1552 rite gave more occasion for the ignorant to equate christening with naming; see Fisher, op. cit., pp. 149–157.

[2] In 1549 this prayer and consignation formed part of the service at the church door, and was therefore distinctly separated from the actual baptism; above, p. 90. When in 1552 the service at the church door was abolished, this consignation was removed from among the introductory prayers, and placed immediately after the baptism itself in such close juxtaposition that it has become possible for the ignorant to mistake it for the essential act of baptism. The vesting in a white robe and the anointing with chrism, which in 1549 followed the actual baptism, were abolished in 1552, as Bucer had recommended; above, pp. 99f.

[3] In 1549 the Lord's prayer was said during the service at the church door: above, p. 92. Here, as in the 1552 order of communion, the Lord's prayer introduces the thanksgiving after the reception of the sacrament.

[4] This prayer was not in 1549.

holy congregation. And humbly we beseech thee to grant that he, being dead unto sin, and living unto righteousness, and being buried with Christ in his death, may crucify the old man, and utterly abolish the whole body of sin, that as he is made partaker of the death of thy Son, so he may be partaker of his resurrection, so that finally with the residue of thy holy congregation he may be inheritor of thine everlasting kingdom: through Christ our Lord. Amen.

At the last end the priest, calling the godfathers and godmothers together, shall say this short exhortation following:

Forasmuch as these children have promised by you to forsake the devil and all his works, to believe in God and to serve him, you must remember that it is your parts and duties to see that these infants be taught, so soon as they shall be able to learn, what a solemn vow, promise and profession they have made by you. And that they may know these things the better, ye shall call upon them to hear sermons: and chiefly ye shall provide that they may learn the creed, the Lord's prayer and the ten commandments in the English tongue, and all other things which a Christian man ought to know and believe to his soul's health: and that these children may be virtuously brought up to lead a godly and Christian life, remembering always that baptism doth represent unto us our profession which is to follow the example of our Saviour Christ, and to be made like unto him, that as he died and rose again for us, so should we which are baptized die from sin and rise again unto righteousness, continually mortifying all our evil and corrupt affections, and daily proceeding in all virtue and godliness of living.

The minister shall command that the children be brought to the bishop to be confirmed of him, so soon as they can say in their vulgar tongue the articles of the faith, the Lord's prayer and the x commandments, and be further instructed in the catechism set forth for that purpose, accordingly as it is there expressed.

21. *Calvin and Baptism*

On 19 April 1538, the Council of Geneva resolved to adopt the more conservative customs of the Church of Berne, and to compel their ministers to conform to them. When Calvin, who had been a lecturer at the cathedral since September 1536, refused to obey, he was banished from the city, and the following August at the invitation of Bucer settled in Strassburg for the time being. From 8 September 1538, Calvin was pastor of a congregation of French refugees at St Nicholas', in January the next year becoming a lecturer in theology.

In 1540 the party in Geneva which had been responsible for Calvin's expulsion lost its control of the city, severe measures being taken against some of its members. Consequently on 22 October that year Calvin was invited to return—a request to which he did not accede until 30 September 1541. Arrived back in Geneva, and in undisputed command, Calvin soon drew up a new ecclesiastical constitution.[1]

The order of baptism to be used in Geneva was included in the *Form of Prayers . . .*, published in 1542.[2] In his letter of farewell addressed to the ministers of Geneva on 28 April 1564, Calvin wrote, "I was constrained also to compile the form of baptism while I was at Strassburg, and they brought to me the children of the Anabaptists from five to ten leagues around to baptize."[3]

This rite of baptism was, as Calvin himself said, his own work, not derived from the rite which Bucer was using in Strassburg in the German speaking Church, nor from any other reformed rite. Although Bucer can hardly have failed to exercise some influence upon Calvin, there is little in Calvin's rite of baptism which can be attributed directly to Bucer's personal influence, unless it be the requirement that baptism should be administered at sermon time when a congregation was present,[4] or the emphasis laid upon the need to do all for the edification of the people.

Although in October 1548 Calvin wrote at great length to the Lord Protector, Somerset, expressing his views on the sacraments and much else, and also wrote to Bucer, now in England, and Cranmer, urging them to abolish all superstitious rites and ceremonies, there is nothing in the orders of baptism in the Prayer Books of 1549 and 1552, which can be shown to be derived from Calvin. Indeed Calvin's rite of baptism, it will be seen, bears no close resemblance to the Anglican or Lutheran rites.[5]

[1] See *Works*, XXI (C.R., XLIX), pp. 204, 224–7, 235, 258, 282.
[2] See W. D. Maxwell, *The Liturgical Portions of the Genevan Service Book* (London 1965), p. 70.
[3] See B. J. Kidd, *Documents illustrative of the Continental Reformation* (Oxford 1911), no. 318, p. 650.
[4] Compare the opening rubrics of the Strassburg rite of 1537; above, p. 38.
[5] See Procter, op. cit., p. 48.

The first English translation of the *Form of Prayers* was made by William Huycke, and published in London on 7 June 1550. We have, however, not reproduced here Huycke's own translation, because he did not translate the first French edition of 1542,[1] which we have preferred to use.

THE FORM OF
PRAYERS AND ECCLESIASTICAL CHANTS
WITH THE MANNER OF
ADMINISTERING THE SACRAMENTS AND
SOLEMNIZING MARRIAGE
ACCORDING TO THE CUSTOM OF
THE ANCIENT CHURCH, 1542

It is to be noted that children must be brought to baptism either on Sunday at the time of the catechism, or on other days at the sermon, so that as baptism is a solemn reception into the church it may take place in the presence of the congregation.

(Huycke's version of this rubric from a later edition is as follows:

Wherein this is to be noted, that they ought to bring the children to be baptized, either, if they happen to be born on the Sunday, to the sermon after dinner which is called the catechism, either, if it be born on the working day, to one of the morning sermons: whereby baptism, as it is a solemn usage and sacrament received in the church, so it may be celebrated in the presence of the congregation. And at such times, the sermon being ended, they present the child or children before the pulpit, where the priest, after the presence of the father demanded, beginneth on this wise:)

The sermon ended, the infant is presented. And then the Minister begins to say:

Our help be in the name of God who has made heaven and earth. Amen. Do you present this child to be baptized?

They reply:

Yes.

The minister:

Our lord shows us in what poverty and misery we are all born, telling us that we must be born again. For if it is necessary that our nature be renewed in order to have admission to the kingdom of God, this is a proof that it is altogether corrupt and accursed. In that, then, he admonishes us to humble ourselves and to be displeased with ourselves: and in this way he prepares us to desire and seek his grace, by which all

[1] See Maxwell, op. cit., p. 71.
[2] From *Calvini Opera* VI, C.R. XXXIV, cols. 185–92.

the corruption and accursedness of our first nature can be abolished. For we are quite incapable of receiving it unless we first be emptied of all trust in our own virtue, wisdom and righteousness, so far as to condemn all that is in us.

But, after he has shown us our wretched condition, he consoles us accordingly by his pity, promising us to regenerate us by his Holy Spirit into a new life, which may be to us for an entry into his kingdom. This regeneration consists in two parts: namely, that we renounce ourselves not following our own reason, our pleasure and own will, but, subjugating and enslaving our desire and our heart to the wisdom and righteousness of God, we mortify all that is of us and of our flesh: and secondly that we follow the light of God to comply with and obey his good pleasure, as he shows it to us by his word, and leads us and directs us to it by his Spirit. The fulfilment of the one and of the other is in our Lord Jesus, whose death and passion has such power and efficacy, that in partaking in it we are as it were buried to sin, so that our carnal desires are mortified. Likewise by the power of his resurrection we rise to a new life which is of God, seeing that his Spirit leads us and governs us, to perform in us the works which are agreeable to him. Always the first and the principal point of our salvation is that by his mercy he remits for us and pardons all our faults, not imputing them to us at all, but blotting out their memory, so that they are in no wise reckoned against us in his judgment. All these graces are conferred on us, when it pleases him to incorporate us in his church by baptism. For in this sacrament he testifies to us the remission of our sins. And for this cause he has appointed the sign of water, to signify to us that, as by this element the bodily defilements are cleansed, so he wishes to wash and purify our souls, so that no more may there appear any stain in them. Again, he there represents to us our renewal, which consists, as has already been said, in the mortification of our flesh, and the spiritual life which it engenders and excites in us.

Thus we receive twofold grace and benefit from our God in baptism, provided that we do not destroy the force of this sacrament by our ingratitude. That is, we have in it sure testimony that God wishes to be a merciful Father to us, not imputing to us all our faults and offences: secondly that he will assist us by his Holy Spirit, so that we can do battle against the devil, sin, and the desires of our flesh, until we have victory over them, so as to live in the liberty of his kingdom, which is the kingdom of righteousness.

Since then it is so, that these two things are accomplished in us by the grace of Jesus Christ, it follows that the truth and substance of baptism consists in him. For we have no other washing but his blood, and we have no other renewal but in his death and resurrection. But as he imparts to us his riches and blessings by his word, so he distributes them to us by his sacraments.

But our good God, not content himself with having adopted us for his children, and received us into the communion of his church, has wished to extend yet more fully his bounty towards us, that is, in promising that he will be our God and the God of our offspring to a thousand generations. However, although the infant children of the faithful are of the corrupt race of Adam, yet he does not at all refuse to accept them, for the sake of his covenant, so as to count them among the number of his children. For this reason he has wished from the beginning that in his church infants should receive the sign of circumcision, by which he represented then all that is today signified to us by baptism. And as he commanded that they should be circumcised, so he owned them for his children, and said that he would be their God, as he was of their fathers.

Now then, since the Lord Jesus has come down to earth not to lessen the grace of God, his Father, but to extend over all the world the covenant of salvation, which was formerly confined to the Jewish people, there is no doubt that our children are heirs of the life which he has promised us. For this reason St Paul says that God sanctifies them from their mother's womb, to separate and distinguish them from the children of pagans and infidels. For this reason our Lord Jesus Christ received the children when they were presented to him, as it is written in the nineteenth chapter of St Matthew: Then were presented to him. . . .

Since he declares that the kingdom of heaven belongs to them, and lays his hands on them and commends them to God, his Father, he teaches us sufficiently that we must by no means exclude them from his church. So following this rule, we will receive this infant into his church to make him a partaker in all the benefits which he has promised to his faithful ones. And first we will present him to God by our prayer, saying from the heart humbly:

Lord God, Father eternal and almighty, since it has pleased thee by thine infinite mercy to promise us that thou wilt be our God and the God of our children, we pray thee that it may please thee to confirm this grace in this present infant, born of a father and mother whom thou hast called into thy church, and, as he is offered and consecrated to thee by us, that thou wouldest receive him into thy holy protection, declaring thyself to be his God and Saviour, remitting to him the original sin of which the whole lineage of Adam is guilty, and then afterwards sanctifying him by thy Spirit, so that when he comes to the age of understanding, he may know and adore thee as his only God, glorifying thee all through his life, so as to obtain evermore from thee remission of his sins. And so that he can obtain such graces, may it please thee to incorporate him in the fellowship of our Lord Jesus to be a partaker of all his benefits, as one of the members of his body. Grant us, Father of mercy, that the baptism which we minister to him according to thine ordinance may bring forth its fruit and virtue, such as has been declared to us by thy gospel:

Our Father, who art in heaven, etc.

Since it is a matter of receiving this infant into the company of the Christian church, do you promise, when he comes to the age of discretion, to instruct him in the doctrine which is received among the people of God, as it is briefly summarized in the confession of faith which we all have.

I believe in God the Father, etc.

You promise then to take trouble to instruct him in all this doctrine, and generally in all that is contained in the holy scripture of the Old and New Testament, to the end that he may receive it as the sure word of God, coming from heaven. Also you will exhort him to live according to the rule which our Lord has set forth for us in his law, which briefly consists in these two points, that we love God with all our mind, our heart and strength, and our neighbour as ourselves. Likewise, according to the exhortations which he has given by his prophets and apostles, that renouncing himself and his own desires, he may devote himself and consecrate himself to glorify the name of God and of Jesus Christ and to edify his neighbours.[1]

After the promise made, the name is given to the child, and then the minister baptizes him:

In the name of the Father and of the Son and of the Holy Spirit.[2]

All is said in a loud voice in the common tongue, so that the people who are present there may be witnesses to what is done there, for which understanding is required, and also so that all may be edified, by recognizing and recalling to memory what is the fruit and use of their baptism.

We know that elsewhere many other ceremonies are used, which we do not deny to have been very ancient; but because they have been invented at will, or at

[1] Edification is one of Bucer's favourite themes; above, pp. 57, 104.
[2] The full formula is given in all editions after 1558.

least for some slight consideration, whatever it may be, since they have not been founded upon the word of God, and furthermore seeing that so many superstitions have arisen out of them, we have had no hesitation in abolishing them, so that there might be no more impediment to prevent the people from going directly to Jesus Christ. First with regard to what is not commanded us by God we are free to choose. Again all that serves in no way to edification must not be received in the church: and if it has been introduced, it must be cast out. For a much stronger reason all that only serves to give offence and is the means of idolatry and false opinions, must not be tolerated at all. But it is certain that the chrism, candle and other such pomps are not of God's ordinance, but have been added by men: and finally they have come to this, that people are more attracted by them and hold them in greater esteem than the ordinances of Jesus Christ. At least we have such a form of baptism as Jesus Christ has ordered, as the apostles have preserved and followed, as the primitive church has used, and we cannot be criticized on any other point, save that we do not wish to be wiser than God himself.

22. Knox and Baptism

When Mary Tudor came to the throne of England in October 1553, John Knox was one of many who fled to the continent to escape persecution for their religious opinions. At first he lived in Frankfurt among a group of about two hundred exiles from England. When in March 1555 his extreme views led to his banishment from Frankfurt, he removed to Geneva, where he received a sympathetic welcome from Calvin. Here in 1556 Knox became the minister of a congregation of refugees from England, continuing in this office until 1559, when the changed religious situation brought about by the accession of Elizabeth to the throne made it safe for him to return to Scotland.[1]

Knox's views on baptism were characterized by a violent aversion to the Latin rite, as the following quotations show.

In 1547 in his *Disputation with Friar Arbuckill* he wrote on the subject of ceremonies: "Such as God has ordained we allow, and with reverence we use them. But the question is of those that God has not ordained, such as, in baptism, are spittle, salt, candle, cuide (except it be to keep the bairn from cold), hards, oil, and the rest of the Papistical inventions."[2]

In his *Answers to some Questions concerning Baptism*, published in 1556, he wrote thus: "The baptism now used in the Papistry is not the true baptism which Christ Jesus did institute, and command to be used in his kirk; but it is an adulteration and profanation of the same, and therefore is to be avoided of all God's children. . . . That it is adulterate, and so consequently profane, is evident: first, for many things be added, besides Christ's institution; and all men's addition in God's perfect ordinance, especially in his religion, are execrable and detestable before him. Secondly, the promises of salvation in Christ Jesus are not in the Papistical baptism lively and truly explained to the people; the word is not preached; yea, that which they read is not understand. The end and use of a true sacrament is not considered, but rather are the people led to put their confidence in the bare ceremony. . . . Yea, farther, who offereth their children to the papistical baptism, offereth them not to God, nor to Christ Jesus his Son, but to the devil, chief author and inventor of such abominations.

"Shall we be baptized again (do some demand), that in our infancy were polluted with that adulterate sign? I answer, Nay, for the spirit of regeneration, which is freely given to us by Christ Jesus our all sufficiency, hath purged us from that poison which we drank in the days of our blindness. The fire of the Holy Ghost hath burnt away whatsoever we received at their hands besides Christ Jesus' simple institution. . . . And in very deed, the malice of the devil could never altogether abolish Christ's institution, for it was ministered unto

---

[1] See Maxwell, op. cit., pp. 3–6.
[2] *Works*, I (1846), *The History of the Reformation in Scotland*, p. 197.

us, 'In the name of the Father, of the Son, and the Holy Ghost'. And yet for that time, I confess, by reason of our blindness, it did not profit us, because it was adulterate, and mixed with men's dreams and fantasies. I confess, for the time it did not profit us; but now, as said is, the Spirit of Christ Jesus illuminating our hearts, hath purged the same by faith, and maketh the effect of that sacrament to work in us without any iteration of the external sign. . . .

"We have some respect also, that no more be given to the external sign, than is proper to it, that is, that it be the seal of justice and the sign of regeneration, but neither the cause, neither yet the effect and virtue. The seal once received is durable, and needeth not to be iterate, lest that by iteration and multiplication of the sign, the office of the Holy Spirit, which is to illuminate, regenerate, and to purge, be attributed unto it. . . ."[1]

During his years in Geneva Knox used an order of baptism plainly derived, and not surprisingly, from Calvin's rite. We give here the text of Knox's rite, as edited by Maxwell;[2] but we have altered the sixteenth-century spelling of words.

THE ORDER OF BAPTISM

First note, that forasmuch as it is not permitted by God's word that women should preach or minister the sacraments:[3] and it is evident that the sacraments are not ordained of God to be used in private corners, as charms or sorceries, but left to the congregation and necessarily annexed to God's word, as seals of the same: therefore the infant, which is to be baptized, shall be brought to the church on the day appointed to common prayer and preaching, accompanied with the father and

---

[1] *Works*, ed. David Laing (Edinburgh 1855), IV, pp. 119–22.

[2] Op. cit., pp. 105–11.

[3] In early times the church of Carthage had a similar objection to baptism by women; see Tertullian, *de Baptismo* 17, ed. E. Evans (London 1964), p. 36. See also *Statuta Ecclesiae Antiqua* (5th century), c. 37, in C. Munier, *Concilia Galliae A. 314–A. 506* (Turnhout 1963), p. 172. The *Sarum Manual* contained a rubric that *"if a man and a woman should be present when the need to baptize a child became urgent, and no other minister more suitable for this task were present, let the man baptize and not the woman, unless the woman happened to know well the sacramental words and not the man, or there were some other impediment"* (tr. Fisher, op. cit., p. 177). A sixteenth-century Council at Malines ordered midwives to see that all children delivered by them were baptized within a week of birth; see Mansi, 36B. 128. See also *Brandenburg–Nuremberg Church Order*; below, p. 135.

Calvin's views about baptism by women were expressed in his *Second Defence of the Sacraments, in answer to the Calumnies of Westphal*, published in 1556. (Joachim Westphal was a minister in Hamburg, who attacked Calvin's sacramental doctrine, accusing him of heresy.) Calvin wrote: "It is here worth while to touch, in passing, on the particular things at which he expressly carps. The first is, that we sometimes allow children to die unbaptized. What is the fault he finds here, but just that we do not resign the office of baptizing to silly women? Assuredly, if any one neglects to present his children early to baptism, he is severely rebuked for his negligence. The church is open every day. If any man's child die without baptism, because he did not embrace the opportunity, he is censured. The only thing wanting to us is, that women do not, without any command from Christ, seize upon the solemn office of pastors. Joachim holds the necessity for baptism to be so absolute, that he would sooner have it profaned by illicit usurpation, than omitted when the lawful use is denied. The thing that offends him he immediately after discloses. It is because we give hopes that infants may obtain salvation without baptism, because we hold that baptism, instead of regenerating or saving them, only seals the salvation of which they were previously partakers." Knox's rubric shows that he shared Calvin's views on this matter.

9—C.I.

godfather.[1] So that after the sermon the child being presented to the minister, he demandeth this question:

Do you present this child to be baptized, earnestly desiring that he may be ingrafted in the mystical body of Jesus Christ?

The answer:

Yea, we require the same.

The minister proceedeth:

Then let us consider, dearly beloved, how almighty God hath not only made us his children by adoption and received us into the fellowship of his church: but also hath promised that he will be our God, and the God of our children unto the thousand generation.

Which thing as he confirmed to his people of the Old Testament by the sacrament of circumcision, so hath he also renewed the same to us, in his New Testament by the sacrament of baptism, doing us thereby to wit, that our infants appertain to him by covenant and therefore ought not to be defrauded of those holy signs and badges whereby his children are known from infidels and pagans. Neither is it requisite that all those that receive this sacrament have the use of understanding and faith, but chiefly that they be contained under the name of God's people: so that remission of sins in the blood of Christ Jesus doth appertain to them by God's promise.

Which thing is most evident by Saint Paul, who pronounceth the children begotten and born either of the parents being faithful, to be clean and holy.

Also our Saviour Christ admitteth children to his presence, embracing and blessing them.

Which testimonies of the Holy Ghost assure us, that infants be of the number of God's people: and that remission of sins doth also appertain to them in Christ.

Therefore without injury they cannot be debarred from the common sign of God's children.

Neither yet is this outward action of such necessity, that the lack thereof should be prejudicial to their salvation, if that prevented by death they may not conveniently be presented to the church.

But we, having respect to that obedience which Christians owe to the voice and ordinance of Christ Jesus, who commanded to preach and baptize all without exception, do judge them only unworthy of any

[1] Notice that a godmother is not required.

fellowship with him, who contemptuously refuse such ordinary means, as his wisdom hath appointed to the instruction of our dull senses.

Furthermore, it is evident that baptism was ordained to be ministered in the element of water, to teach us that like as water outwardly doth wash away the filth of the body, so inwardly doth the virtue of Christ's blood purge our souls from that corruption and deadly poison wherewith by nature we were infected. Whose venomous dregs, although they continue in this our flesh, yet by the merits of his death are not imputed unto us, because the justice of Jesus Christ is made ours by baptism.

Not that we think any such virtue or power to be included in the visible water or outward action (for many have been baptized and yet never inwardly purged) but that our Saviour Christ, who commanded baptism to be ministered, will by the power of his Holy Spirit effectually work in the hearts of his elect in time convenient all that is meant and signified by the same. And this the scripture calleth our regeneration, which standeth chiefly in these two points, in mortification, that is to say, a resisting of the rebellious lusts of the flesh: and in newness of life, whereby we continually strive to walk in that pureness and perfection wherewith we are clad in baptism.

And although we in the journey of this life be encumbered with many enemies, which in the way assail us, yet fight we not without fruit. For this continual battle which we fight against sin, death and hell is a most infallible argument that God the Father, mindful of his promise made unto us in Christ Jesu, doth not only give us motions and courage to resist them, but also assurance to overcome and obtain victory. Wherefore, dearly beloved, it is not only of necessity that we be once baptized, but also it much profiteth oft to be present at the ministration thereof, that we, being put in mind of the league and covenant made betwixt God and us, that he will be our God, and we his people, he our Father, and we his children, may have occasion as well to try our lives past as our present conversation: and to prove ourselves, whether we stand fast in the faith of God's elect, or contrariwise have strayed from him through the incredulity and ungodly living: whereof if our consciences do accuse us, yet by hearing the loving promises of our heavenly Father, who calleth all men to mercy by repentance, we may from henceforth walk more warily in our vocation.

Moreover ye that be fathers and mothers may take hereby most singular comfort to see your children thus received into the bosom of

Christ's congregation, whereby you are daily admonished that ye nourish and bring up the children of God's favour and mercy, over whom his fatherly providence watcheth continually.

Which thing as it ought greatly to rejoice you, knowing that nothing can chance unto thee without his good pleasure, so ought it to make you diligent and careful to nurture and instruct them in the true knowledge and fear of God. Wherein if you be negligent, ye do not only injury to your own children hiding from them the good will and pleasure of almighty God their Father, but also heap damnation upon yourselves, in suffering his children bought with the blood of his dear Son so traitorously for lack of knowledge to turn back from him.

Therefore it is your duty with all diligence to provide that your children in time convenient be instructed in all doctrine necessary for a true Christian, chiefly that they be taught to rest upon the justice of Christ Jesus alone, and to abhor and flee all superstition, papistry, and idolatry. Finally, to the intent that we may be assured that you the father and the surety consent to the performance hereof, declare here before God and the face of his congregation the sum of that faith, wherein you believe, and will instruct this child.

Then the father or in his absence the godfather shall rehearse the articles of his faith, which done, the minister exhorting the people to pray, saith in this manner or such like kneeling:

Almighty and everlasting God, which of thy infinite mercy and goodness hast promised unto us that thou wilt not only be our God but also the God and Father of our children, we beseech thee that as thou hast vouchsafed to call us to be partakers of this thy great mercy in the fellowship of faith: so it may please thee to sanctify with thy Spirit, and to receive into the number of thy children, this infant, whom we shall baptize according to thy word, to the end that he coming to perfect age may confess thee only the true God, and whom thou hast sent Jesus Christ: and so serve him and be profitable unto his church in the whole course of his life, that after this life ended, he may be brought as a lively member of his body unto the full fruition of thy joys in the heavens, where thy Son our Christ reigneth world without end. In whose name we pray as he hath taught us:

Our Father, etc.

When they have prayed in this sort, the minister requireth the child's name, which known, he saith:

N., I baptize thee in the name of the Father and of the Son and of the Holy Ghost.

And as he speaketh these words, he taketh water in his hand and layeth it upon the child's forehead, which done he giveth thanks, as followeth:

Forasmuch, most holy and merciful Father, as thou dost not only beautify and bless us with common benefits, like unto the rest of mankind, but also heapest upon us most abundantly rare and wonderful gifts, of duty we lift up our eyes and minds unto thee, and give thee most humble thanks for thy infinite goodness, which hast not only numbered us amongst thy saints, but also of thy free mercy dost call our children unto thee, marking them with this sacrament as a singular token and badge of thy love. Wherefore most loving Father, though we be not able to deserve this so great a benefit (yea if thou wouldest handle us according to our merits, we should suffer the punishment of eternal death and damnation) yet for Christ's sake we beseech thee that thou wilt confirm this thy favour more and more towards us, and take this infant into thy tuition and defence, whom we offer and present unto thee with common supplications, and never suffer him to fall to such unkindness whereby he should lose the force of his baptism, but that he may perceive thee continually to be his merciful Father, through thy Holy Spirit working in his heart: by whose divine power he may so prevail against Satan that in the end, obtaining the victory, he may be exalted into the liberty of thy kingdom.[1]

---

[1] If this seems to be an abrupt conclusion, it should be remembered that baptism was administered in the course of the morning service, and there was more to follow, including a blessing. See Maxwell, op. cit., p. 120.

23. *The Book of Discipline*

In 1560 there appeared the first *Book of Discipline*, the object of which was to describe the manner in which the Reformed Church of Scotland should be governed. Although it lacked official authority, having been passed neither by the General Assembly nor by Parliament, it has a section on baptism, which throws further light on the state of contemporary opinion. It is published in Knox's *Works*, ed. Laing, II (1848), pp. 186, 211, 239f.

THE SECOND HEAD; OF SACRAMENTS

To Christ Jesus his holy evangel truly preached of necessity it is that his holy sacraments be annexed and truly ministered as seals and visible confirmations of the spiritual promises contained in the word: And they be two, to wit, baptism and the holy supper of the Lord Jesus: which are then rightly ministered, when by a lawful minister the people before the administration of the same are plainly instructed, and put in mind of God's free grace and mercy, offered unto the penitent in Christ Jesus; when God's promises are rehearsed, the end and use of the sacraments declared, and that in such a tongue as the people does understand; when farther to them is nothing added, from them nothing diminished, and in their practice nothing changed besides the institution of the Lord Jesus and practice of his holy apostles.

And albeit the Order of Geneva, which now is used in some of our kirks, is sufficient to instruct the diligent reader, how that both these sacraments may be rightly ministered, yet for one uniformity to be kept, we have thought good to add this as superabundant.

In baptism we acknowledge nothing to be used except the element of water only (that the word and declaration of the promises ought to precede we have said before). Wherefore whosoever presumeth in baptism to use oil, salt, wax, spittle, conjuration, or crossing accuseth the perfect institution of Christ Jesus of imperfection; for it was void of all such inventions devised by men. And such as would presume to alter Christ's perfect ordinance you ought severely to punish. . . .

A certain time must be appointed to reading and to learning of the catechism, and certain time to the grammar and to the Latin tongue, and certain time to the arts, philosophy and to the (other) tongues, and a certain to that study in which they intend chiefly to travel for the profit of the Commonwealth. Which time being expired, we mean in every course, the children must either proceed to farther knowledge, or else they must be sent to some handicraft, or to some other profitable exercise: provided always that first they have the form of knowledge of Christian religion, to wit, the knowledge of God's law and commandments, the use and office of the same, the chief articles of our belief, the right form to pray unto God, the number, use and effect of the sacraments, the true knowledge of Christ Jesus, of his office and natures, and such others [other points], as without the knowledge whereof neither deserveth any man to be named a Christian, neither ought any to be admitted to the participation of the Lord's Table. And therefore these principals ought and must be learned in the youth-hood. . . .

It appertaineth to the policy of the church to appoint the times when the sacraments shall be ministered. Baptism may be ministered whensoever the word is preached; but we think it more expedient that it be ministered upon the Sunday, or upon the day of prayers, only after the sermon, partly to remove this gross error by the which many deceived think that children be damned if they die without baptism; and partly to make the people assist the administration of that sacrament with greater reverence than they do. For we do see the people begin already to wax weary by reason of the frequent repetitions of these promises.

We think that none are apt to be admitted to that mystery (i.e. holy communion) who cannot formally say the Lord's prayer, the articles of belief, and declare the sum of the law.

24. Zwingli and Baptism

Zwingli (1484–1531) came to Zurich in 1518 as people's priest at the Great Minster, where his exposition of the New Testament aroused wide interest. Zurich was not openly won over to the Reformation until 1523, when Zwingli produced his Sixty-Seven Theses, and the Town Council decided to give him its support, with the result that the canton of Zurich broke away from the jurisdiction of the Bishop of Constance.

Among a number of reforms introduced that year was an order of infant baptism in the vernacular, first used by Leo Jud on 10 August. It will be seen that it retained many of the ceremonies of the old Latin rite to which the Reformers objected on the ground that they possessed no scriptural authority. No doubt it was deemed politic to introduce this fairly moderate measure of baptismal reform first as a preparation for something more drastic later.

A short and public form for the tender in faith for the baptism of children. Also other prayers to God to be used publicly in the Christian congregation.[1]

When anybody wishes to baptize a child, he breathes under his eyes and says:

Be gone, thou unclean spirit, and give place to the Holy Spirit, the Comforter.

Then he signs the child on the forehead and breast and says:

Accept the sign of the holy cross on thy forehead and breast, receive faith in the heavenly precepts, and so behave thyself that thou mayest be a temple and dwelling place of God.

A prayer.

Let us pray.

O almighty God, Father of our Lord Jesus Christ, who wouldest look upon this thy servant (*handmaid*), N., whom thou hast called to instruction in the faith, take away all blindness of heart from him: break all the snares of the devil with which he is bound: O Lord, open to him the door of thy goodness so that he, signed with the sign of thy wisdom, may be rid of the stench of all evil desires, and according to the sweet savour of thy commandments may joyfully serve thee in thy church [*Christenheit*], and may daily grow so that he may be made meet to

[1] *C.R.* 91, pp. 710–13.

come to the grace of thy baptism, to receive thy medicine: through Christ Jesus our Lord. Amen.

Then the priest puts salt in the child's mouth and says:

Receive the salt of wisdom, so that Christ may bring thee to eternal life. Peace be with thee and with thy spirit.

Let us pray.

Almighty, eternal God, who hast through the flood according to thy just judgment condemned the unbelieving world, and didst save faithful Noah the eighth person (2 Pet. 2.5), and didst drown hardhearted Pharaoh with all his in the Red Sea, and didst lead thy people Israel through it with dry feet, by which thou didst prefigure this bath of baptism: we pray thee of thine infinite mercy that thou wouldest graciously look upon this thy servant, N., and give the light of faith to his heart, that through this saving flood all that is born in him from Adam may be drowned and engulfed, that he, taken from the number of the unbelievers and children of wrath, may be graciously received by thee, O heavenly Father, for a child of thine, that, incorporated in thy Son by the cross and daily suffering, and buried with him, in fervent charity, firm hope and true faith he may without fear overcome death and come to eternal life: through the same our Lord Jesus Christ. Amen.

And therefore, thou accursed devil, acknowledge thy judgment, and give glory to the living God, give glory to his Son, Jesus Christ, and to the Holy Spirit, and begone from this N., whom God and our Lord Jesus Christ has called to his grace and faith and to the fount of baptism. And this sign which we make on his forehead thou shalt nevermore dare to violate: through our Lord Jesus Christ. Amen.

The Lord be with you.
Answer: And with thy spirit.
This is the gospel which Mark wrote (Mark 10.13–16).
Glory be to thee, O God.

It came to pass at a certain time that they brought little children to the Lord Jesus, that he might lay his hands upon them. But the disciples rebuked them for bringing them to him. When Jesus saw it, he was displeased, and said to them, Suffer the little children to come to me, and forbid them not: for theirs is the kingdom of heaven. Verily I say to you: Whoever does not receive the kingdom of God as a little child, he shall not enter therein. And so he took them in his arms, laid his hands on them and blessed them and let them go.

Here the priest spits in his hand and takes the spittle, and first touches the right ear and says:

Hipatha, thou shalt be opened.

Then the nostrils and says:

Unto a good odour.

Then on the left ear and says:

But thou, devil, begone and flee, for the kingdom of God is coming.

Then the minister speaks to the godfathers, who answer on behalf of the child:

Dost thou renounce the devil? Yes.
And all his works? Yes.
And all his pomps? Yes.

Then he asks the child's name and says:

Dost thou believe in God the Father almighty, one maker of heaven and earth?

They say:

Yes, I believe.

Dost thou believe in Jesus Christ, his only Son, our Lord, that he suffered for sins, died and rose again from the dead?

Yes, I believe.

Dost thou believe in the Holy Spirit, one holy universal Christian church, the communion of saints, the forgiveness of sins, the resurrection of the flesh, and after death an eternal life?

Yes.

Then the child is brought into the church, and the priest says:

The Lord bless thy going in and coming out from henceforth and for ever.

Then he anoints the child with oil on the breast and between the shoulders, and says:

I anoint thee with holy oil in Christ Jesus our Lord,
and asks:
Wilt thou be baptized?

They answer:

Yes.

Name the child.

Then the priest takes the child and dips him in the water, saying:

N., I baptize thee in the name of the Father, the Son and the Holy Spirit.

Then the priest takes chrism and makes a cross on the top of the child's head, and says:

The almighty God and Father of our Lord Jesus Christ, who has regenerated thee from above by water and the Holy Spirit, and has forgiven thee all thy sins, anoint thee with holy oil unto eternal life. Amen.

As he vests him in his christening robe, he says:

Receive now a white and spotless robe, which thou shalt bring undefiled to the judgment seat of Christ. Amen.

End of the order of baptism.

THE SECOND REVISION OF THE ZURICH ORDER OF BAPTISM

If Zwingli's doctrine of baptism can be summed up in one sentence, it would be in a sentence which he wrote in 1525, "So baptism must be an outward sign that we have been engaged to a new life and incorporated in Christ."[1] Similarly he wrote, "We receive in baptism a sign that we are about to fashion our life according to the rule of Christ."[2] He rejected the doctrine that the sacraments convey the grace which they signify, "for by that argument restriction would have been placed on the liberty of the divine Spirit, who distributes to every man as he will, that is, to whom and when and where he will".[3] The interior baptism of the Spirit, he said, was possessed by all who had faith in Christ, and was so necessary "that unless it is given, nobody is saved, for nobody is saved except by faith: and faith is not born except by the teaching of the Holy Spirit".[4] This would seem to suggest that baptism in water was totally unnecessary, and infant baptism indefensible. Indeed Zwingli once asked, "Why does he need baptism who has already been assured by faith in Christ that his sins are done away?"[5]

Moreover at one time Zwingli had disapproved of infant baptism. "In 1523, on Philip and James's day", declared Hubmaier two years later, "I conferred with you [i.e. Zwingli] in Graben Street upon the scriptures relating to baptism. Then and there you said I was right in saying that children should not be baptized before they were instructed in the faith."[6] Moody quotes from two letters which Zwingli wrote in June 1523 and October 1524 respectively: "It is useless to wash a thousand times in the baptismal water him who does not believe"; and "God has commanded to baptize those who have previously believed."[7]

[1] *Von der Taufe, von der Widertaufe, von der Kindertaufe*, C.R. 91, p. 245.
[2] *de Vera et False Religione* (Tigur), p. 202.
[3] Ibid., p. 200.   [4] Ibid., p. 207.   [5] Ibid., p. 201.
[6] B. Hubmaier, *Conversation on Infant Baptism*, quoted in Kidd, op. cit., pp. 451f.
[7] Dale Moody, *Baptism: Foundation for Christian Unity* (Philadelphia 1967), pp. 45f.

But by May 1525, to the chagrin of the Anabaptists in Zurich, Zwingli had had second thoughts, writing, "For some time I myself was deceived by the error, and I thought it better not to baptize children until they had arrived at the age of discretion."[1] Elsewhere he argued that the words of Mark 16.16 applied only to those who could hear, and therefore infants were not excluded from the common salvation, "especially those born of faithful parents: for otherwise their state would be worse than that of Israel after the flesh. If, therefore, the children of Christians are not less children of God than are the children of the Israelites, who, in the words of Peter, can forbid them to be baptized?"[2] While Zwingli's argument may succeed in showing that infants are eligible for baptism, it hardly proves that they need it.

Zwingli's drastically revised rite of baptism came into use in May 1525.[3] The reason for its brevity and simplicity is given in the title.

Now follows the form of baptism which is now used in Zurich, and all the additions, which have no foundation in the word of God, have been removed.

The minister of the church first says:

In the name of God. Amen. Our help standeth in the name of the Lord, who hath made heaven and earth.

Then he asks the godfathers and godmothers:

Will ye that this child be baptized with the baptism of our Lord Jesus Christ?
Answer: Yea.

Then the priest says:

Name this child.

The godmothers say:

N.

Then the priest says:

Let us then all pray God together: O almighty and eternal God, who through the flood didst by thy mighty judgment condemn the unbelieving world and thyself deliver of thy great mercy faithful Noah: who didst drown obdurate Pharaoh with all his host in the Red Sea, and didst bring thy people Israel through the same dry-shod, figuring thereby this bath of baptism: We pray thee, of thine unmerited mercy, that thou wouldest graciously look upon this thy servant, *N.*, and kindle the light of faith in his heart whereby he may be incorporate into thy Son, and with him be buried in death and raised again to newness of life; that so, following him daily, he may joyfully bear his cross, and

---

[1] C.R. 91, p. 228; tr. Moody, op. cit., p. 46.   [2] *de Vera et False Religione*, pp. 220f.
[3] C.R. 91, pp. 334ff. English translation in Kidd, op. cit., pp. 423f.

hold fast to his with true faith, firm hope and fervent charity: and that
for thy sake he may so manfully quit this life, which is naught else but
death, that at the last day he may appear with boldness at the general
judgment of thy Son. Grant this through the same thy Son our Lord
Jesus Christ, who liveth and reigneth with thee in the unity of the Holy
Ghost, one God. Amen.

The minister says:

The Lord be with you.
Answer: And with thy spirit.

The minister says:

That which now followeth standeth in the gospel of Mark in the tenth
chapter at the thirteenth verse.
Answer: Glory be to thee, O Lord.

The minister:

It came to pass upon a time that they brought, etc. . . . blessed them.
    Thanks be to God. He willeth to forgive us all our sins through his
Son.

Then the minister takes the child and says:

Will ye that this child be baptized?
Answer: Yea.

The minister says:

Name this child.
Answer: N.

The minister says:

N., I baptize thee in the name of the Father and of the Son and of the
Holy Ghost.

At the bestowal of the chrisom:

God grant thee that as thou art now clothed bodily with a white robe,
so at the last day thou mayest appear before him with a clean and open
conscience. Amen.

The Lord be with you. Go in peace.

PRIVATE BAPTISM

25. The Brandenburg–Nuremberg Church Order of 1533

After infant baptism had become normal, almost the only occasions when baptism was required in great haste were the tragically frequent cases of newly born infants who were not expected to survive. The rubrics of the *Sarum Manual* ordered the parochial clergy frequently to teach their people the trinitarian formula so that they might know how to baptize in case of need: if anybody baptized in emergency recovered, he was to be brought to church to receive the catechisms, exorcisms, and unctions that had been omitted.[1] In the sixteenth century this office of private baptism was known to the Germans by two names, *iachtauf* or sudden baptism, and *nottauf* or baptism in necessity. On this subject there is a relevant passage in the *Brandenburg–Nuremberg Church Order* of 1533. It can be read in German in Sehling, op. cit., XI, p. 177 and in an English translation in Goode, op. cit., pp. 9f.

And inasmuch as a laudable and well-grounded custom has hitherto been observed among Christian people, that in case of necessity any Christian person, but especially the midwives, have baptized young children, which has been called private baptism,[2] pastors ought most diligently to instruct and warn midwives, that they take baptism in hand seriously and in the fear of God, but chiefly that they know how to recite the word (I baptize thee in the name of the Father and of the Son and of the Holy Ghost) quite distinctly and orderly. And moreover those women who attend upon pregnant and lying-in women, and are also present at the private baptism, should be admonished to pay careful and reverent attention to the matter, in order to guard against all impediment or error. And whosoever has received the private baptism above mentioned ought to rest therein, and there is no need to baptize him a second time (*sub conditione*), according to the needless abuse of former times, chiefly to avoid giving great occasion thereby to the error of the Anabaptists.

Pastors and preachers ought also to instruct women in childbed, that they are not under the power of the devil, as has hitherto been imagined, not without singular prejudice to consciences, and with gross error. And although they are more liable than other sick persons to strange

---

[1] See Fisher, op. cit., pp. 175f.   [2] Literally, "hasty baptism".

visions and dreams, yet this ought not by any means to terrify them, for such may be the effect of remaining weakness of body. And although perhaps Satan may presume to assail women in childbed more than other people, he does so no doubt, as his manner is, in order thereby to bring into contempt the estate of matrimony which God has blessed, and God's work, as though it were impure, whereas on the contrary it is holy, and even the principal vocation of women, by which they please God, as Paul speaks: "She shall be saved in childbearing, if she continue in faith and love and holiness, with sobriety" I Tim. ii.

Therefore also the benediction after childbed is unnecessary.[1] For it springs from mere superstition, just as if they were desecrated by the birth, which comes from God's blessing. Yet they should nevertheless keep at home for a proper time, that they may avoid injuring themselves or the infants in their health, which is not well pleasing to God.

---

[1] That is to say, the service for the Purification of Women is abolished.

26. The Saxon Church Order, 1539

While George, Duke of Albertine Saxony, was alive, Lutheran reforms were kept out of his dominions. But on his death in 1539 his brother, Henry, who succeeded him, immediately invited a commission from Wittenberg to carry out the reformation of the Saxon Church. That same year there was drawn up a Church Order, which amongst other things included an order of baptism according to Luther's second *Taufbüchlein* of 1526, and an order of baptism in time of need. We omit the former here, because it does not contain anything strikingly unusual in a work of this kind, but include the latter because it was one of the sources which Bucer used in compiling the *Consultation* for Hermann of Cologne. The German text is found in Sehling, op. cit., I, pp. 264–8.

The pastors shall in their sermons instruct the people that they shall not lightly have recourse to emergency baptism, but, when the gravest need shall require that baptism should and must be given, that those who are at hand should first of all call upon the Lord our God, and pray an Our Father, and that done should baptize forthwith in the name of the Father and of the Son and of the Holy Ghost, and that none should doubt that the child is properly and sufficiently baptized, so that it is unnecessary for him to be baptized again in church or anywhere else.

Yet if it be desired that such a child, when he survives, be brought to church, the pastor shall ask the people whether they are sure that the child is properly baptized, and in what manner and with what words he has been baptized; and if they then say that in necessity they called upon God on behalf of the child and after prayer made they have baptized him in the name of the Father and of the Son and of the Holy Spirit, and that they do not doubt but are as sure as can be that, if the little child had died at once, he was thereby completely baptized, then shall the pastor not baptize him again, but shall allow such a baptism to stand, and shall receive him into the congregation and number of true Christians, and read over the child the Gospel, Mark x, which is customarily read at baptism, and commend him by prayer to almighty God, and allow them to depart in the name of the Lord, as follows:

The pastor shall ask thus:

Dear friends of Christ, since we were all together born in sins under God's wrath to eternal death and condemnation, and have no other

137

means by which we may be released from our sins before God, justified and saved, except through our only Mediator and Saviour, Jesus Christ, and since this little child here present also lies in such peril, I ask you whether he was brought to the Lord Christ and also incorporated into him through baptism, or not.

If they answer "Yes", then the pastor shall ask further:

Through whom was this done and who was present thereat?

Someone will say:

Such and such a person, N. and N. were present, and one of them gave the child baptism.

Then shall the pastor ask again:

Did you call upon the name of the Lord and pray?

And if they answer, "Yes, we called upon God and prayed the holy Our Father", then he shall ask again:

With what did you baptize?

One of them answers:

With water.

Then he shall ask:

With what words did you baptize?

Then one of them says:

I baptize thee in the name of the Father and of the Son and of the Holy Spirit.

Finally he shall ask:

Do you know that you used the words in accordance with the command of Christ?

And if they thereupon answer, "Yes, we know it", then he says:

Now, my dear friends, because you have done all this in the name and at the command of our dear Lord God, so I tell you that you have acted properly and well, since the poor little children are in need of grace and our Lord Jesus Christ does not refuse them the same, but calls them to it in the kindliest fashion, as the following text of the holy gospel surely proves, which the evangelist has written thus:

Mark, chapter x: At that time they brought little children to Jesus, etc.

And because from the words of our Lord Christ which we have just heard we are sure and certain that this little child is also received into the kingdom of grace, we shall pray that he may also be continually preserved therein to eternal blessedness.

And let us pray.

The almighty God and Father of our Lord Jesus Christ, who has regenerated thee by water and the Holy Spirit, and has forgiven thee all thy sins, strengthen thee with his grace to eternal life. Amen.

Peace be with thee.

But if the people, when they bring a little child to baptism, give uncertain answers to the pastor's questions, and say that they do not know what they thought, still less what they said or did, in this great emergency (as is often wont to happen on such occasions), you shall not hold a long discussion but shall take the child as unbaptized and proceed to baptism in the same way as one normally proceeds to baptism and to baptize all unbaptized persons.

And when the prayers together with the exorcisms have been said, and the children through their godparents have renounced the devil and made confession of the faith, then shall the pastor baptize the children without condition in the name of the Father and of the Son and of the Holy Spirit.[1]

---

[1] The Lutherans did not approve of conditional baptism. Luther himself had written, "About the question proposed to me in your last letter, about conditional baptism, I conferred with Master Philip [i.e., Melanchthon], and after careful consideration we decided that conditional baptism must be abolished from the church, and where it is either doubtful or unknown whether a person is baptized, then he should be simply baptized unconditionally as if he had never been baptized. And our reason is this, that conditional baptism asserts nothing, it neither denies nor affirms, it neither gives nor takes away. Take somebody conditionally baptized. He will afterwards be compelled to say thus: I am now just as ignorant whether I have been baptized as I was before, and with me all who baptized me. For if my first baptism was a true one, which is bound to be unknown, in any event, then my second baptism (because conditional) is nothing. If the first baptism was not a true one, the second one is still nothing, because it is a doubtful one all the time that the first is doubtful, since as conditional it will depend upon the first which remains doubtful. . . . Therefore it is safer to sin by rebaptizing in such a case, if it is a sin at all, which we do not believe, than to give an uncertain baptism, in which case there is without doubt sin. . . . Nor are we made into raving Anabaptists: for they, as you know, openly condemn the first sure baptism, and are unwilling that it should be called baptism." (Ep. 104, Vinceslao Linck, written at Wittenberg in 1529, in Supplementum Epistolarum Martini Lutheri, ed. J. F. Buddeus (Halae 1703), pp. 78f.)

27. Hermann's Consultation[1]

HOW BAPTISM MUST BE ADMINISTERED
AT OTHER TIMES

But if the infants be weak so that it is to be feared that they will not live to the next Sunday or holy day, or if for weighty matters baptism cannot be ministered upon those days, the pastors shall warn the people that yet they bring their children to be baptized at those hours when after the custom the people resort together to hear the Lord's word.

But if that thing cannot be done neither, baptism in the mean while must not be denied to the infants offered thereunto, whensoever they be brought, for, as much as lieth in us, we must not suffer that any depart out of this life without the sacrament of baptism. For the Lord instituted baptism that it may be to us a sacrament of regeneration and washing of sins from which in this life no man is free, no not an infant one day old.[2] For it is our part to do in all things after the Lord's word, and to receive his gifts and benefits that way that he himself hath appointed to us.

When baptism then shall be ministered upon working days, let the pastors join together in order the catechism, exorcism and baptism, and they shall moderate their exhortations and prayers according to the company and strength of the child.

For if they see that the child is in danger of life, and that the company is small, they shall be short in all things. And they shall use only the first part of the admonition which we willed to be said before the catechism unto these words, *Wherefore, we exhort, and pray you, beloved,* etc. So they shall use the first part only of the demands of every article, and in the exorcism they shall use only one prayer with the Lord's prayer, the creed and the gospel. Which things premised, let them baptize the infant forthwith, and let them exhort the parents, godfathers and other that stand by, that they determine certainly that the infant, whether he live or die, is the son of God, and heir of everlasting life; and if he live, that they procure him to be brought up unto religion and God's glory, according to the exhortation set before, which beginneth, *After that, beloved,* etc.

OF BAPTISM MINISTERED TO CHILDREN
AS SOON AS THEY BE BORN FOR DANGER OF LIFE

The people shall be taught and warned in sermons that they presume not lightly to minister privately this most divine sacrament, for it is worthy to be ministered in the congregation and by peculiar ministers, with all gravity and reverence: and that maketh much for this purpose, that it may be wholesomely ministered, and received. But if extreme necessity press us, that they that be present with the child being in danger, may enjoy themselves together in the Lord, and lift up their minds religiously unto God, let them call for his mercy promised, and exhibited in

---

[1] Above, p. 54; tr. Daye (1548), folios clxvii–clxxi.

[2] This is a reference to Job 14.4f, which Origen quoted in the Septuagint version to prove that there is in infants an innate corruption, and which Augustine used as one of his proof texts to sustain his theory of original guilt. See N. P. Williams, *The Ideas of the Fall and of Original Sin* (London 1927), pp. 224n, 378f.

Christ Jesus our Lord upon the infant; and when they have said the Lord's prayer, let them baptize him in the name of the Father, the Son and the Holy Ghost.

Which done, let them not doubt but that their infant is truly baptized, washed from sins, born again in Christ and made the son and heir of God: let them then give thanks to God for this his so great benefit, and let them not think that baptism must be renewed in children so baptized. For in all points, so much as we may, we must so do all things as the Lord hath appointed. If any godly man be present when the infant is in extremity, let his ministry be used to baptism.

Further, if it chance that the infant so baptized at home do live, it is convenient that he be brought afterward to the temple of his parents, kinsfolks and god-fathers, which must come with a good company and religiously, as men that ought to give thanks for this exceeding great benefit of regeneration ministered to their infant, to offer him to God and his Saviour in the congregation. The pastors then shall ask these men after what sort, and with what words they baptized the infant, whether they did baptize him as the Lord commanded in water, and in the name of the Father, the Son and the Holy Ghost, which if they shall answer that they called God upon the child, and prayed for him, and baptized in the name of the Father, the Son and the Holy Ghost, and that they believe that he is truly cleansed from sins and born again to God, the pastors must confirm them in this belief, and in no wise baptize such an infant again. And that men may be more comforted, and the celebration of so great a sacrament more augmented, and the benefit of Christ bestowed upon the child through baptism more commended, the preachers shall allow the same in the congregation, using a lesson of the holy gospel and prayer after this sort.

The pastor when they be come which bring such an infant unto the Lord shall first demand of them:

Beloved in Christ, forasmuch as we be all born in sin and the wrath of God, guilty of eternal death and damnation, and can by none other means get remission of sins, righteousness and everlasting life than through faith in Christ, and forasmuch as also this infant is born subject to these evils, I mean of death and the wrath of God, I ask of you whether he were offered to Christ and planted in him through baptism?

If they answer that they so believe, he shall ask them further, by whom it was done, and who were present. And when they have named them, he shall ask him which by their relation baptized the child, if he be present, or other which then were present, whether the name of the Lord were called upon him and prayer made for him. If they answer that they did so, he shall ask how the child was baptized. If they then answer, *In water and with these words I baptize thee in the name of the Father, the Son and the Holy Ghost,* he shall ask them last of all whether they certainly know that they have rightly used the word of God, and if they answer that they know and remember that they did so, let the pastor say[1] this moreover:—

Forasmuch as, beloved in Christ, I hear that all things concerning the baptism of this infant have been done in the name of God and according to his institution, I pronounce in the name of Christ that ye have done well. For infants want the grace of God, which our Saviour denieth not unto them, whensoever it is asked for children, according to his word; for he hath not bound the benefit of his redemption to any

[1] Latin: *addat.*

places, times or persons. For in what place soever they that believe in him come together in his name, he is present in the midst of them; and when he is called upon through faith, he worketh in his word and sacraments, and he performeth in deed[1] whatsoever he offereth in his sacraments, and promiseth in his words. And to confirm this faith, and that we may stir up ourselves to thank the Lord for this his so great benefit ministered to this infant by baptism, let us hear out of the gospel how the Lord will have children brought unto him, and how he will bounteously bless them that be offered unto him.

And they brought children unto him that he might touch them, etc.

By these words of Christ we be certified that as many infants as be offered unto Christ according to his word pertain to the kingdom of God, be the children of God, the members of Christ, that the angels be present with them as ministers, and that all the creatures of God be subject unto them, to do them good. Wherefore we must minister to such with singular diligence, that they may be well brought up in Christ and grow in him, and this charge pertaineth to you[2] parents, kinsfolks, godfathers and all other friends which be of the body of this our congregation. I commend then this infant, the son and heir of God, the brother and co-heir of Christ, the member of Christ, and your member in Christ, to your faithfulness, and charge that ye procure him with all diligence to be nourished, brought up and instructed to the Lord, to whom he is born again, and to the kingdom of God, to which he is born again, every man according to his vocation and power, that as soon as he can for his age he may learn to keep all those things that Christ commanded to be kept. Wherefore it pertaineth to you chiefly parents, godfathers and kinsfolk, though all other in this congregation,[3] and all Christian men to whomsoever he shall come ought not to deny their labour and help to procure that this infant as soon as he may for his age be brought to the school and to the congregation, and be instructed in the mysteries of God with all faithfulness, that he may learn to acknowledge and magnify the most ample benefits of God received in baptism, that afterward he may profess his faith himself in the congregation, that with his own voice he may renounce Satan and the world with all his enticements and works before the holy congregation, that he may bind himself to Christ and to his congregation unto all obedience, and continue in the same unto the end as a lively

[1] Latin: *praestat solide.*
[2] Latin: *quicunque Christi sunt, quibus illos Dominus peculiariter copulavit.*
[3] Latin: *qui in hac Ecclesia vivunt.*

member of Christ and a branch continuing in Christ, and bring forth plentiful fruit unto the praise and glory of God and edification of his church.

After this let him say, laying his hand on the child:

The Lord be with you.

Answer: And with thy spirit.

Let us pray.

Lord God, the Father of our Lord Jesus Christ, who hast begotten again this infant of water and the Holy Ghost, and hast given him in holy baptism remission of all sins, confirm the same with thy grace, and guide and further this new life, which thou hast given and finish it up whereunto thou hast bound the infant with this holy sacrament. Grant also to his parents and to us all that we may faithfully and diligently serve thee in taking charge of him, that through him and us all thy name daily be more and more sanctified and thy kingdom promoted unto the full fruition of blissfulness;[1] through Christ our Lord. Amen.

But if they which offer the infant cannot answer sufficiently to the said demands, so that they grant that they do not well know what they thought or did in baptizing, being sore troubled with the present danger, as it often chanceth, then, omitting curious disputations, let the pastor judge such an infant not to be yet baptized, and let him do all those things that pertain to this ministration, as we described before, that is to say, let him use an admonition and catechism to them that bring the child, and an exorcism of the child, the common confession of the faith, and all other things, which done let him baptize the infant without condition, in the name of the Father, the Son and the Holy Ghost.

[1] See Strassburg rite, above, p. 39.

28. The Prayer Book of 1549

OF THEM THAT BE BAPTIZED IN
PRIVATE HOUSES IN TIME OF NECESSITY

The pastors and curates shall oft admonish the people that they defer not the baptism of infants any longer than the Sunday or other holy day next after the child be born, unless upon a great and reasonable cause declared to the curate and by him approved.

And also they shall warn them that without great cause and necessity they baptize not children at home in their houses. And when great need shall compel them so to do, that then they minister it on this fashion.

First let them that be present call upon God for his grace and say the Lord's prayer, if the time will suffer. And then one of them shall name the child, and dip him in the water, or pour water upon him, saying these words:

N., I baptize thee in the name of the Father and of the Son and of the Holy Ghost. Amen.

And let them not doubt but that the child so baptized is lawfully and sufficiently baptized, and ought not to be baptized again in the church. But yet nevertheless if the child which is after this sort baptized do afterward live, it is expedient that he be brought into the church, to the intent the priest may examine and try whether the child be lawfully baptized or no. And if those that bring any child to the church do answer that he is already baptized, then shall the priest examine them further:

By whom the child was baptized?
Who was present when the child was baptized?
Whether they called upon God for grace and succour in that necessity?
With what thing, or what matter, they did baptize the child?
With what words the child was baptized?
Whether they think the child to be lawfully and perfectly baptized?

And if the ministers[1] shall prove by the answers of such as brought the child that all things were done as they ought to be, then shall not he christen the child again, but shall receive him as one of the flock of the true Christian people, saying thus:

I certify you that in this case ye have done well, and according unto due order concerning the baptizing of this child, which being born in original sin, and in the wrath of God, is now by the laver of regeneration in baptism made the child of God and heir of everlasting life:[2] for our Lord Jesus Christ doth not deny his grace and mercy unto such

[1] 1559: "minister".
[2] 1552 and 1559: "received into the number of the children of God and heirs of everlasting life".

144

infants, but most lovingly doth call them unto him, as the holy gospel doth witness to our comfort on this wise:

At a certain time they brought children unto Christ. . . .

After the gospel is read, the minister shall make this exhortation upon the words of the gospel:

Friends, ye hear in this gospel the words of our Saviour Christ, that he commanded the children to be brought unto him, how he blamed those that would have kept them from him, how he exhorted all men to follow their innocency; ye perceive how by his outward gesture and deed he declared his good will toward them, for he embraced them in his arms, he laid his hands upon them, and blessed them. Doubt you not, therefore, but earnestly believe that he hath likewise favourably received this present infant, that he hath embraced him with the arms of his mercy, that he hath given unto him the blessing of eternal life, and made him partaker of his everlasting kingdom. Wherefore we being thus persuaded of the good will of our heavenly Father, declared by his Son, Jesus Christ, towards this infant, let us faithfully and devoutly give thanks unto him, and say the prayer which the Lord himself taught; and in the declaration of our faith let us also recite the articles contained in our creed.

Here the minister with the godfathers and godmothers shall say:

Our Father which art in heaven, hallowed be thy name, etc.

Then shall they say the creed, and then the priest shall demand[1] the name of the child, which being by the godfathers and godmothers pronounced, the minister shall say:

N.,[2] dost thou forsake the devil and all his works?

Answer: I forsake them.

Minister: Dost thou forsake the vain pomp and glory of the world with all the covetous desires of the same?

Answer: I forsake them.

Minister: Dost thou forsake the carnal desires of the flesh, so that thou wilt not follow and be led by them?

Answer: I forsake them.[3]

---

[1] 1552 and 1559: "Then the priest shall demand the . . .".

[2] The name was omitted in 1559.

[3] 1552 and 1559 put the three questions together: "Dost thou in the name of this child forsake the devil and all his works, the vain pomp and glory of the world with all covetous desires of the same, the carnal desires of the flesh, and not to follow and be led by them?" *Answer:* "I forsake them all." The phrase "in the name of this child" is inserted here, although it did not occur in the corresponding place in the 1552 service of public baptism.

Minister: Dost thou believe in God the Father almighty, maker of heaven and earth?

Answer: I believe.[1]

Minister: Dost thou believe in Jesus Christ, his only begotten Son, our Lord, and that he was conceived by the Holy Ghost, born of the Virgin Mary, that he suffered under Pontius Pilate, was crucified, dead and buried, that he went down into hell, and also did arise again the third day, that he ascended into heaven, and sitteth on the right hand of God the Father almighty, and from thence shall come again at the end of the world to judge the quick and the dead, dost thou believe this?

Answer: I believe.

Minister: Dost thou believe in the Holy Ghost, the holy catholic church, the communion of saints, remission of sins, resurrection of the flesh[2] and everlasting life after death?

Answer: I believe.

Then the minister shall put the white vesture, commonly called the chrisom, upon the child, saying:

Take this white vesture for a token of the innocency which by God's grace in the holy sacrament of baptism is given unto thee, and for a sign whereby thou art admonished so long as thou shalt live, to give thyself to innocency of living, that after this transitory life thou mayest be partaker of the life everlasting. Amen.[3]

Let us pray.

Almighty and everlasting God, heavenly Father, we give thee humble thanks that[4] thou hast vouchsafed to call us to the knowledge of thy grace and faith in thee: increase[5] and confirm this faith in us evermore: give thy Holy Spirit to this infant that he being born again, and being made heir of everlasting salvation through our Lord Jesus Christ, may continue thy servant, and attain thy promises[6] through the same our Lord Jesus Christ, thy Son, who liveth and reigneth with thee in unity of the same Holy Spirit everlastingly. Amen.

---

[1] 1552 and 1559 begin, "Dost thou in the name of this child profess this faith to believe in...". By combining the three interrogations in one, they abandon the traditional and primitive threefold form of questions. Some other slight verbal alterations were made in 1552. In 1552 and 1559 the reply to the single question was "all this I stedfastly believe".

[2] "of the flesh" was omitted in 1552, but restored in 1559.

[3] This prayer was omitted in 1552, as the giving of the chrisom was then abolished; above, p. 110.

[4] 1552 and 1559: "for that".

[5] 1552 and 1559: "increase this knowledge and...".

[6] 1552 and 1559: "promise".

Then shall the minister make this exhortation to the godfathers and godmothers:

Forasmuch as this child hath promised by you to forsake the devil and all his works, to believe in God, and to serve him, you must remember that it is your parts and duty[1] to see that this infant be taught, so soon as he shall be able to learn, what a solemn vow, promise and profession he hath made by you, and that he may know these things the better, ye shall call upon him to hear sermons: and chiefly ye shall provide that he may learn the creed, the Lord's prayer and the ten commandments in the English tongue, and all other things which a Christian man ought to know and believe to his soul's health, and that this child may be virtuously brought up to lead a godly and a Christian life, remembering alway that baptism doth represent unto us our profession, which is to follow the example of our Saviour Christ, and to be made like unto him, that as he died and rose again for us, so should we which are baptized die from sin, and rise again unto righteousness, continually mortifying all our evil and corrupt affections, and daily proceeding in all virtue and godliness of living.

Etc. As in public baptism.

But if they which bring the infants to the church do make an uncertain answer to the priest's questions, and say that they cannot tell what they thought, did or said in that great fear and trouble of mind (as oftentimes it chanceth), then let the priest baptize him in form above written concerning public baptism, saving that at the dipping of the child in the font, he shall use this form of words:

If thou be not baptized already, N., I baptize thee in the name of the Father and of the Son and of the Holy Ghost. Amen.

The principal source of this rite is the *Consultation*: but what is there prescribed has been very considerably abbreviated. The post-baptismal unction found in the 1549 rite of public baptism is omitted here. Again, whereas Luther (above, p. 139) disapproved of conditional baptism, the English rite of 1549 and the revisions of 1552 and 1559 retained it.

---

[1] 1552 and 1559: "your part and duty . . .".

THE
BLESSING OF
THE FONT

29 The Missale Mixtum and the Missale Gallicanum Vetus

In the earlier baptismal liturgies, such as that in the *Gelasian Sacramentary* (see Whitaker, op. cit., pp. 176ff), the form for the blessing of the font was included together with the order of baptism itself among the material for Easter Eve. Since in Rome at that time the administration of baptism except in cases of sickness was restricted to the paschal and pentecostal vigils, obviously the font would be blessed on those days. In the *Sarum Manual*, published in England in the early sixteenth century at a time when baptisms took place on any day of the year, the blessing of the font was still included with the order of baptism; but the rubrics make it clear that the font was not blessed before every baptism, the consecrated water being reserved for future use, and only renewed when it grew stale.[1] In the Book of Common Prayer of 1549, which permitted the consecrated water to be reserved for up to a month, the blessing of the font comes after the order for private baptism. But the form provided in 1549 seems to have been derived in part from the *Missale Mixtum* and the *Missale Gallicanum vetus*. The former is a Spanish book, which was edited in 1500 by Cardinal Ximenes, the Latin text being available now in Migne, *P.L.*, 85.464ff. The latter, originating in Gaul shortly before the time of Charlemagne, has been edited by L. C. Mohlberg in the series, *Rerum Ecclesiasticarum Documenta, Fontes III* (Rome 1958), the relevant passage being on page 41. In both cases the text is in an unsatisfactory state.

MISSALE MIXTUM

I exorcize thee, creature of water, through God the Father almighty and the founder of all things, who commanded thee to be consecrated for the begetting of the human race and through the office of our humility: and through Jesus Christ our Lord, Son of God and Son of Man, who walked upon thee on foot and presented himself for our salvation to be baptized in thee by John and through the Holy Spirit, who appeared upon him in the form of a dove in Jordan: that all the evil of the spirit of wickedness being expelled from thee, those who shall be washed by us in thee or from thee, and

---

[1] See Fisher, op. cit., pp. 165ff.

MISSALE MIXTUM

baptized in the name of the triune majesty having received divine grace may be found worthy to be enrolled in the number of the faithful.
R. Amen.
Our God through thy mercy, etc.
Humble yourselves for the blessing.
The Lord be ever with you.
R. And with thy spirit.

God who alone hast immortality, and, that thou mightest not alone possess it, didst impart it to us also by our new birth through Jesus, who hast wished by the washing of baptism to refashion for better the human race after the entrance of the sin of the first birth,

be present, we pray thee, at the invocation of thy name
R. Amen.
Sanctify ✠ this font, thou ✠ sanctifier of the human race,
R. Amen.
Be this place made worthy that the Holy Spirit may flow into it.
R. Amen.
Here be that old Adam buried, and the new Adam rise.
R. Amen.
Here may everything die that is of the flesh, and everything rise that is of the spirit.
R. Amen.
May the old clothing be put off and the most foul vices and crimes be put away, so that the garments of thy splendour and immortality may be put on.
R. Amen.
Whosoever are baptized in Christ, may they put on Christ.
R. Amen.
Whosoever here renounce the devil grant them to triumph over the world.

R. Amen.

MISSALE GALLICANUM VETUS

It is meet and right.
It is very just and right that we should give thanks to thee, Lord God eternal, who alone hast immortality, and, that thou mightest not alone possess it, didst impart it to us also by the renewing of our age, who, when the human race had by transgression lost the dignity of its first origin, didst wish to refashion it for better by the office of baptism both precious and blessed:

be present, we pray thee, at the invocation of thy name,

sanctify this font, thou sanctifier of the human race;

be this place made worthy that the Holy Spirit may flow into it;

here be that old Adam buried, and the new Adam rise;

may everything die that is of the flesh, and everything rise that is of the spirit;

may the clothing defiled with vices be put off and its crimes be done away, so that the garments of splendour and immortality may be received;

whosoever shall be baptized in Christ, may they put on Christ;

whosoever here shall have renounced the devil, grant them to triumph over the world;

Whosoever in this place shall have confessed, do thou recognize him in the kingdom.
R. Amen.
So be all sins drowned in this font, that they may never rise again.
R. Amen.
May the benefits of this water so avail that the flames of eternal fire be quenched.
R. Amen.
May the fonts admit to thine altars those whom the altars shall admit to thy kingdom.
R. Amen.
Here may all fear of death perish.
R. Amen.
Whosoever here shall have denied himself, may he gain thee.
R. Amen.
Whosoever here shall have begun to be thine, may he not cease to be thine.
R. Amen.
So that consecrated to thee by our ministry, he may be consecrated unto eternal virtues and eternal rewards.

R. Amen.
Through the mercy of our God himself who is blessed and lives and governs all things world without end.
R. Amen.
The Lord be ever with you.
R. And with thy spirit.

who shall have called upon thee in this place, do thou know him in the kingdom;

so be sins drowned in this font, that they may not rise again;

may the benefit of this water so avail that it may quench the flame of eternal fire;

may the fonts admit to thine altars those whom the altars shall admit to thy kingdom;

here may all fear of death perish;

whosoever here shall have begun to be thine, let him not cease to be thine;

whosoever shall have denied himself, may he gain thee;

and may the people that is consecrated to thee by our ministry and thy mystery be consecrated unto thee unto eternal rewards:

through our Lord Jesus Christ.

30. The Prayer Book of 1549

In the Prayer Book of 1549 the blessing of the font, included immediately after the order for private baptism, appears to be derived from the *Missale Mixtum* and the *Missale Gallicanum vetus*. But doubts have been expressed whether it was possible for Cranmer to have read both these works. The case for his having read the *Missale Mixtum* has been argued in *Church Quarterly Review*, XXXI (January 1891), Art. "Capitulum Coloniense: An Episode in the Reformation", p. 430n. Frere wrote, "It is clear that the Mozarabic Missal was accessible at the time of the revision, for it was printed by Ximenes in 1500, and it may very easily have been known to Cranmer; on the other hand the Ms. of the *Missale Gallicanum* was not discovered and printed till the end of the seventeenth century. So it is probable that Cranmer had some other Gallican Order of Service before him which has not so far been identified" (F. Procter, *A New History of the Book of Common Prayer*, revised and rewritten by W. H. Frere (London 1965), pp. 571f.)

We have printed in italics the petitions and phrases in the 1549 rite which appear word for word in one of these earlier works. The footnotes will make it evident that neither of these can claim to be the sole source used by Cranmer. The parts which are enclosed in brackets were omitted in 1552.

The water in the font shall be changed every month once at the least, and afore any child be baptized in the water so changed, the priest shall say at the font these prayers following:[1]

O most merciful God, our Saviour Jesu Christ, who hast ordained the element of water for the regeneration of thy faithful people, *upon whom, being baptized in the river of Jordan, the Holy Ghost came down in the likeness of a dove*, send down, we beseech thee, the same thy Holy Spirit to assist us, and to be present at this our invocation of thy holy name: *Sanctify*✠[2] *this fountain* of baptism, *thou that art the sanctifier of all things,*

---

[1] The reservation of the consecrated water for use on future occasions is in accordance with the rubrics of the *Sarum Manual* (see Fisher, op. cit., pp. 165f, 171). While the rubric of 1549 requiring the water to be changed once a month, though not necessarily more frequently than that, was withdrawn in 1552, nothing was then said as to how often this should be done. Procter (op. cit., p. 380) considered that the words, "grant that all thy servants which shall be baptized in this water . . .", implied that the same water was used for baptism on a number of occasions. Since the revision of 1552 carefully avoided any suggestion that the water was consecrated, there would have been no objection on doctrinal grounds to its reservation for future use.

[2] There is a consignation at this point only in the *Missale Mixtum*.

154

that by the power of thy word all those that shall be baptized therein may be spiritually regenerated, and made the children of everlasting adoption. Amen.

O merciful God, grant *that the old Adam* in them that shall be baptized in this fountain *may be so buried* that *the new man may be raised up again.* Amen.[1]

Grant *that*[2] *all carnal affections may die* in them, *and that all things belonging to the spirit may* live and grow in them. Amen.

Grant (to *all them which* at this fountain *forsake the devil* and all his works) that they may have power and strength to have victory and *to triumph against* him, *the world*, and the flesh. Amen.

(*Whosoever shall confess thee*,[3] O Lord, *recognize him also in thy King-dom.* Amen.

Grant that *all sin* and vice here *may be* so *extinct* that they never have power to reign in thy servants. Amen.

Grant that *whosoever here shall begin to be of thy* flock *may* evermore *continue in the same.* Amen.

Grant that *all they which* for thy sake in this life *do deny* and forsake *themselves may win* and purchase *thee*, O Lord, which art everlasting treasure. Amen.[4])

Grant that whosoever *is* here *dedicated* to thee *by our* office and *ministry* may also be endowed *with heavenly virtues, and everlastingly rewarded* through thy mercy, O blessed Lord God, *who dost live and govern all things world without end.*[5] Amen.

(The Lord be with you.

Answer: And with thy spirit.)[6]

Almighty everliving God, whose most dearly beloved Son Jesus Christ, for the forgiveness of our sins did shed out of his most precious side both water and blood, and gave commandment to his disciples that they should go teach all nations, and baptize them in the name of the Father, the Son and the Holy Ghost, regard, we beseech thee, the supplications of thy congregation, and grant that all thy servants which

---

[1] For the version of such of these prayers as were retained in 1552 see above, p. 109.
[2] "here" is omitted, as in *Gallicanum vetus*.
[3] "thee" is found only in *Gallicanum vetus*.
[4] The order of this and the previous prayer is inverted in *Missale Mixtum*, but not in *Gallicanum vetus*.
[5] These last words are only in *Missale Mixtum*.
[6] Only in *Missale Mixtum*.

shall be baptized in this water (prepared for the ministration of thy holy sacrament)[1] may receive the fulness of thy grace, and ever remain in the number of thy faithful and elect children, through Jesus Christ our Lord.[2]

[1] These words in brackets were removed in 1552 in order to avoid even the remotest suggestion that the water was consecrated; above, p. 109.
[2] For the new position of this prayer in 1552 see above, p. 109.

CONFIRMATION

31. The Situation Confronting the Reformers

The doctrine of confirmation prevalent in the West on the eve of the Reformation can be illustrated from the following documents:

THE DECREE FOR THE ARMENIANS (1439)

The second sacrament is confirmation; its matter is chrism, made from oil—which signifies the lustre of conscience—and from balsam—which signifies the fragrance of a good reputation—blessed by a bishop. The form is: "I sign thee with the sign of the cross, and I confirm thee with the chrism of salvation, in the name of the Father and of the Son and of the Holy Ghost."

The ordinary minister is the bishop. Now, although a simple priest has the power to confer other anointings, no one but a bishop should confer this anointing. For we read that it was only the apostles, whose place the bishops hold, who were accustomed to give the Holy Spirit through an imposition of hands, as is clear from the Acts of the Apostles [Acts 8.14ff is cited]. Now in place of that imposition of hands there is given in the church confirmation. True, we read that by way of dispensation of the apostolic see, which is given for a cause that is reasonable and urgent, a simple priest has conferred this sacrament, using chrism that has been consecrated by the bishop.

The effect of this sacrament is that in it the Holy Spirit is given, as he was given to the apostles on the day of Pentecost, to strengthen Christians to confess fearlessly the name of Christ. . . .[1]

Appeal is made to the laying on of hands by St Peter and St John at Samaria to provide scriptural justification for the custom, already long established in the West, of restricting the administration of confirmation, except in rare circumstances, to a bishop. But it is noteworthy that, whereas early writers such as Tertullian[2] and Cyprian[3] laid great emphasis on hand-laying as the sacramental means by which the Holy Spirit was imparted in initiation, by the fifteenth century the emphasis was placed entirely on the anointing of the forehead with chrism, and the hand-laying, if it had not disappeared from the rite altogether,

---

[1] Tr. P. F. Palmer, *Sacraments and Worship* (London 1957), pp. 146f. On this interpretation of the effect of confirmation see Fisher, op. cit., pp. 63f, 134f.
[2] *de Baptismo* 8; ed. E. Evans, *Tertullian's Homily on Baptism* (London 1964), p. 17.
[3] *Ep.* 69.11 and 73.6; *C.S.E.L.* III, pp. 760, 783.

was no longer doctrinally important. If the laying on of the bishop's hand had continued to have the significance which Tertullian and Cyprian saw in it, it would have been correspondingly easier to answer the criticism of the Reformers that the Latin rite of confirmation lacked any biblical authority.

THE FALSE DECRETALS AND GRATIAN

The *False Decretals* are a collection of papal pronouncements and conciliar decisions purporting to have been made by Isidore, Bishop of Seville from 600 to 636. In fact, however, they were published about the year 850;[1] and those decretals which concern confirmation are in large part pronouncements of a much later age, which the unknown compiler, pseudo-Isidore, has attributed to popes of the pre-Nicene Church. The first persons to suspect their authenticity were Nicholas of Cusa (d. 1464) and Juan Torquemada (d. 1468). Although Cassander and Erasmus rejected them, they were frequently quoted as if genuine in the controversy over confirmation in the early years of the Reformation period.[2]

We are concerned here with five passages in these Decretals, three of which also found their way into the Canon Law, being quoted in part, as if genuine, by Gratian in his *Decretum*, published about 1140.[3] We give here the relevant excerpts from the *False Decretals* with the parts quoted by Gratian in italics.

(A) LETTER FALSELY ASCRIBED TO URBAN I, POPE FROM 222 TO 230

For all the faithful must through episcopal impositions of the hand receive the Holy Spirit after baptism, so that they may be full Christians, because when the Holy Spirit is poured into a man the faithful heart is enlarged to prudence and constancy. We receive of the Holy Spirit, so that we may become spiritual, because the natural man does not perceive the things which are of the Spirit of God. We receive of the Holy Spirit, so that we may have sense to distinguish between good and evil, to love what is just, to spurn what is unjust, to fight against malice and pride, to resist luxury and manifold snares and foul and unworthy desires. We receive of the Holy Spirit that inflamed with the love of life and the desire of glory we may be able to lift our mind from earthly things to the things above and divine things.[4]

The real source of the first sentence is, according to Hinschius, the Council of Aix la Chapelle of 836,[5] and of the rest a sermon preached at Pentecost by a Gallican bishop, for long known as pseudo-Eusebius of Emesa, but now identi-

---

[1] See E. H. Davenport, *The False Decretals* (Oxford 1916), pp. 92–7.
[2] See A. Boudinlon, Art. "Decretals", in *Encyclopaedia Britannica* (11th edn), VII, p. 916.
[3] Ed. A. Friedberg, *Decretum Magistri Gratiani*. Leipzig 1879.
[4] P. Hinschius, *Decretales Pseudo-Isidorianae* (Leipzig 1863), p. 146.
[5] Mansi 14.681.

fied with Faustus of Riez.[1] This homily is dated by Van Buchem between the years 451 and 470,[2] two hundred years after the time of Urban I.

(B) LETTER FALSELY ASCRIBED TO MELCHIADES, POPE FROM 310 TO 314

Concerning those matters about which you asked to be informed, that is, whether the laying on of the hand of the bishops is the greater sacrament or baptism, know that each is a great sacrament; and just as the one is given by greater ministers, that is, by the chief pontiffs, and cannot be performed by lesser ministers, so it must be venerated and held in greater veneration: but these two sacraments are so closely connected that they are in no wise to be separated save by the intervention of premature death, and one cannot rightly be performed without the other. For when death intervenes one can save without the other, but the other cannot. Wherefore it is written: In those days, says the Lord, I will pour out of my Spirit upon all flesh. Let us notice the riches of supreme goodness. That which in the confirming of neophytes the imposition of the hand conveys to each, that the descent of the Holy Spirit upon the companies of believers then gave to all. But because we have said that the laying on of the hand and confirmation can confirm something to him who has been now regenerated in Christ, perhaps somebody may think to himself. After the mystery of baptism what does the ministration of him who confirms profit me? Or as far as I can see, we have not received all from the font, if after the font we need the addition of something new in kind. It is not so, most beloved: let your charity attend to me. Just as military order requires that when a commander has received any one into the number of his soldiers, he should not only put a mark on him when he has been received, but also issue him with suitable weapons so that he may fight, so in the case of a person baptized that blessing is a protection. You have found a soldier: find him the equipment for warfare. Is it any use if any parent conferred a large property on his little child, if he did not take care also to provide a tutor? Therefore the divine word says, Except the Lord keep the city, the watchmen wake in vain. *Therefore the Holy Spirit who comes down upon the waters of baptism with his saving descent confers in the font all that is needed for innocence, in confirmation he provides*

[1] See A. Souter, "Observations on the Pseudo-Eusebian Collection of Gallican Sermons", in *Journal of Theological Studies*, XLI (1940), p. 47; B. Leeming, "The False Decretals, Faustus of Riez and the Pseudo-Eusebius", in *Studia Patristica*, II, part 2 (Oxford 1955), pp. 125ff.
[2] See L. A. Van Buchem, *L'Homélie Pseudo-Eusébienne de Pentecôte* (Nijmegen 1967), p. 113.

an increase in grace. Because those who will live in this world must walk all their lives among invisible enemies and perils, in baptism we are regenerated to life, after baptism we are confirmed to combat. In baptism we are washed, after baptism we are strengthened, and if for those who will pass hence at once the benefits of regeneration suffice, yet for those who will live the helps of confirmation are necessary. Regeneration by itself saves those who are presently to be received into the peace of the world of bliss, but confirmation arms and equips those who are to be reserved for the contests and battles of this world. He who after baptism with his acquired innocence comes unspotted to death is confirmed by death, because he cannot sin after death. If perhaps we may here wish to ask this also, After the passion and resurrection of Christ what would the coming of the Holy Spirit profit the apostles, the Lord himself clearly expounds this. What I tell you, he says, you cannot bear now; but when he, the Spirit of truth, has come, he will teach you all truth. You see that *when the Holy Spirit is poured into a man, the faithful heart is enlarged to prudence and constancy.* So before the descent of the Holy Spirit the apostles are scared even to the point of denial, but after his visitation they are armed even to the point of martyrdom despising their safety. According to this we are redeemed by Christ, but by the Holy Spirit we are illuminated with the gift of spiritual wisdom, we are edified, taught, instructed, perfected, so that we can hear that voice of the Holy Spirit: I will give thee understanding and I will instruct thee in this way wherein thou shalt go.[1]

(c) LETTER FALSELY ASCRIBED TO EUSEBIUS
POPE FOR A FEW MONTHS, 309 OR 310.

Similarly we, adhering to the rule of the Roman Church, order that all heretics, who by the grace of God are converted and, believing in the Name of the Trinity, have been baptized, be reconciled by the imposition of the hand. The sacrament of the laying on of the hand is to be held in great veneration, which cannot be performed by others than the chief priests. Nor in the time of the apostles is it read or known that it was performed by others than the apostles, nor can it ever be performed or ought to be by others than those who hold their place.[2]

---

[1] Van Buchem, op. cit., pp. 61–4. The quotation from Joel is the text of Faustus' Whitsun sermon; and all that follows is from that sermon, which is to be dated a century and a half after the time of Melchiades. The passage quoted by Gratian is in Friedberg, op. cit., p. 1413.

[2] Hinschius, op. cit., p. 242. Hinschius thought that part of this passage came from the letter of Innocent I to Decentius of Gubbio in 416; see Whitaker, op. cit., p. 218.

(D) EPISTLE 4 FALSELY ASCRIBED TO CLEMENT OF ROME

Hasten together therefore to these waters, for they are the only waters which can quench the heat of the fire to come. He who delays to come to them, certainly the idol of unbelief remains still in him. For whether a man be just or unjust, baptism is above all things necessary, to the just that perfection may be completed in him and he may be regenerated, and to the unjust that there may be given to him remission of the sins which he has committed. Therefore all must hasten without delay to be reborn to God and at length to be sealed by a bishop, that is, to receive the sevenfold grace of the Holy Spirit, because the end of every man's life is uncertain. But when he has been regenerated by water and afterwards confirmed by a bishop with the grace of the sevenfold Spirit, as has been said, because otherwise he cannot at all be a perfect Christian nor have his abode among the perfect, if he has remained so not from necessity but from carelessness or deliberate choice, as we have learned from the blessed apostle Peter, and the other apostles by the Lord's command taught, and finally that he show by his good works the likeness in him of the Father who begat him.[1]

(E) LETTER TO ALL THE BISHOPS
FALSELY ASCRIBED TO POPE FABIAN (D. 250)

In your letter we find included among other things the point that certain bishops in your area diverge from your and our practice, and do not make chrism every year on Maundy Thursday, but reserve the chrism once made for two or three years. For they say, as we have found in the above mentioned prelates, that they cannot find balsam every year, and that it is not necessary to make chrism every year, and while one supply of chrism lasts, it is not necessary to make another. For they are in error who think such things, and they reason foolishly rather than correctly when they say these things. For on that day the Lord Jesus, after having supper with his disciples and washing their feet, as our predecessors received from the holy apostles and handed on to us also, taught that chrism should be consecrated; for the washing of our feet itself signifies baptism, when it is performed and confirmed with the anointing of holy chrism. For just as the solemnity of the actual day is to be

---

[1] The text is somewhat confused. The real author is not Clement of Rome who died about A.D. 99, but the unknown fourth-century writer of the *Clementine Recognitions* (*P.G.* 1.1353), except that into his text Pseudo-Isidore has inserted the reference to episcopal sealing and receiving the sevenfold Spirit. See Hinschius, op. cit., p. 63.

celebrated every year, so the actual making of holy chrism is to be performed every year, and renewed year by year and delivered to the
faithful, because the new chrism is consecrated every year and is to be
renewed on the aforementioned day, and the old chrism is to be burnt
in the holy churches. We have received all this from the holy apostles
and their successors, and we command you to adhere to it. These
customs the church of Rome and the church of Antioch have preserved
from the time of the apostles; these customs are maintained by the
churches of Jerusalem and Ephesus, in which the apostles who presided
over them taught that the old chrism must be burnt, and did not allow
it to be used for more than one year, and gave orders that then new and
not old chrism must be employed.[1]

DIONYSIUS AREOPAGITICUS
DE ECCLESIASTICA HIERARCHIA

II.7: The priests taking him [i.e. the candidate] hand him to the sponsor
and minister of the reception; and together with him they clothe the
man being perfected with a robe and conduct him again to the hierarch.
The latter, having sealed the man with the divinely consecrated ointment, finally makes him a partaker in the eucharist which consummates
the holy rites.[2]
II.8: The perfecting unction with the ointment makes him that has been
perfected of a sweet odour; for the holy perfecting of the divine birth
unites that which is perfected with the divinely ruling Spirit.[3]

If Dionysius the Areopagite, mentioned in Acts 17.34, were the real author
of this treatise, we should have here irrefutable evidence of confirmation with
chrism as far back as the time of St Paul. But the real author, whose identity has
never been discovered, was a Syrian writer of the fifth century.[4]

---

[1] *P. L.*, 130, 154; Hinschius, op. cit., pp. 106f. Hinschius thought that a possible source
of part of this letter was canon 46 of the Council of Meaux, held in 845.
[2] *P.G.* 3.396.   [3] *P.G.* 3.404.
[4] See G. Dix, *The Shape of the Liturgy* (London 1943), p. 445, n. 2, and the authorities
there cited.

32. The Origin of the Reformed Doctrine of Confirmation

WYCLIFFE

Over a century before Luther there began to appear another view of confirmation, of its origin and its significance. In his *Trialogus*, published in 1383, Wycliffe strongly criticized the medieval doctrine, stating his own views in the form of a conversation between Alithia and Phronesis (iv.14, ed. G. Lechler (Oxford 1868), pp. 292ff).

Alithia: "Tell me, I pray, about the third sacrament which is commonly called confirmation, and first of all about its foundation in the teaching of scripture. For its foundation does not seem to me sufficiently proved from Acts viii. . . . From that text it is generally concluded that besides the baptism with which people are baptized, there ought to be added as well apostolical confirmation, because the apostles acted thus. But this confirmation seems to be too uncertain, since it could probably be said, that, although baptism in the name of Jesus Christ was at the time valid, in so far as that name had been sufficiently proclaimed, yet, when the proclamation of the name had been accomplished, it was necessary to return to the form of words in the gospel, and so those who had thus only been baptized in the name at Samaria had to be baptized lawfully, just as those baptized with the baptism of John or another unlawful baptism had without danger to be baptized again. And it is established from this that we say that our baptized normally receive the Holy Spirit from the very fact that they are lawfully baptized: much more then was this true in the primitive church. But in that text it is said that Peter and John laid their hands on them and they received the Holy Spirit, and if they had not received him before, how had they before been lawfully baptized? . . . And as for the oil with which they anoint children, and the linen band which is wound round their heads, it seems that this is a frivolous rite which cannot be derived from scripture. So too it seems that that confirmation which was introduced apart from the apostles is a blasphemy against God, because it continually asserts that bishops give the Holy Spirit anew or strengthen and confirm the gift. . . . But the apostles do not dare to speak thus, but they prayed for them that they might receive the Holy Spirit from God." . . .

Phronesis: ". . . it seems to some that that frivolous and brief confirmation of the bishops with its additional rites was introduced at the prompting of the devil to this end that the people should be deceived in their faith in the church and the dignity and necessity of bishops should be the more accepted."

THE BOHEMIAN BRETHREN

The influence of Wycliffe's ideas was strongly felt by John Huss (d. 1415), who, it may be noted, translated the *Trialogus* into Czech. Among the followers of Huss in Central Europe were the Bohemian Brethren, whose treatment of confirmation must be noticed next. Amos Comenius, 1592–1671, himself one of their bishops, wrote a history of the Bohemian Brothers, in which he included a form for the reception of novices into the Church. At the end of the order of baptism he wrote, "Finally an exhortation is addressed to the parents and godparents that, remembering their obligation, they carefully instruct the child until they can with approval set him, religiously educated and rightly brought up, in the presence of the church, and commend him to the pastoral care of the ministers. Last of all the rite is concluded with the prayer of divine blessing."[1] This emphasis on post-baptismal instruction was fully in accord with the ideas of Wycliffe. There were two ways of receiving novices into the brotherhood, an order for adults who wished for admission and an order for the children of faithful parents, who had been baptized in infancy. The procedure for the latter was as follows:

But the juniors, having been taught the main points of religion by their parents and sponsors or by their teachers in school, are publicly in church committed to the care of the pastors, before the celebration of the holy supper (most frequently at the time of the visitation by the seniors themselves) in this rite:

1. There are first read the words of Christ: *Come unto me, etc.* (Matt. xi.28) with the addition of a very brief exegesis.

2. The boys and girls selected for this, after having been examined for some time previously by the pastor, are placed in order in the middle of the church.

3. Then they are asked whether they wish to renew the covenant entered into with God in their baptism, Deut. xxix.10, etc., Josh. xxiv,22, Isa. xliv.5.

4. When they assent, the main points of the covenant are explained

---

[1] *Historia Fratrum Bohemorum* (Halae 1702), p. 34.

according to the form prescribed by the apostle, Titus ii.11,12,13, and they are ordered openly before the church to renounce Satan, the world, the flesh, etc.

5. A confession of faith is demanded of them: so together they all in a loud voice recite the apostles' creed.

6. Then kneeling, the minister going before them, they pray God that he will forgive the sins of their youth, and will strengthen them with his Holy Spirit that they may do what is pleasing to his will: which later the whole congregation also does, praying for them.

7. In the prayers there is proclaimed to the novices as also to the whole church absolution and the right of the children of God to take their place at the table of the Lord.

8. Finally, there is added also the apostolic rite of the laying on of hands, Mark x.16, Heb. vi.2, Acts viii.16,17, with an invocation of the divine name upon them for strengthening their hope of heavenly grace.[1]

Thus it was the practice of the Bohemian Brethren to baptize in infancy the children of their members, to require them to receive instruction as they became older, and when they had been sufficiently instructed to confess their faith in person in front of the whole congregation. This was in essence a coming of age ceremony, in which those baptized in infancy personally took upon themselves their obligations; and it also conveyed the privilege of admission to holy communion. Although the prayers offered for them include a petition for the strengthening of the Holy Spirit, and although reference is made to Acts 8.16f, the final hand-laying seems to be regarded as a solemn blessing rather than as a sacramental means of grace. The emphasis is mainly on the manward side of things, the personal confession of faith, rather than on the conferring of a gift by God.

The information supplied by Comenius is corroborated in earlier writings emanating from the Brotherhood, from which we quote the following:

(A) A NOTE APPENDED TO THE SECTION ON BAPTISM
     IN A SHORT CONFESSION OF FAITH
     IN A BOOK DATED 29 JULY 1468[2]

Again there should be three sureties for the child, so that if the father and mother are somewhat negligent or dead, the sureties themselves may take charge of the children to guide them to what is good. And

---

[1] From Amos Comenius, op. cit., pp. 34ff.
[2] See G. Rietschel, Lehrbuch der Liturgie (Berlin 1909), p. 147.

when he is grown up and has come to understanding, so that he can answer for himself, they should then bring him to the pastor, and give testimony concerning him how he has been preserved in the power of baptism, and has received instruction. Also he should be questioned whether he will so persevere in the faith of the Lord Christ and in the Christian doctrine preached by the apostles. And when it is known that he is of age reckoned according to the testimony of his sureties and his own confession by word of mouth, he shall receive him into the congregation and by laying on of hands confirm him, and pray that God will give him strength from on high with perseverance. And in the old church he was given a blow on the cheek as a sign that he must suffer for Christ, and this was called strengthening, whether of old or young. But today in the Roman Church they call it confirmation.[1]

(B) FROM "A CONFESSION OF FAITH SENT
BY THE MORAVIANS, OR WALDENSES,
TO VLADISLAV, KING OF HUNGARY, IN 1504"

Our faith being taken from the sacred scriptures, we profess that the practice was observed in the times of the apostles. Whoever did not receive the promised gifts of the Holy Spirit in the years of youth received them for the confirmation of faith by prayer and the laying on of hands in this manner. So also we feel with regard to infants. Whoever being baptized has come to the true faith and purposes to pourtray it in action, in adversities and reproaches, to the intent that the new birth may be seen revealed in his spirit and life of thankfulness, such a one ought to be brought to the bishop, or priest, and be confirmed. And being questioned with regard to the truths of the faith and the sacred precepts, and also with regard to his good will, his firm purpose and works of truth, he shall testify and declare that he has all such things. Such a one should be confirmed in the hope of the truth he has attained, and in deed aided by the prayers of the church, so that there may come to him an increase of the gifts of the Holy Spirit for steadfastness and the warfare of the faith. Finally, by the laying on of hands to confirm the promises of God and the truth held in virtue of the name of the Father and of his Word and the kindly Spirit, let him be received into the fellowship of the church.[2]

[1] Tr. W. Lockton, "The Age for Confirmation", in *Church Quarterly Review* (April 1925), pp. 42f.
[2] *Confessio Fidei Fratrum Waldensium*, tr. Lockton, op. cit., p. 43.

(C) FROM "A DEFENCE OF THE TRUE DOCTRINE OF THOSE
WHO ARE COMMONLY CALLED WALDENSES, OR PICARDS,
WHO HAVE RETAINED THE DOCTRINE OF JOHN HUSS
IN AGREEMENT WITH HOLY SCRIPTURE", PUBLISHED IN 1538

And so when they have come to years of discretion, and understand
the reason of their faith, and have begun seriously to love Christ, we
bring them to a profession of whatever things they have been taught by
their parents or godparents, or by the ministry of the church, that all
those things they themselves of their own accord and quite freely and
before the whole church for their own personal salvation may profess
in the celebration of the rite of the laying on of hands. And this being
done their confirmation follows.[1]

ERASMUS

This rite of admission to full church membership after careful instruction was
known to Erasmus, whose approval it clearly received (see Lockton, op. cit.,
p. 47; Rietschel, op. cit., p. 147). There follows here an important passage from
Erasmus' *Paraphrase on St Matthew's Gospel*, published in 1522, translated by
Lockton, op. cit., p. 47. See also *Desiderii Erasmi Roterodami Opera Omnia* (Lug-
duni Batavorum 1706), tom. VII, and E. C. Achelis, *Lehrbuch de Praktichen
Theologie*, II (Leipzig 1911), p. 309.

It seems to me that it would be not moderately conducive to this matter
if boys who are baptized, when they arrive at puberty, were ordered to
be present at discourses of this sort, in which it is clearly declared to
them what the baptismal profession involves. Then they should be
carefully examined in private by approved men whether they sufficiently retain and remember the things which the priest has taught. If
they be found to retain them sufficiently, they should be asked whether
they ratify what their godparents promised in their name in baptism. If
they answer that they ratify them, then let that profession be renewed
in public at a gathering of their equals, and that with solemn ceremonies,
fitting, pure, serious, and magnificent, and such things as become that
profession, than which there is none more sacred. . . . These things
indeed will have greater authority if they are performed by the bishops
themselves, not by the parish priests, or by hired suffragans.

Erasmus, it will be noted, laid great weight upon the need to instruct in the
faith those baptized in infancy, and to require from them when they were of an
age a personal confession of their faith. It may be that he included the laying on

---

[1] *Apologia Verae Doctrinae*, tr. Lockton, op. cit., p. 44.

of hands among the solemn ceremonies which he thought should accompany
the profession of faith. But he did not say that it should be linked closely with
admission to communion.

These words of Erasmus are of importance because they became known to the
Reformers, including Bucer, and so influenced them when they addressed
their minds to the reform of confirmation.

33. Luther and Confirmation

Luther expressed his views on confirmation at greatest length in his *Babylonian Captivity*, published in 1520. The following excerpt is from Woolf's translation, op. cit., pp. 290ff.

It is difficult to understand what the Romanists had in mind when they made the sacrament of confirmation out of the laying on of hands. We read that Christ touched the children in that way, and by it the apostles imparted the Holy Spirit, ordained presbyters, and cured the sick; as the apostle wrote to Timothy: "Lay hands suddenly on no man." Why have they not made a "confirmation" out of the sacrament of the Lord's Supper? It is written in Acts 9, "And he took food and was strengthened"; and, in Psalm 104, "And bread strengtheneth man's heart." On this reasoning, confirmation would include three sacraments—the supper, ordination, and confirmation itself. But this argument suggests that anything whatever that the apostles did was a sacrament; but, in that case, why did the Romanists not make a sacrament of preaching?

I am not saying this because I condemn the seven sacraments as usages, but because I deny that it can be proved from scripture that these usages are sacraments. O would that there were in the church the kind of laying on of hands that obtained in the time of the apostles, whether we preferred to call it confirmation or healing! But nothing of this remains nowadays except what the Romanists have devised to embellish the duties of bishops, lest they be entirely without function in the church ... our present inquiry has to do with the nature of the sacraments of divine institution, and we find no reason for enumerating confirmation among them. What is required above all else for constituting a sacrament is that it should be accompanied by a divine promise, and this, of itself, calls for our faith. But nowhere do we read that Christ gave a promise in regard to confirmation, although he placed his hands on many people. Among other relevant passages, we read in Mark 16, "They shall lay hands on the sick and they shall recover." But no one has turned this into a sacrament, because it is impossible.

For these reasons, it is enough to regard confirmation as a rite, or ceremony, of the church, like the other ceremonies of the consecration of water, and similar things. If in all other cases physical objects may be sanctified by preaching and prayer, surely there is greater reason for thinking that a man may be sanctified by them. Nevertheless, since sermons and prayers for these purposes are not mentioned in scripture as accompanied by a divine promise, they cannot be called sacraments in which we must have faith; nor are they helpful in promoting salvation from sin. On the other hand, by their very nature, sacraments save those who believe the divine promises always attaching to them.

Thus according to Luther the test of a sacrament is whether our Lord in words recorded in the New Testament promised that a certain act would be the outward sign and vehicle of a particular inward grace; and confirmation, whether by hand-laying or sealing with chrism, fails this test. Not being a sacrament, confirmation was in Luther's judgment in no sense necessary to salvation.

In 1522, two years later, Luther referred again to confirmation in expounding Titus 3.5. The following passage is in *Kirchenpostille: Epistel in der Fruh—Christmas, D. Martin Luthers Werke* (Weimar 1907), Band X, 1.i, p. 117.

You hear: *the water*, that is the bath: you hear: *to be born again*, that is the regeneration and the renewal, and the Spirit, whom here St Paul interprets as the Holy Spirit. And here it is to be noticed that the apostle knows nothing of the sacrament of confirmation. For he teaches that the Holy Spirit is given in baptism, as Christ also teaches, indeed, in baptism we are reborn by the Holy Spirit. We read in the Acts of the Apostles that the apostles laid their hands on the heads of the baptized, so that they might receive the Holy Spirit, which is analogous to confirmation; but there it happens that the Holy Spirit is given with outward signs and causes men to speak in many tongues in order to preach the gospel. But this was a temporary measure and does not continue any more.

In a sermon on the subject of impediments to matrimony, preached the same year, Luther poured scorn on episcopal confirmation as no more than fraudulent juggling, on the ground that it had no foundation in scripture, and that the bishops deceived the people with their lies that it bestowed grace and character.[1] Nevertheless in another sermon delivered that same year, although he regarded it as no better than monkey play, Luther expressed a willingness to see confirmation continue on certain conditions: "I allow that confirmation be administered provided that it is known that God has said nothing about it, and knows nothing of it, and that what the bishops allege about it is false. They mock our God in saying that it is a sacrament of God, when it is a merely human invention."[2] In the spring of the next year, 1523, Luther said, again in a sermon:

[1] *Welche Personen verboten sind zu ehelichen*, ed. cit., Band X, ii, p. 266.
[2] *Von ehelichen leben*, ed. cit., p. 281.

"Confirmation should not be observed as the bishops desire it. Nevertheless we do not find fault if every pastor examines the faith of the children to see whether it is good and sincere, lays hands on them, and confirms them."[1] That is to say, the confirmation which Luther was prepared to tolerate consisted in a solemn blessing of children who had been previously instructed in the faith, such as we have seen was practised among the Bohemian Brethren.

Now whatever Luther wrote about confirmation, the fact remains that he composed no order of confirmation in German. In producing the two editions of his *Taufbüchlein*, and his Longer and Shorter Catechisms, Luther showed what he thought to be essential, namely, that the children of the faithful should be baptized in early infancy and afterwards fully instructed in the faith before they were admitted to adult membership of the Church with the right to participate in the Holy Communion. The rites of confirmation subsequently used in Lutheran Churches are not derived from Luther himself.

Osiander, too, compiled an order of baptism but no order of confirmation, while the *Brandenburg–Nuremberg Church Order* of 1533, largely his work, included no rite of confirmation as such. On the subject of admission to full membership this latter work said:

When the people present themselves, the ministers shall discreetly ask them, as they have opportunity, whether they know the ten commandments, the creed and the Lord's prayer, whether they have a right understanding of the holy sacrament and know what it will profit them if they receive it worthily, but, more particularly, whether they have hatred or enmity towards any man, for nothing is more opposed to this holy sacrament than disunity. They shall further enquire whether the people understand all these things, so that they may discover whether they are being improved through the preaching of the catechism. They shall gently and kindly teach them those things of which they are ignorant, and they are to take particular care that they cause neither young nor old to feel so ashamed because of their questions that they are driven to remain long without the holy sacrament.

And when they see and recognize that somebody has an understanding of the Christian faith and leads a virtuous life, it is not necessary that such a person should be questioned afresh every time as though he were a stranger, but he may be allowed to come to the holy sacrament whenever he presents himself without being questioned again.[2]

---

[1] *Predigt am Sonntag Lätare Nachmittags*, ed. cit., Band XI, p. 66; tr. A. C. Repp, *Confirmation in the Lutheran Church* (St Louis 1964), p. 17; on pp. 15–20 of this work is a full and valuable discussion of Luther's views on confirmation, to which the present writer is much indebted.

[2] Sehling, op. cit., XI, p. 186.

34. *A Strassburg Order of Confirmation*

When Bucer came to Strassburg in 1523, he found the peace of the Church there greatly disturbed by the activities of the Anabaptists and the followers of Caspar Schwenkfeld. Hence he was made acutely aware of the need to defend against the charge of moral laxity a Church which admitted to baptism persons too young to have personal faith. He believed that he could draw the sting of this criticism if for children baptized in infancy and subsequently well instructed he provided an order for public confession of the faith with hand-laying and prayer, to which they could be brought at the age when the children of the Anabaptists received baptism.

But there is reason to doubt whether Bucer succeeded in introducing such a rite into Strassburg while he was a pastor there. Although in a letter in 1548 he wrote, "This is the gospel and this is the doctrine which we taught for twenty eight years and proposed to the people",[1] there is no clear evidence for the existence of a rite of confirmation consisting in hand-laying and prayer in Strassburg as far back as the year 1520, or, with one exception, during the sixteenth century at all.[2]

This one exception is a rite of confirmation used in the church of St Nicholas in Strassburg about the year 1550, after Bucer had left the city, and during the time that Marbach was superintendent.[3] While there is no certain evidence that this rite is the rite which Bucer himself used some twenty years earlier, it breathes the spirit of Bucer.

ON THE CONFIRMATION OF CHILDREN
(FIRMUNG)

Among other reasons why the Anabaptists reject infant baptism is this, that (as they claim) through the introduction of infant baptism the order and discipline of the church are bound to fall into decay, and that these will never be rightly restored without the abolition of this infant baptism. For as long as everyone is baptized in infancy but not everyone has faith, since many are called but few are chosen, voluntary submission to the obedience and discipline of the church is not practised, and no distinction can be drawn or preserved between true and genuine Christians who are such by a conscious act of their own will and false Christians who are Christians in name only. Indeed the latter, even if they live a life of open sin and wickedness deserving the church's ban, cannot be excluded, as was once the church's practice; hence everyone who has been baptized claims to be and to be called a Christian by virtue of his baptism alone. If, however, baptism was postponed and delayed until each person came to the age of reason, and then baptism was only administered to those who had professed their faith and voluntarily sub-

---

[1] See Rietschel, op. cit., pp. 152f.
[2] Ibid., pp. 151f; see also Repp, op. cit., p. 31, n. 73.
[3] See Hubert, op. cit., p. 132.

mitted to the discipline and correction of the church, it would be possible to watch over these people afterwards, and, if they fell into sin and wickedness, to discipline and warn them in accordance with the teaching of Christ.

But it is not the fault of precious infant baptism to which they do such violence and wrong, rather the fault lies in the fact that in the Popish church and among us supposed Evangelicals, as also among them, the Anabaptists, the catechism is neglected and not conducted with diligence, and that when children grow up and come to the age of reason they are not urged to make a public confession of their faith in the presence of the church and to submit themselves gladly to the discipline and admonitions of the church and of all faithful Christians; the result has been that, when children have fallen into bad ways, been brought up without any fear of God, and have neither known nor understood the principal articles and the foundation of the Christian religion, it has been impossible for the parish priests and curates to induce even a modicum of discipline and order into the lives of such rough and uncomprehending people, so that the church may be preserved from open crimes and sins.

Now there is an old practice customary among God's people in the Old Testament, as also in the early Christian church immediately after the apostles' time, that children after receiving circumcision and baptism in their infancy were afterwards instructed and taught with a special care and earnestness in the law by the Levites in their synagogues, and Christian children, as soon as they came to the age of understanding, were taught and instructed by the catechists in the chief articles of Christian doctrine, which they then openly in the Temple in Jerusalem at the three great festivals, and baptized children in the congregations and churches where they received holy baptism, confessed and recited, immediately after which as Jewish children by sacrifice and other ceremonies so also Christian children with hand-laying and the Christian prayer of God's people and the Christian congregation were received and confirmed.

Such a Christian and altogether necessary ceremony is once more provided in the church, whereby baptized children after they have now learned the catechism are openly brought before the church and after an open and voluntary confession submit to the discipline and obedience of the church with hand-laying and faithful prayer to commend them to the Lord our God and his dear congregation.[1]

First, the week before the Sunday on which the children are to be presented they come to church for an hour each day and there recite the whole catechism in order, so that, well practised, they may not falter anywhere: and then on the Sunday morning in the sermon the pastor gives notice that any children who have now learnt their catechism will in the afternoon make profession of their faith, and admonishes the whole congregation diligently to come to hear them, but in particular he admonishes the children's parents and their godfathers and godmothers who had them at their baptism and in their name promised and vowed that when they had grown up and come to the age of reason they would make such a profession of their faith before the church.

Secondly, about one o'clock in the afternoon one of the church bells is rung for a quarter of an hour for a first warning, after which the church minister reads two or three chapters of the bible together with the summaries of Veit Dietrich from the altar.

Thirdly, when the reading is over, the bells are rung together. In the meanwhile the boys and girls who are being presented should already have assembled, and each one should modestly have taken the place appointed and assigned to him during the previous week.

Fourthly, after the bells have rung, the whole congregation present sings "Come, Holy Ghost". Then the pastor says from the altar the prayer beginning, *Almighty God, merciful Father, who hast thy holy angel* ... together with the *Our Father.*

Fifthly, the pastor says:

Dear friends, you have already heard sufficiently in today's sermon why

---

[1] The last paragraph is cited in Lockton, art. cit., p. 46.

we have come together at this time, namely, to present some of your dear children, who will openly profess their faith, which they hold about God and the right and true Christian religion, and afterwards, provided that their profession is honest and in accordance with the holy and divine scripture, to commend them with our prayer to almighty God, the Father of our Lord Jesus Christ. Therefore be silent, sit down, so that none may disturb his neighbour, and diligently give attention.

Sixthly, the pastor goes from the altar to the children who are being presented, and addresses them all together in these words:

Dear children, you are born of Christian parents, who have made you, like all other children, members of the church and of our Lord Jesus Christ through holy baptism, where they together with your godfathers and godmothers promised and vowed to bring you up at home in the fear of God, and to teach you, as soon as you were of an age to understand, the ten commandments, the articles of the Christian faith, the holy Our Father and all other things which every true Christian ought to believe and know,[1] and further that when you had learnt the same they would present you to the church again, so that you might confess your faith publicly and so submit yourselves willingly to the discipline and order of the church as devout children; since therefore the congregation is now assembled to hear each of you, give me your answers in all modesty to the questions which I shall now put to you in turn.

Now, my dear son, tell me, are you a Christian?

Here the pastor first asks the six questions as they are printed at the beginning of the catechism without any further exposition, and when seven or eight boys have recited the answers to these, each in his turn, he begins again at the first one with the ten commandments, and makes him thoroughly recite the exposition of each article.

Seventhly, when both boys and girls have recited and given the exposition of all the articles of the catechism in turn, the pastor continues thus:

Dear children, you have now recited the summary and the principal articles of Christian teaching duly and correctly, but you should not imagine that you now know and understand everything and have no further need of learning and studying. This is only the beginning and the proper foundation of the knowledge of God and of that true godliness to come. Hence in the first place it is necessary that you should come to the children's catechism on Sunday even more diligently than before, so that you may become well versed in those things which you have now recited, and also learn your duty to your neighbour: for these things are easily forgotten if they are not constantly practised.

[1] Compare this with the exhortation to the godparents in the Prayer Book of 1549; above, p. 95

Once they have been truly grasped, however, they are of the highest use and value to a man all his life long in everything that he begins and undertakes; you will be able to remember and understand all the better everything else that you hear preached, to read the holy scriptures for yourselves at home with greater profit and benefit, and to recognize and discern all false doctrine. And secondly, since there is only one Christian church which has God's word pure and undefiled together with the true use of the holy sacraments, into which you were incorporated in holy baptism, and in which you are now to be confirmed as its true members through the laying on of hands, you shall promise and vow that you will always cleave to this Christian church, hate and shun the Popish church, and keep yourselves from all other assemblies and sects and everything that is contrary to sound doctrine. Thirdly, dear children, since, as the apostle says, it is not the hearers of the law but the doers who are justified, it is not sufficient for you to know and understand the catechism and the principal articles of Christian doctrine, but you must faithfully act and live in accordance with them that whatever you do or do not do may be in conformity with them, so that you may never become a stumbling-block to anybody or set them a bad example, but may always be found to be true and fruitful members of the Christian church and obedient children of God. Fourthly and lastly, since no man can be without sin and even the holy children of God sometimes stumble and fall, more particularly, however, because young people lack knowledge and therefore need to be instructed and encouraged to do what is good while they are growing up for their own highest good, you must freely and gladly submit yourselves and allow yourselves to be directed, instructed, and taught by your parents, lords, masters, and mistresses in your homes, showing and displaying to them obedience and all respect in everything that is meet; and if you do what is wrong and commit sin—from which may God the Lord graciously preserve you—you must surrender and submit yourselves first to the discipline, warning and punishment of those who are your proper masters, and also to that of the church and its elders and proper ministers. If you are now prepared to do this with the grace of God, then give your answer.

Here the children say one after another:

Yes, sir, with the help and grace of our Lord Jesus Christ.

Eighthly, the pastor turns from the children and addresses the congregation, thus:

Dear friends, you have now heard how these children who are being presented have made a profession of their faith which is in all points in accordance with holy scripture, and also how they have freely submitted and offered themselves to the church and to you all. Therefore you shall henceforth accept and recognize them as fellow members and heirs with yourselves of the Christian church and of eternal life to come, and since you have the advantage over them in virtue of your years and greater understanding, you must pay particularly diligent attention to them and watch over them, so that they may faithfully live out and practise what they have publicly promised and vowed here in the presence of their dear church. You must also take heed to yourselves lest by wicked actions and a careless life you become the cause of their sin and wrongdoing, but if they do what is wrong and commit sin you shall zealously punish and correct them and encourage them to do what is good.

Whatever help we ministers may be able to give you in this through our office by special exhortations and admonitions out of God's word, we will be ready to offer both now and at all times.

But in order that God the Lord may grant his grace and his Holy Spirit to this work, let us earnestly call upon him with our whole heart and make our prayer to him.

Here the priest kneels down before the altar with the two assistants and says in a loud voice:

Almighty, merciful God, who alone beginnest and confirmest every good work in us . . .[1]

At the end of this prayer the priest turns round to the children, stretches out his hand over them and says:

O Lord Jesus Christ, Son of God, who hast said, If we who are evil can give good gifts to our children . . .

When the prayer is ended, the service is concluded with the singing of a psalm, such as "Keep us, Lord, to thy word" or the Magnificat, "My soul doth magnify the Lord", or some other, and then the pastor dismisses the people with the blessing.

The children who were presented, however, are kept behind afterwards until their names and the names of their parents have all been entered in the church register, and they are then admonished to come to the catechism with even greater diligence than before and to learn the duty to one's neighbour as well as the six articles of the catechism.

The confirmation of children normally takes place twice in the year in spring and autumn, depending on whether a sufficient number of children have learnt the catechism.

---

[1] This prayer is also in the *Cassel Church Order*; below, p. 180.

35. *Ziegenhain and Cassel*

Whether or not he was able to persuade the church in Strassburg to accept a rite such as this, Bucer was able to put into effect his ideas about confirmation when in 1538 the Landgrave Philip summoned him to Hesse to assist in the reformation of the church there. That year there was drawn up at Ziegenhain an Order of Church Discipline in which the following are the regulations concerning confirmation:

Such children who through catechetical instruction are sufficiently advanced in Christian knowledge to be permitted to go to the Lord's table shall on a high festival such as Christmas, Easter and Pentecost, at the instance of the elders and preachers, be presented by their parents and sponsors to the pastors in the presence of the congregation in a place designated in the churches for that purpose. The elders and all other ministers of the word shall stand about the pastor, who shall then examine these children in the chief articles of the Christian faith. When they have answered the questions and publicly surrendered themselves to Christ the Lord and his churches, the pastor shall admonish the congregation to ask the Lord, in behalf of the children, for perseverance and an increase of the Holy Spirit, and conclude this prayer with a collect.

Finally, the pastor shall lay his hands upon the children, thus confirming them in the name of the Lord, and establish them in Christian fellowship. He shall thereupon also admit them to the table of the Lord, adding the admonition that they continue faithfully in the obedience of the gospel and readily receive and faithfully heed Christian discipline and reproof, especially from the pastors.[1]

This rite of confirmation, drawn up by Bucer, was not entirely original. For Bucer was already well acquainted with the rite used by the Waldenses, who in 1530 had addressed certain questions to him, and in his reply he had asserted that scriptural justification for his rite of confirmation with hand-laying and prayer was to be found in our Lord's blessing of the little children in Mark 10: "[the church] has appointed for us for all initiatory ceremonies one baptism, unless you wish to add imposition of hands and solemn blessing such as Christ

---

[1] German text in Sehling, op. cit., VIII, p. 104; translation, Repp, op. cit., p. 32.

gave to the children brought to him, whom the disciples wished to send away"
(quoted in Rietschel, op. cit., p. 153). The public ratification of the faith was
derived by Bucer from the Waldenses and also from Erasmus, while the associa-
tion of confession of the faith with first communion had already been made by
Luther.

In 1539 the regulations of the synod of Ziegenhain were incorporated in the
Church Order of Cassel. But there is no certain evidence that the order of confirmation in this church order was for the time being used in any part of Hesse
except Cassel itself. In its "Order of Confirmation (*Firmung*) and Hand-Laying" Bucer issued these instructions: "This shall take place at Christmas,
Easter and Pentecost at the time of the public preaching: and one shall make an
announcement to the people eight days beforehand and signify the hour, so
that the congregation may be present at the appointed time.

"The ministers of the word shall in the preceding weeks prepare the children
who are to be confirmed in the church. And the children shall also each for
himself with his own mouth before the minister of the word and their parents
rehearse the following confession.

"Also so that the children on whom the hand is laid may go on the same day
to the holy supper of Christ, it shall be held on the same appointed feast day in
all parishes, and therefore on these days one shall come to church one hour
earlier."[1]

There follows a series of questions addressed to the children together with the
answers required from them. Since Bucer used these questions and answers and
the collect again without much alteration when he compiled the section on
confirmation in the *Consultation*,[2] we have not reproduced them here. These
questions deal with the apostles' creed, baptism, and the supper. The children
promise to continue in the fellowship of the Church, attending the common
prayers and bringing their offerings and alms for the poor, and giving humble
obedience to the elders of the Church.

After the questioning comes a long collect, followed by the actual hand-laying with its accompanying formula, "Receive the Holy Spirit, protection and
guard against all evil, strength and help to all goodness from the gracious hand
of God the Father, Son and Holy Spirit. Amen."

How far Bucer intended that the hand-laying should be regarded as a sacramental act conveying the gift of the Holy Spirit is open to dispute. The fact that
he includes this hand-laying among the sacramental ceremonies of the Church
has to be interpreted in the light of Luther's comparison of confirmation with
the ceremony of blessing water.[3] Furthermore, it is possible that Bucer's own
views on this subject underwent a change, because, whereas in his Strassburg
Catechism (1534) he had expressed the opinion that our Lord regarded his
blessing of the little children as a sacrament of the same standing as baptism, yet
in his Catechism of 1543 he said that, although our Lord had not ordered the
use of hand-laying in confirmation, nevertheless the Church did well to continue the practice since it was a proved means of blessing.

Again, the formula in *Cassel*, "Receive the Holy Spirit", could be interpreted

[1] Sehling, op. cit., VIII, p. 124.   [2] See below, pp. 197–201.
[3] See above, p. 172.

as implying that through prayer and imposition of hands an objective gift of the Holy Spirit was imparted. For Erasmus Sarcenius (1501–59) thought it necessary to alter the formula to read, "Strengthen this N. with thy Holy Spirit", and Bucer himself in the *Consultation*[1] used this formula, "Confirm (*sterck*) this thy servant with thy Holy Spirit".[2]

---

[1] See below, p. 202.
[2] On this subject we are much indebted to the full discussion of it in Repp, op. cit., pp. 38–42.

36. The Brandenburg Church Order of 1540

There was no chance for Lutheran reforms to be introduced into Electoral Brandenburg while Joachim I was Elector; but when he died in 1535, he was succeeded by his son, Joachim II, who was prepared to welcome a limited measure of ecclesiastical reform. So it came about that the order of confirmation in the *Brandenburg Church Order* of 1540 was more conservative than many Lutheran rites of confirmation. The German text is in Sehling, op. cit., III, p. 59.

ON CONFIRMATION OR STRENGTHENING
(CONFIRMATION ODER FIRMUNG)

Although all sorts of abuses and frivolity have invaded this rite through lack of understanding and it has been used and interpreted in a completely different way from when it was first instituted, it can still be seen that its primary purpose was this: that those who had accepted the Christian faith and been baptized should afterwards be examined by the bishops at their visitation, and if they found that they had truly embraced the faith, the bishops prayed to God to confirm, preserve and strengthen them in the same and laid their hands upon them. They also made a cross on their foreheads as a token that they should confess their faith openly without shame or fear, signifying thus that they should take upon themselves the cross of Christ and not be ashamed of it.

If, however, the bishops discovered that they were not sufficiently instructed in the faith, they seriously reproved the parish priests and the godparents and earnestly exhorted them to instruct them afterwards, as the godparents had promised to do at their baptism and as the parish priests were bound to do in virtue of their office.

Consequently, so that this rite shall not be disdained but that young people may hereby advance in knowledge of the faith and Christian life and obtain profit and gain, it is our will that confirmation be retained in accordance with the old practice, namely, that when those who have been baptized come to an age when they know what they should believe and how to pray, and also know how they should lead a Christian life and behave honestly, as it is set out in the catechism, they are to be summoned before the bishop at his visitation and examined, and if it is found that they have a good understanding of the faith and Christian life, the bishop shall, as we said above, lay his hands upon them and pray to almighty God that they may remain constant in the faith and may be preserved and strengthened yet more in the same, and then confirm them.

If, however, some are found who have grown up and yet have not been sufficiently and properly instructed in the faith, the bishops shall seriously reprove the pastors and the godparents and command them most sternly to instruct the children of their parishes and their god-children diligently afterwards, so that they may have a better knowledge of what they ought to believe and how they ought to conduct themselves, which can be done if the catechism is diligently preached and conducted.

Since there are many people—praise God—in our lands but few bishops, with the result that it would be too much for the bishops to examine and to instruct each person themselves, they may order the pastors to do this. But it seems good to us that every time confirmation is administered by a pastor the bishops should have one of their learned men present to see that the pastors do all things correctly and do not make confirmation into an abuse and an empty ceremony again, as happened in the past. And so that the pastors and those who are to be confirmed may be the better prepared, it seems fitting to us that this examination, instruction, and confirmation should always take place at Easter and Pentecost, but if there is an obstacle to this in any place, confirmation may be administered at another more convenient time.

[This church order required confirmation to be administered by the laying on of hands with prayer, and if possible by a bishop: but the use of chrism was not enjoined. Nevertheless, this same church order had retained the anointing with chrism at baptism:]

Because it is an ancient traditional ceremony to use chrism in baptism we wish to retain its use, but it is to be understood in the following way.

As the use of chrism is a traditional ceremony, so it has a particular significance. In the Old Testament only kings and priests were commanded by God to be anointed, but we Christians are spiritually anointed by our Lord Jesus Christ with the Holy Spirit to be a royal priesthood, and are therefore called Christians, that is, the anointed, after Christ. To show this the fathers used this external ceremony at baptism and anointed the Christians with chrism, to signify that they were anointed spiritual kings and priests by the Holy Spirit, as various Easter collects show.

Since a ceremony of this kind is not harmful or detrimental to faith but a good reminder, we wish it to continue, but the people must be duly instructed that it is the Holy Spirit who anoints us in baptism and makes us Christians and not the chrism which is only a sign of this, and that those who are not anointed with chrism are none the less fully Christians and suffer no loss without it.[1] Therefore, it is also unnecessary for children who were baptized in need and in haste by women or otherwise to be anointed with chrism afterwards, for this would then be regarded as a necessary part of baptism.[2]

---

[1] This is a deliberate contradiction of what was written by "Urban I"; above, p. 160.
[2] The *Brandenburg Church Order* of 1540 is, therefore, at one with the English Prayer Book of 1549 in retaining the use of chrism in baptism but abolishing it in confirmation.

37. The Council of Cologne 1536[1]

Cap. VIII Again, when the sacrament of confirmation is conferred, our vicars will teach what is done in the Pontificals, namely, that there is sought there the grace of the Holy Spirit by which the novice is confirmed against the temptations of Satan, and is strengthened, so that what he believes in the heart to righteousness he may also openly confess with his mouth to salvation. Wherefore it is customary for that tender age to be fortified by it, which is more inclined to wickedness than to piety, so that that inclination may be reduced, and docility towards piety may be increased. All the faithful (says Urban the Roman pontiff) through the laying on of the bishops' hand. . . .[2] But more about this in another place.

Cap. IX Whether it is expedient to follow the custom whereby confirmation is given not only to adults but also to infants, and that not fasting, we do not here pronounce: although what was sanctioned at the Council of Orleans has pleased us more, namely, that persons should come fasting to confirmation, and of a perfect age, so that they may be admonished to make sacramental confession before they come to it, whereby purified they may be worthy to receive the gift of the Holy Spirit.[3] For since this sacrament is not of absolute necessity, it will be given more conveniently and more profitably, if a little admonition may be added. But before an infant has advanced beyond the seventh year of his age, he will understand, not to say remember, too little or nothing of those things that are done.

Cap. X Just as in baptism there are sponsors, so here there are those who present the person to be confirmed, and set him in the presence of the bishop: and that for a not entirely different reason, except what some people say, that it is fitting that those who have not yet been strengthened against the temptations of the flesh, the world, and Satan

---

[1] Above, p. 43.   [2] For the real source of this quotation see above p. 160.
[3] The reference is to a canon which Gratian (ed. Friedberg, p. 1414) included in his *Decretum*, attributing it to the Council of Orleans of 511. Whatever its real source, this canon has been misinterpreted here, because it did not intend that all confirmation candidates must be of perfect age, but that candidates who were of perfect age must make their confession before their confirmation.

should be presented to the bishop by persons who have been confirmed for some time and have their senses exercised, to whom the faith of the person to be confirmed is known and has been examined, Wherefore they are also to be advised of their duty, and care must be taken that the receiving of so great a sacrament should be carried out worthily and reverently, as we read was done in the primitive church.

Cap. XI In certain places, more by reason of ambition than of piety, when each of the sacraments of baptism and confirmation is administered, those who are called godparents try each to surpass the other in the price of the gift which children raised from the font and presented to the bishop are given. Furthermore, especially after baptism, conversations break out at the very time when conversations should be avoided. Wherefore the people are to be warned that they only study those things which are worthy of these sacraments, and that other things they should either restrain or entirely cut out. For we could not offend God more seriously than by treating his most holy mysteries unworthily.

Cap. XII In addition the parish priest shall teach the people what the chrism means, and why it is made of olive oil and balsam, as the *Enchiridion* will explain.

38. The Enchiridion of Cologne[1]

ON THE SACRAMENT OF CONFIRMATION

Since in baptism not only all sin, both actual and original, is remitted, but also the Holy Spirit, regenerating us to a new creature, is given, who also thus weakens the tinder of concupiscence (that is, the disorder of the appetite and the foolishness of corrupt nature, which remains in us after baptism), that it cannot hurt us, unless we again assent to sin, it follows that if immediately after receiving baptism we had to depart from this world, baptism alone would suffice and regeneration by itself would save those soon to be taken into the peace of the world of bliss. For he who after baptism comes with his acquired innocence spotless to death, is confirmed by death itself, because he cannot sin after death.[2] But now we after crossing the Red Sea have to enter the vast desert of this world and without respite contend with enemies within and without, before we can come to the land of promise, namely, with the flesh, the world, and the devil, whose force is so great that nobody can safely boast that he while in this body of sin can be without sin, because human desires and the remains of old sin lurking in our bosom never cease to cause rebellion against the Spirit. The world also assails us with all its devices while we are still laden with this mortal body. . . .

What are the other sacraments of the church? First of all confirmation and the eucharist. Now we must speak about confirmation. In baptism we are reborn as sons of God, and we receive the promise of the heavenly inheritance, but in order that we may keep it, the pupils need a tutor. Hence Christ did not think it sufficient that in baptism should be imparted to use the renewing Spirit without also there being conferred upon us through the sacrament of confirmation the protecting and defending Spirit, who, however, is not another Spirit, but is the same Spirit as was given in baptism, each according to the various bestowals of graces and spiritual gifts. For in that he is given in confirmation, he is the Comforter, who to the regenerate in Christ is guardian and consoler and tutor. Therefore the Holy Spirit who comes

[1] Above, p. 45. [2] From pseudo-Melchiades; above, p. 162.

upon the waters of baptism in a saving descent in the font gives beauty[1] to innocence. In confirmation he provides an increase to grace, because those who are to live to a full age in this world have to walk among invisible foes and perils, wherefore the Spirit has appeared in more than one form.

In baptism he descends in the form of a dove and testifies to the innocence into which he regenerates. But on the day of Pentecost he fell upon the disciples in fiery tongues, with which the apostles without fear spoke of the great deeds of God.

So in baptism we are regenerated to life: after baptism we are confirmed for battle. In baptism we are washed; after baptism we are strengthened; in baptism we are received as soldiers of Christ and signed. In confirmation we who are to be kept for the struggles and battles of this world are equipped with suitable weapons in order to fight.

Therefore each is a great sacrament, and although the one is closely connected with the other,[2] nevertheless in the gospels and apostolic epistles they are so distinguished that not one but two sacraments plainly appear. After Christ at the last supper had washed the apostles' feet, and had said, "He who is washed . . ." (John 13.10), at length after much else he added, "But when the Comforter is come . . ." (John 15.26). And again, "I have still many things . . ." (John 16.12f).

Then after his resurrection, although the Lord had breathed on the apostles, saying, Receive the Holy Spirit, yet when about to ascend into heaven he promised another gift to the apostles, and through the apostles to all the regenerate: "I", he said, "will send the promise of my Father to you, but you remain in the city until you are clothed with power from on high." And again, "You shall receive power . . ." (Acts 1.8): this promise he most clearly fulfilled later with a visible sign on the day of Pentecost, so that what we see happened once to the apostles in visible form we should be in no doubt at all was done to us by the sacrament of confirmation. For what in the primitive church the descent of the Holy Spirit gave to whole peoples that believed, this in the confirmation of neophytes the laying on of the hand of the bishops bestows on individuals, but to everyone according to the measure of the gift of Christ. . . .

So that this may be made more manifest, at least two most clear pieces of scriptural evidence must be examined [Acts 8.14–17 and

---

[1] Not quite what pseudo-Melchiades wrote; above, p. 161.   [2] Above, p. 161.

19.1–6 are quoted]. Both of these passages all catholic writers refer to the sacrament of confirmation. . . .

Peter, the chief of the apostles, saw Christ, he tasted of his glory on the mountain, he heard the voice of the Father, he saw the wonderful works with his own eyes, he himself also performed miracles. He walked on foot on the waters: he talked on most familiar terms with the Lord. When he had been washed by the Lord and pronounced clean, he declared that he was ready to go with him both to prison and to death. But what happened? Frightened at the voice of a slave girl, he immediately denied him. There came another slave girl, and again he denied him. How could Peter have stood before kings and princes when he could not stand among women? Moreover, after the resurrection even after he had seen Christ, and received a great consolation, he lay hid with the rest of the apostles for fear of the Jews, and more, when with the others he had seen Christ so gloriously ascending and had been comforted with a vision and consolation of angels, he still did not dare to go out in public but waited for the promise of the Father, the Holy Spirit. But as soon as the Spirit came, then at once he and the other apostles all together began to speak with great confidence, and with great power gave their testimony of Christ's resurrection, and were so unafraid of the chief priests and kings of this world that they gloried even in their tribulations and went out from the presence of the council rejoicing that they had been counted worthy to suffer for the name of Jesus.

So in the sacrament of confirmation it happens that the Holy Spirit whom we received in baptism for purification and cleansing we receive for strength also and an increase of power, by which we are confirmed against the assaults of sins, the world, and the devil, and becoming fearless are able to be broken by no disturbances, to yield to no tribulations and lastly to be separated by no terrors or tortures from Christ, claiming with Paul to say, "God forbid that I should glory except in the cross of our Lord Jesus Christ, through which the world is crucified to me and I to the world." This strength of the Holy Spirit is that charity of God which is poured into our hearts by the Holy Spirit, who assures us that neither death nor life nor angels nor principalities nor powers nor present things nor future things nor depth nor height will be able to separate us from the charity of God which is in Christ Jesus. Since it seemed good to Christ to impart this grace to his holy apostles with a certain visible sign immeasurably glorious, how much more was it necessary that the same grace should be transmitted to us who are so much weaker by a certain visible sign for confirming in us our faith in the word?

The word with which this sacrament is conferred is this, I sign thee with the sign of the cross and confirm thee with the chrism of salvation in the name of the Father and of the Son and of the Holy Spirit. We have dealt above with the promise with which this word is associated and the source from which it is derived.

The material of this sacrament is chrism, which is applied by the bishop's hand to the forehead of him that is to be confirmed. In the church of God three kinds of oil are consecrated by the bishops on Maundy Thursday, the oil of the sick, the oil of the catechumens, and the chrism which is composed of olive oil and balsam, and that not without a notable mystery. And it must not be thought that the introduction of holy chrism is new, since it is possible to learn and see from Dionysius,[1] Clement,[2] Fabian,[3] Tertullian,[4] Cyprian,[5] Jerome,[6] Augustine,[7] and the other catholic writers that we have received the consecration of chrism from the apostles, and that the same practice has been received not only in the Roman church but throughout the whole catholic church. For although the ceremonies of the Old Law vanished away when the light of Christ dawned, nevertheless the Christian religion did not disdain the mystery of unction, but rather what had usually been peculiar to kings and priests in that people alone from which Christ was to spring became common among every catholic people that, just as Christ was so called from the chrism, inasmuch as God anointed him with the oil of unique excellence, the Holy Spirit, above his fellows, so also those who participate in him, however many they are, are sharers in the act and in the name and from Christ are called Christians, so that under his leadership they may be his rulers and leaders, and offer to God spiritual sacrifices, being ordained by God priests of holiness, as Peter addressing all Christians says, "You are a chosen generation, a royal priesthood, a holy nation, a people of God's possession." So the external unction with chrism signifies the internal unction of the Holy Spirit, which we receive from Christ, which teaches us about all things.

Now the enemies of the church try to take away its honour from the

---

[1] Above, p. 164.   [2] Above, p. 163.
[3] Above, pp. 163f; these first three references are all spurious.
[4] de Baptismo 7, ed. Evans, p. 16.   [5] Ep. 70.2, C.S.E.L. III, p. 768.
[6] Dialogus c. Luciferianos 9, P.L. 23.165.
[7] Among numerous references by Augustine to the use of chrism are c. Litt. Petil., ii. 104, P.L. 43.342; Sermo 227, P.L. 38.1100; de Civitate Dei 17.9, P.L. 41.532.

chrism on the ground that in the Acts of the Apostles we do not read that the apostles in confirming the baptized used chrism, but only laying on of hands and prayer: and they do it in their own manner, degenerate sons, desiring to make mother church, the pillar of truth, a liar for asserting that the consecration of chrism has been handed down to us through the apostles; but she conquers and will always conquer, because not even the gates of hell will prevail against her. But you wish to know why we do not read that Christ anointed the apostles with chrism, nor that the apostles in the first beginnings of the church anointed the people that were to be confirmed: then notice that there was no need of the external unction of chrism, which symbolised the invisible unction of the Holy Spirit, all the while that the Holy Spirit descended on the confirmed with a visible sign; this we read consisted in the laying on of the hands of the apostles in those first beginnings of the church, but later when the church of God had spread, since there was no longer need of that visible sign of speaking in different tongues, those to be strengthened and confirmed with the Holy Spirit were anointed with chrism so that they might both themselves be admonished by the outward sign, and stirred to faith in the inward mystery and contemplation of it, since the blessed Augustine says that the sacrament of chrism is in the class of visible signs,[1] as is baptism itself. For, as he says elsewhere,[2] "The Spirit is now given through the laying on of the hand without the attesting evidence of temporal and visible miracles, as he was formerly given with them for the commendation of a rude faith and the enlarging of the church. For who now expects this, that those on whom the hand is laid that they may receive the Holy Spirit should suddenly begin to speak with tongues, but invisibly and secretly through the bond of peace the divine charity is seen to be poured into their hearts, so that they can say, For the charity of God has been poured into our hearts through the Holy Spirit who has been given us."

Therefore our rivals must be confronted with the universal agreement of the church of all ages, a most sure testimony, that this ordinance is apostolical, especially when at one and the same time—and that not long after the death of the apostles—in almost all churches it is preserved and approved as an apostolic usage. For so Fabian has it. . . .[3]

Nor must we omit to say here that the chrism is administered one way in baptism and another way in confirmation. For he who has been baptized is signed with chrism by the priest on the top of the head, but

---

[1] *c. Litt. Petil.*, ii, 104, *P.L.* 43.342.   [2] *de Baptismo c. Donat.*, 3.16.21, *P.L.* 43.149.
[3] Above, p. 163.

by the bishop on the forehead, so that in the former unction may be signified the descent of the Holy Spirit upon him to consecrate a dwelling place for God, but in the latter so that the sevenfold grace of the same Spirit may be shewn to come upon a man with all the fulness of holiness and knowledge and power,[1] which the prayers which are said at each unction make sufficiently clear. In confirmation the bishop amongst other things prays thus over the person to be confirmed: Send upon him thy Holy Spirit of sevenfold grace, the Comforter, from heaven, the Spirit of wisdom and understanding, the Spirit of counsel and strength, the Spirit of knowledge and piety, and fill him with the Spirit of thy fear, and sign him with the sign of the holy cross for a propitiation and may he not lose the Holy Spirit but keep him to eternal life. Therefore Dionysius testifies that this sacrament was called by the apostles *Telotes*, that is, perfection and absolution of spiritual power. . . .[2]

Now we will proceed to the explanation of the signs and rites. What the chrism means we have said above, although it is made specially of a mixture of olive oil and balsam. For oil represents the richness of grace, the splendour of faith, and the warmth of charity, and balsam the sweetness of the Spirit by which Christ draws us to himself, and by the reception of which we say, We are the good odour of Christ. For we are confirmed to this end that we remember that we must fearlessly confess the faith, and surround ourselves with the good odour of deeds for the edification of our neighbour.

But he who is to be confirmed is signed with the sign of the cross on his forehead, which is the place of modesty, so that we may be admonished that we have received the sign of our Emperor Christ, whom, putting away all fear and shyness, we must openly and everywhere confess, as Paul said, "God forbid that I should glory save in the cross of our Lord Jesus Christ."

After confirmation the confirmed person is struck a blow that he may remember that he henceforth will gladly suffer insult for the name of Jesus, and to him who strikes him on the right cheek will also offer the left.

Finally, at the end of the divine prayers and invocations which are made over the confirmed, the sponsors or godparents are enjoined to

---

[1] Rabanus Maurus, *de Clericorum Institutione* 1.30, P.L. 107.314, quoted in Gratian, ed. cit., p. 1414.
[2] Above, p. 164.

instruct the confirmed person in the faith, that he turn from evil and do good, and teach him the Lord's prayer.

The effect of the sacrament is more than sufficiently revealed in what has been said already, namely, that it is given in order to impart the gift of the Holy Spirit, by whom we are confirmed against all the temptations of the flesh, the world, and the devil, by whom we are strengthened in faith to confess and glorify the name of our Lord Jesus Christ, by whom finally we receive an increase of charity and perseverance in good works. So the mystery of this sacrament is to be called to mind all through life, so that the Christian may reflect that he is Christ's standard bearer, that he carries the arms of Christ on his forehead, that in the Crucified he will conquer every adverse power, that he will have to be counted a deserter, if he runs away from these standards to the camp of the enemy, that is, the devil, that he is not to be crowned unless he has striven lawfully, that finally he is to be lost unless he has stood loyally by his commander in all actions, tribulations, and hardships. Hence there is scarcely any ceremony in the church which more effectively encourages us to constancy in all temptations, perseverance, and patience. The disposition of him who comes to participate in this sacrament will be this, that he believes that he will receive the Holy Spirit, the pledge of salvation. Moreover, he will confirm his faith from the passages of scripture cited above, mindful of the word of the Saviour, which Christ said to the apostles (of whom the bishops in the church are the successors): As the living Father sent me, I also send you. For as the divine Ambrose says,[1] This is not the work of man, nor is he given by man, but invoked by the priest the Spirit is given by God, in which the function of God is the ministration of the priest.

Finally, the minister of this sacrament is the bishop. For as we read in the Acts, Philip the deacon, although he converted the Samaritans by the word of God and baptized them, did not however administer this sacrament, but the apostles sent to them Peter and John who when they had come down, prayed for them that they might receive the Holy Spirit, which now is done by the bishops who are the successors of the apostles.

[1] de Spiritu Sancto 7.

39. *Hermann's Consultation*[1]

OF THE
CONFIRMATION OF CHILDREN BAPTIZED
AND SOLEMN PROFESSION OF
THEIR FAITH IN CHRIST,
AND OF THEIR OBEDIENCE TO BE SHOWED TO
CHRIST AND TO HIS CONGREGATION

This custom hath been observed in the old and new testament, of the institution of God, that those, which in their first infancy were received into the grace of the Lord, among the old people by circumcision, and in the new people by baptism, as soon as they had understanded this benefit of God, which they had received, and as soon as they had afore conceived faith in God, they themselves should profess their faith in the congregation, and they themselves should bind themselves to the obedience of God, and of the congregation.

At which confession of faith and profession of obedience in the congregation they were to be solemnly confirmed of the congregation in religion through prayer and some token of God's confirmation, which under Moses consisted in sacrifices and oblations and, in the time of the gospel, in laying on of hands and participation of the supper of the Lord. For this is the nature of true and lively faith, that every man desireth to set forth, and magnify the benefits, that God hath showed him, and for his part to offer, and consecrate himself, to the glorifying of his name with all offices of godliness. Whereof Psalm xxii singeth, "Of thee is my praise in the great congregation", Psalm xxxv, "I will give thanks unto thee in a great assembly", etc.

Furthermore, we are so grafted in Christ through baptism, and so made the members of his body, that is to say, of the congregation, and so joined in Christ to other members of Christ, that we must serve all them, with whom we have any acquaintance any participation of kindness, chiefly for the furtherance of godliness and religion, and afterward also in things necessary for this present life, I mean that one

[1] Above, p. 54; tr. Daye (1548), folios clxxi–clxxv.

194

of us acknowledge another, and embrace one another in Christ with sincere love. And first that we teach one another, warn, correct, comfort, and exhort in those things that pertain to a new life in Christ. Secondly, that we also help one another in things necessary for this present life with counsel, work, and service. Therefore the communion of both lives in Christ the Lord, and the recompensation of good turns one to another, requireth that every man openly offer and give himself to this fellowship of the outward and inward man, and to this charge and recompensation of benefits. Seeing then that this confession of faith and giving of ourselves to the obedience of Christ and commendation of his church, which the very nature of faith and necessity of this communication of Christ requireth, cannot be done in baptism, when infants be baptized it must needs be done of them that were baptized in their infancy, when they be meetly well instructed of religion, and when they somewhat understand those great benefits that be given in baptism.

But when they solemnly profess their faith and obedience before the congregation the very nature of faith requireth again that the congregation pray for them solemnly and desire for them the increase of the Holy Ghost that he will confirm and preserve them in the faith of Christ and obedience of the congregation, and that he will ever lead them into all truth. And forasmuch as such prayer made in the name of Christ and trust of his promises cannot be but effectuous, it pertaineth to the ministry of the congregation to strengthen them with the confirmation of the Holy Ghost, for whom the church hath prayed. Therefore our elders following the example of Christ and the apostles, did use laying on of hands as a sign at this confirmation.

This ceremony then observed in the faith of Christ (because it is undoubtedly the office of faith and Christian love, agreeable all manner of ways to the words and institutions of the Lord, and edifying of the religion of Christ) we will that it be restored in the congregation to a godly and a wholesome use, all abuses removed that have crept into the place of this ceremony, which how shameful and noisome they were to our religion every Christian man may easily judge.

Heretofore this ministry of confirmation was a peculiar work of a suffragan. But forasmuch as all things in the church must be referred, ordained, and done for the common profit of Christian men, we will that hereafter this ministry of confirmation, if it cannot be done commodiously by a suffragan, or not as it ought to be done, shall be done by visitors, twice a year in principal solemnities. For whereas at

the beginning the office of confirmation was only committed to
bishops, bishoprics were not so large as they be now, neither were their
dioceses greater than that the bishops might visit once a year every
parish and hear himself, and confirm the children being catechized or
instructed. But now the world is otherwise, and bishoprics be after
another fashion, so that it is impossible that one bishop or suffragan
may with convenient leisure administer this confirmation in his
diocese. For every year there grow up some in every church whom it
shall become to profess their faith, and to be solemnly confirmed.
Wherefore forasmuch as every congregation hath need of yearly looking to, and visitation and solemn profession of faith and confirmation
of them, who in age and knowledge of Christ be grown so far, the
necessary procuration of the Lord's flock committed unto us con-
straineth us, that we provide that the congregation want not meet
ministers for this purpose. For the health of the sheep of Christ must
not serve the persons of the ministers but the persons of the ministers
must serve to their health, that all things may be done according to this
saying, All are yours whether it be Paul or Apollos or Cephas, 1 Cor. iii.

And as St Jerome witnesseth, this confirmation was not therefore the
proper office of bishops in old time because it was not lawful for other
to administer the same seeing that even common ministers, yea every
Christian man, if ordinary ministers wanted, might minister baptism, a
much more excellent sacrament, but it was committed to bishops
peculiarly for this cause, that the bishops of every congregation might
attain more certain knowledge, and might have more wholesome care
and charge while they themselves inquired every year with what
faithfulness and diligence the pastors had instructed both the rest and
chiefly the young children of Christ.

It holp also to greater consent of religion and reverence and obedience
towards the holy ministry, when everyone professed his faith and
obedience of Christ to one bishop.

But forasmuch as so many congregations be committed to the charge
of one bishop that everyone cannot be visited by one bishop or suffragan, we must needs procure that this office of examination and confirmation, which cannot be deferred more than a year without the
great incommodity of the congregations and peril of religion, be
executed by more persons, seeing that it cannot be done by one;
howbeit the parish priests in every congregation with their companions
certain days before the coming of the visitors, shall diligently prepare
the children, whom they propose to offer to confirmation to make

their confession of faith and profession of Christian communion and obedience decently and seemly, which must be done of them after this sort.[1]

The demand: Dost thou profess thyself to be a Christian?

Answer: I profess.

Demand: What is it to be a Christian?

Answer: To be born again in Christ, and to have remission of sins and participation of everlasting life through him.

Demand: Whereby trustest thou that these things be given thee?

Answer: Because I am baptized in the name of the Father, the Son and the Holy Ghost.

Demand: What believest thou of God the Father, the Son and the Holy Ghost?

Answer: The same that the articles of our creed do comprehend.

Demand: Rehearse them.

Answer: I do believe in God the Father almighty, maker of heaven, etc.

Let the child in this place recite all the articles of the creed plainly and distinctly.

Demand: What understandest thou, when thou sayest, I believe in God the Father, in the Son and in the Holy Ghost?

Answer: That they be three persons of one being and power, and yet but one God.

Demand: Why sayest thou God almighty maker of heaven and earth?

Answer: Because I believe that God, as he made all other things, so he made me of nothing by his only Son, our Lord Jesus Christ, and preserveth and governeth through the same Jesus Christ alone, and is present in every place, and worketh all good things in all men, through his only ever wise purpose and righteous will.

Demand: How dost thou understand the second article of Christ our Lord?

Answer: I acknowledge thereby that our nature through the fall of Adam is so corrupted that no angel nor man could purge our sins and satisfy for them, so that it was necessary that the eternal Word, the Son of God, should be made man, conceived of the Holy Ghost and born of the substance of the Virgin Mary, a very man undoubtedly but without sin, who through his death satisfied for our sins, and

---

[1] The series of questions and answers which follows here is derived from the *Cassel Church Order* of 1539, which also was the work of Bucer. A great many of them are taken almost word for word from *Cassel*; some are paraphrased. But in the *Consultation* Bucer added some further questions and answers which were not in *Cassel* at all. These latter are in italics.

through his resurrection and ascension into heaven hath set us with himself in heavenly things, to whom the Father hath given all power in heaven and in earth, that he may govern us and restore in us his own image, and at length, when he shall come to judge the quick and the dead, that he may raise us from the dead, and that he may give to us, which were perfectly framed again to his own image, the inheritance of eternal blissfulness in heaven, and deliver other to be punished in everlasting fire, which have obstinately despised him.

Demand: What is the meaning of the third article?

Answer: Thus, that Christ the Lord hath given the Holy Ghost to us, who through the ministry of the gospel gathereth together the faithful into his congregation, wherein they must be ever stirred up unto repentance, and unto faith, and to receive remission of sins by the word of God, *and sacraments of the communion of Christ, and so in leading a life holy, godly and profitable to their neighbours, with a good conscience,* that they look for Christ the Saviour, who shall take them up to himself in heaven out of this world, and shall raise up again their bodies in the day of judgment unto an heavenly life.

Demand: *Dost thou then surely believe all these things?*

Answer: *I believe them all, and I pray God that he will vouchsafe to increase this faith in me.*

Demand: *What ought this faith to work in thee?*

Answer: *That I doubt nothing but that God and the Father of our Lord Jesus Christ, which with this his Son, sent us his word and gave us all things, is the only true God, that he made all things of nothing, that he only worketh, and giveth all good things, and that he will show himself a Father unto me also for the same his Son's sake our Lord Jesus Christ, that he washed me from sins with Holy Baptism, that he gave me his Holy Spirit, that he incorporated me to his dear Son, and so received me into his church and adopted me to be his son and heir, that also he will keep me in his congregation, give me in the same repentance and remission of sins and the communion of his Son that through him I may ever call upon his name with children's trust, and that in the renewing of myself I may profit daily unto his image: furthermore I believe that through his word and sacraments he will confirm and increase the same in me so that I shall study continually to sanctify his name, and to serve his congregation with all manner of good works, till he take me out of this world unto heavenly joys and the blessed resurrection. All which things I acknowledge that they be performed unto me, and shall be through the only free mercy of the heavenly Father, and through the estimable merit of his Son our Lord Jesus Christ.*

Demand: God and our heavenly Father increase and confirm this thy faith, through his Son, our Lord Jesus Christ. Amen.

Dost thou think, then, and dost thou acknowledge in this faith that thou art verily the son of God and his heir, the brother and joint-heir of our Lord Jesus Christ, and therefore a member of his body, which the congregation is?

Answer: I think so and acknowledge trusting in the most certain promise of God's benevolence and in the merit of our Lord Jesus Christ.

Demand: Doth that please thee then, and dost thou allow it, and wilt thou continue in the same, that thy godfathers promised and professed in thy name at holy baptism, when in thy stead they renounced Satan and the world, and bound thee to Christ and to this congregation that thou shouldest be thoroughly obedient to the gospel?

Answer: I allow these things, and by the help of our Lord Jesus Christ I will continue in the same unto the end.

Demand: Dost thou thyself renounce Satan and all his works with thy heart and mouth here in the sight of God and before his holy congregation?

Answer: I renounce.

Demand: And the world and all his concupiscences?

Answer: I renounce.

Demand: And dost thou wholly give thyself unto all obedience of Christ and his congregation?

Answer: I wholly give over myself thereunto.

Demand: How wast thou first adopted of God to be his son and to be received into his congregation?

Answer: By holy baptism.

Demand: What is baptism?

Answer: The laver of regeneration, whereby I am washed from sins, and grafted in Christ the Lord, and have put him upon me.

Demand: Wilt thou continue in this communion of Christ *unto the end*?

Answer: I will, by the help of our Lord Jesus Christ.

Demand: What requireth this communion of Christ?

Answer: That I continue in this doctrine *that I have confessed, and in all the articles of our faith, and that I believe that I have remission of sins in Christ the Lord, and that I am justified, acceptable to God and heir of everlasting life for his dear beloved Son's sake, and not through mine own merit of righteousness, further that I study to live according to all the*

commandments of God. And that I may go forward in this knowledge
of God, and obedience it requireth that I diligently hear the word of
God by the ministers chiefly upon the Sundays and holy days, and if
the elders of the congregation, or other that will show me such love,
do reprove me of sin, that I take it in good part, and amend my life,
that I also through a sincere zeal of Christ and their health warn my
neighbours living ill and inordinately, and amend them if I can, but,
if I cannot, that I take other with me, which I think may do more
with them, and if they will not hear them neither, that I bring the
whole matter before the elders of the congregation, whom if they
despise to hear, and be therefore excommunicated, that I take them
for heathen and publicans, and avoid their companies as much as my
vocation will suffer, and civil business with them, and their necessity
according to the word of God.

Demand: What doth the communion of the congregation of Christ
require beside?

Answer: It requireth also that I receive the supper of the Lord with
other Christian men, to whom I come, and with whom I dwell, as
one that is one bread and one body with them in Christ.

Demand: What is this sacrament?

Answer: It is the communion of the body and blood of Christ,
which in the Lord's supper, when it is celebrated according to the
institution of the Lord, be truly exhibited with the bread and wine.

Demand: To what use dost thou receive the body and blood of the
Lord?

Answer: *That my faith in him and trust of the new and eternal testament of
the grace of God, redemption of Christ and communion with him may be
confirmed in me more and more,* and that I may live less to myself and
more in him, and that he may repair a new and holy life in me. For
as concerning mine own flesh and blood I can do nothing but sin and
live an ungodly life.

Demand: What more doth the communion of the congregation
require?

Answer: That I add my prayers to the common prayers of the church,
that I come together with them, and give there oblations and alms
liberally to the use of the poor, and so behave myself in all things as a
member of Christ joined in Christ, and cleaving together with all
godly men, and that I acknowledge and reverently use in all things
those whom the Lord made feeders of his congregations, curates of
souls and elders, *as it becometh an obedient son of God, finally, that I be*

thankful for these exceeding benefits, the gospel and communion of his Son our Lord Jesus Christ.

Demand: Wilt thou faithfully perform and observe all these things, as thou hast now professed?

Answer: I will by the help of our Lord Jesus Christ.

After that one of the children hath rehearsed a full confession of his faith, and hath professed the obedience of Christ before the whole congregation, it shall be sufficient to propound questions to the other children after this sort.

Demand: Dost thou also *my son* believe and confess, and wilt thou wholly give over thyself unto the communion and obedience of Christ and his congregation, as thou heardest even now this child to believe and confess that he would bind himself to the obedience of Christ and his congregation?

Here it shall suffice that every one answer thus for himself.

I believe *and confess the same and yield up myself to Christ and his congregation trusting in the grace and help of our Lord and Saviour, Jesus Christ.*

But where children be not so exercised in the knowledge of religion, that they can answer by heart according to the prescribed form the visitor who shall administer the confirmation must read all the answers to such children, and it shall be sufficient if they answer simply that they believe the things that were read. Howbeit he shall labour to declare all things unto them, that they may understand what they go about and what they confess, and profess. Howbeit they must be diligently warned that they remember that they stand in the sight of God, whom they cannot deceive, who beholdeth the heart. And that therefore they must procure with all reverence that they declare the same thing in their life that they profess with their mouth and think in their heart.

But, as we warned before, all the children one by one must be exercised and prepared hereunto and diligently examined the week before, by the ministers and elders of every congregation, and the pastors and elders must bring no children before the visitor to be confirmed, but such as they trust know the sum of religion and believe truly in Christ. It is not to be required precisely that the children answer featly concerning the words, for it chanceth often, that they which be well instructed in the knowledge of faith cannot very handsomely utter the things that they mean, chiefly in an open place, either for shame or some other weakness of mind. Wherefore we must more regard which children truly understand the things that pertain to religion, than which can featly declare them with words, wherein those excel more often which have less godly minds. Now further when the children which shall be confirmed have confessed their faith, and professed the obedience of the gospel, the congregation must be warned that they humbly pray for these children. Whose prayer the pastor shall offer to the Lord, with such a Collect.

The Collect.[1]

Almighty and merciful God, heavenly Father, which only workest in us to will and to perform the things that please thee, and be good indeed, we beseech thee for these children whom thou hast given to

---

[1] This is substantially the prayer in *Cassel* with some additions.

thy church, and hast begotten again to thyself by holy baptism, and in whom thou hast poured that light that they acknowledge and confess before the congregation thy grace and benefits towards themselves and their redemption in Christ Jesu, *and will wholly give over themselves to thee and thy congregation to be obedient to thy commandments*, confirm this thy work, which thou hast wrought in them, increase in them the gift of thy Spirit that ever going forward in the knowledge and obedience of the gospel in thy congregation they may continue to the end, and that they go nowhere aside from that faith and obedience of the gospel, which they have now confessed and professed, being seduced through some perverse doctrine or driven forth by the lusts of the flesh. Grant them that they luckily springing up in thy Son, our Lord Jesus Christ, the head of us all, may grow into him till they come to man's age fully and perfectly in all wisdom, holiness, and righteousness, that they may more fully know and more perfectly love thee, the Father and thy Son, our Lord Jesus Christ, and that they may confess, exalt, and magnify the same more earnestly and effectuously before their neighbours, both in words and deeds. And as thou hast promised us that thou wilt give us whatsoever we shall ask of thee in the name of thy dear Son, *and as thy Son promised us that thou wouldest give us, requiring thee a good spirit much more promptly than any father giveth his children good things, when they pray him: so give these children the thing that we pray thee for, through thy Son Christ, that* when we shall now lay our hands upon them in thy name *and shall certify them by this sign, that thy fatherly hand shall be ever stretched forth upon them, and that they shall never want thy Holy Spirit to keep, lead, and govern them in the way of health, and in a very Christian life:* grant thou, I say, unto them that they may acknowledge these things with true faith, and that they may certainly believe that thou wilt defend them with thy almighty right hand, and keep them from all evil, and deliver them, and lead them to all good works. Finally, that thou wilt never take thy Holy Spirit from them: through our Lord Jesus Christ.

Here the pastor, laying his hands upon them, shall say:

O Lord Jesu Christ, the Son of God, which saidst in the gospel, If you then being evil can give good gifts to your children, how much more shall my Father give the Holy Ghost to them that ask him, item, If two consent together upon the earth, . . .etc.: Confirm this thy servant with thy Holy Spirit, that he may continue in the obedience of thy gospel, and strongly resist the devil and his own weakness, and not grieve the Holy Ghost, or trouble or offend thy church with slanders, but that his whole life may serve to the praise of thy glory, his own health and common profit of thy congregation, as thou hast prescribed to us, and as thou hast promised that thou wilt give to them that ask thee. Amen.

After this let the hymn be sung, "*Now all thanks*", etc.

Now a good while sithence the sign of oil was wont to be used in confirmation but because they abused this sign most superstitiously, and forasmuch as also among Christian men signs and shadows of spiritual things ought not to be so much regarded as the thing and truth itself, the sign of laying on of hands shall be sufficient in this ministration, which the apostles and old fathers thought sufficient, And that this ceremony may be handled with greater gravity and reverence and with more fruit both of the children and of the whole congregation the deans with the visitors, or parish priests, of every congregation shall choose out such a place in the temples from whence the confession and profession of the children and other things that must be done therewithal may be clearly heard and perceived of the whole congregation.

40. Cologne—The Antididagma[1]

The treatment of confirmation in the *Consultation* was strongly criticized in the *Antididagma*, where the claim was made that "the confirmation of the baptized, which is performed by the imposition of episcopal hands and the marking of the sign of the cross with holy chrism on the forehead of the baptized, was celebrated from the time of the apostles in the catholic church as a great sacrament".[2] In order to defend this claim appeal was made to the much quoted passages in Dionysius Areopagiticus, Clement of Rome, Urban, and Melchiades,[3] and to passages in Basil, the Council of Laodicea, Augustine, Prosper, and Eusebius. While all the authorities quoted attest the use of chrism or hand-laying or both in confirmation, those that are genuine do not prove their use before the fourth century. While Gropper may be excused for not knowing that the tradition to which he appealed was not as primitive as he thought, the fact that his appeal was only to tradition and not primarily to the text of Scripture must have rendered his argument quite unconvincing to Bucer and all who took the Reformed position.

In defending episcopal confirmation, Gropper wrote briefly, "For proof of this what is read in Acts 8 will suffice for all devout Christians."[4] He also cited the Councils of Orange and Meaux and the letter of Melchiades.[5] However, the laying on of hands in Acts 8 had been used from the time of Cyprian onwards as scriptural authority for restricting the administration of confirmation to bishops, but it could hardly be adduced to afford scriptural warrant for confirmation with chrism.

The following excerpt sums up the complaint made in the Antididagma:

That book [i.e. the *Consultation*] lest it should go too little against ecclesiastical traditions, abolishes entirely the consecration and the use of chrism, folio 94, the first side.

It denies that confirmation is a divine sacrament. It only requires a public confession of faith before the church. It says that confirmation is not a function which belongs peculiarly to the bishop. It concedes the right to confirm to some visitors and in general to the other pastors, but not according to the form and ancient custom handed down by the catholic church.

Moreover, not only is the chrism traduced as being a useless sign, on the ground that it has been the centre of great superstition, but also the marking of the holy cross on the forehead is here plainly omitted,

[1] Above, p. 70.   [2] Ed. cit., p. 62.   [3] Above, pp. 160–4.
[4] Ed. cit., p. 62.   [5] Above, p. 161.

and, as it appears, this catholic custom is reckoned a useless tradition. For this book wishes each and every ancient ordinance to yield to the reform which is here instituted, folio 90, first and second sides.

In this connection very many questions are piled together in the book. But what those who have invented them mean by questions of this kind the prudent reader understands well enough. But one of them reads thus:

Does that please you, and do you wish to continue in it, that your godparents at holy baptism on your behalf renounced the devil and the world? which you find on folio 90, the first side.

It is not catholic, and so far has never been heard in the catholic church. God preserve us from giving to Christians once baptized a free choice whether they wish to continue in that which their godparents professed in their name in baptism. For baptism must be more highly esteemed and valued among Christians than circumcision among Jews. Now whether in Judaism before the coming of Christ the choice was given to Jews, after they had come to years of discretion, whether they wished to remain in the covenant of God sealed in circumcision or not everybody knows who is even a little versed in scripture. Such a question and such a liberty (as is probably to be feared) could in these most dangerous times provide great occasion for rebaptism and for the embracing of other heresies. Therefore those who have with evil information presented this book to our most clement Lord and Prince Elector, endowed with singular integrity, have either dealt with the subject imprudently or contrived some perfidy.

The final criticism was grossly unfair, because those to whom this question was addressed were expected to answer in the affirmative; and if they were not willing so to reply, they would not have been presented for confirmation. Furthermore, it was clearly intended that all baptized children should, when old enough, learn the catechism and then personally confess their faith and their intention to persevere in it.

41. Confirmation in England—Henry VIII

In his *Babylonian Captivity*, published in 1520, Luther denied that there were seven sacraments, and consequently also denied that confirmation was a sacrament; above, p. 171. This provoked a sharp rejoinder from King Henry VIII, who in his *Assertio Septem Sacramentorum*,[1] published in 1521, defended the traditional view of confirmation. Cranmer had this book in his library.

CAP. X. ON THE SACRAMENT OF CONFIRMATION

So far is he from receiving confirmation as a sacrament that he says that he even wonders what entered into the mind of the church to make confirmation a sacrament, and in a matter so sacred that most frivolous man jests and frivols, asking why they do not also make three sacraments out of bread, on the ground that they have in scripture some opportunities for so doing. The church does not do this for this reason that it does not seize an opportunity from any words of scripture whatsoever to appoint other sacraments than those which Christ instituted and sanctified with his blood, just as on the other hand she omits none of those which have been handed down from Christ and the apostles through their hands, although nothing be written about them anywhere: for in asserting that confirmation effects no salvation and rests upon no promise of Christ, he only says this, but he proves nothing, even if he denies everything.

But when Luther himself deals with certain passages from which, although Luther pours scorn upon it, the sacrament of confirmation could not unreasonably have its origin, why does he make so malicious a judgment about the whole church, as if she founded a sacrament gratuitously, because he finds no word of promise in these passages? As if Christ has promised, said or done nothing at all except what the evangelists include. By this argument if only the gospel of John was extant, he would have denied the institution of the sacrament in the supper of the Lord, about which institution nothing at all is written by John, who by the same counsel of God has not referred to that point that all have omitted many other things which Jesus did, "which", as

---

[1] Ed. L. O'Donovan (New York 1908), pp. 355–63.

206

the evangelist says, "have not been written in this book, and which the whole world could not contain". Therefore some things were revealed to the faithful through the mouths of the apostles, and thereafter were preserved in the perpetual faith of the catholic church; and why should you not believe her in certain matters, although they are not mentioned in the gospels, since, as Augustine says, "without the tradition of the church you could not know what gospels there are". If none of them had ever been written, yet the gospel would have remained written in the hearts of the faithful, and this was prior to the manuscripts of all the evangelists; and the sacraments would have remained, which themselves I doubt not are older than all the books of the evangelists, so that Luther should not think it an effective argument that a sacrament has been received in vain if he does not find it instituted in the gospels. Furthermore, if he accepts nothing at all which he does not read so clearly in scripture that there is no chance of prevarication, how does he believe (if indeed he does believe, who believes hardly anything) the perpetual virginity of Mary?

[After quoting John 15.26f and 16.13] Therefore since the church has had so many and such counsellors, so many living evangelists, and that Spirit who inspires truth, will she be thought to have instituted a sacrament gratuitously and to have set her hope in an empty sign? Will she not rather be thought to have learnt this from the apostles, will she not rather be thought to have learnt it from the Holy Spirit?

[After quoting passages from Hugh of St Victor and Jerome attesting the episcopal anointing and hand-laying after baptism] Thus far Jerome whose opinion is supported not only by many other passages of scripture but also much the most clearly by him who declares in the Acts of the Apostles that the people who were previously baptized in Samaria, when Peter and John went down to them and laid their hands on them, received the Holy Spirit. I am astonished therefore what has come into Luther's mind that he should maintain that confirmation is to be regarded as only a rite and a ceremony, and deny that it should be regarded as a true sacrament; for not only by the testimony of holy doctors and by the faith of the whole church, but also in the clearest passages of holy scripture it is shown by the visible sign of the hand of the bishops to confer not only grace but also the Spirit of grace himself. Therefore let Luther cease to despise the sacrament of confirmation, which the dignity of the minister and the authority of the church and the usefulness of the sacrament itself commend.

42. The Convocation of 1537

Hence in 1521 the Sovereign was opposed to any change in the doctrine and practice of confirmation. But in the following years the views of the German Reformers began to penetrate into England. Luther's writings began to reach England from 1520 onwards, and were widely read, amongst others by the King himself. Unsuccessful attempts were made to suppress them.[1] In 1536 the Lower House of Canterbury Convocation found it necessary to present to the Upper House "The Protestation of the clergy of the Lower House within the province of Canterbury, with declaration of the faults and abuses which heretofore have, and now be within the same, worthy special reformation". Among the sixty-seven propositions which they repudiated were three which had a bearing on confirmation:

iv, *Item*, That children ought not in any wise to be confirmed of the bishops afore they come to the age of discretion.

v, *Item*, That all ceremonies accustomed in the church, which are not clearly expressed in scripture, must be taken away, because they are man's inventions.

vi, *Item*, That hallowed oil is no better than the bishop of Rome his grease or butter.[2]

In 1536 the *Ten Articles* were issued by order of the King. Since the only sacraments with which they dealt were baptism, the Eucharist, and penance, they must be taken to imply that Henry had abandoned the position which he took up in 1521, and had moved a long way towards the standpoint of Luther in the *Babylonian Captivity*.[3]

One result of the publication of the *Ten Articles* was that the next year Convocation was specially summoned to consider the four sacraments which had not been mentioned. Hence what was said in this Convocation affords a good picture of the state of opinion concerning confirmation at this time.

The first question about confirmation was whether it was a sacrament of the New Testament, instituted by Christ, or not. The replies, which reveal a large measure of disagreement, are to be found in J. Strype, *Ecclesiastical Memorials*, I, part 2, pp. 340–63.

[1] See T. M. Lindsay, *A History of the Reformation* (Edinburgh 1934), pp. 320f.
[2] See T. Fuller, *Church History of Britain*, ed. J. S. Brewer (Oxford 1845), III, pp. 129, 131.
[3] Above, p. 171.

LEE, ARCHBISHOP OF YORK, 1531–44. That the sacrament of confirmation was institute by Christ, we be induced to think, for so much
as the apostles used the same, and that with diligence, as appeareth in
the Acts, the 8th and the 19th chapters, and gave the same by tradition
to the church. And that the apostles durst not have taken upon them,
as of themself, to institute any sacrament. And this is the opinion of
St Clement in the fourth epistle. . . . By which words of St Clement
the first question is answered, that is, That this sacrament is institute by
command of the Lord.

GOODRICH, BISHOP OF ELY, 1534–54 As touching this sacrament of
confirmation, as it is now used, there is no express mention made in the
New Testament of the institution thereof by Christ. But the holy and
ancient fathers have taken it for a sacrament of the New Testament,
grounding themselves upon the Acts of the Apostles.

HILSEY, BISHOP OF ROCHESTER, 1535–9 And for this was imposition
of hands ordained, not to continue in that effect as it did in the beginning of the infant church, but to bring baptized people unto a ready
disposition to receive the gifts of the Holy Ghost in visible signs. The
which visible signs are now so far out of sight, that we neither see them,
neither feel them by any confirmation, that we receive now in the
church. . . . Wherefore as Christ moved this question to the high priests
and scribes, so is this question purposed unto us, Whether that confirmation in oil, with this word, *I sign thee*, etc. be of Christ's or of
man's teaching. If it be of Christ's, believe in it; if of man's teaching,
say not, We fear the people. For truth must be truth, and though the
world wholly resist it, and the heeders of that truth that God teacheth
cannot escape just judgment . . .
    But he [i.e. Thomas Aquinas, *S.T.*, Q. 72, a. 1, ad. 7] allegeth the
Acts of the Apostles, that Peter and John laid their hands upon the
people of Samaria that had received baptism, and therewith they received the Holy Ghost. Truth it is that they did so; and so was the
Holy Ghost given: but there is no promise that as often as we do this
that then he or she, that we do so unto, forthwith all shall receive the
Holy Ghost with such gifts as the Samaritans did. And yet it is necessary
that we have such promise afore that we should make a doctrine to the
people, that they shall believe, that every man that is confirmed shall

inevitably (all things done that is used to be done by ministers of the church) receive the Holy Ghost in such effects.

More, if we stand in contention herein, and say that though we have no express written word for this, yet we have the unwritten verity: surely then have we a large garden to gather what we list, and approve all things for sacraments that the fathers hath received, and beareth a signification of holiness: as holy ashes, holy palm, holy water, etc., and shall so increase to an infinite number without need of sacraments.

[After quoting the reference to chrism in Dionysius Areopagiticus] I grant that Denys there speaketh of the cream, but not of such sacrament of cream, that the church now useth. Wherefore I grant that the use of cream came from the apostles, but not with doctrine that whosoever receiveth it, receiveth in it the sevenfold Spirit.

Wherefore I suppose that this holy rite and godly ceremony began by holy fathers, to examine the faith of them that were baptized infants, when that they should come to years of discretion, as my Lord of Hereford's book more evidently [sheweth]; and then, through the word and prayer and imposition of hands, confirmed that faith which they did confess with their mouths. And this is in my judgment not to be despised, but to be allowed and approved, yea although that such ministers take thereunto holy oil, as they do now at this day.

LONGLAND, BISHOP OF LINCOLN, 1521-47   Confirmation is a sacrament of the new law, and instituted by Christ. Proof: first the testimony of the martyr Fabian, Clement and Dionysius.

CAPON (SALCOT), BISHOP OF BANGOR, 1534-9, OF SALISBURY, 1539-57 This sacrament is a sacrament of the New Testament; thus meaning instituted (since the time of the New Testament preached), not of Christ, so far as we can know by scripture, but of the fathers of the church.

STOKESLY, BISHOP OF LONDON, 1530-9   The first question . . . To this I answer that it is.

CRANMER, ARCHBISHOP OF CANTERBURY, 1533-56   There is no place in scripture that declareth this sacrament to be instituted of Christ. First, for the places alleged for the same be no institutions, but acts and deeds of the apostles. Second, these acts were done by a special gift given to the apostles for the confirmation of God's word at that time.

Thirdly, the said special gift does not now remain with the successors of the apostles.

WOTTON, SOMETIME DEAN OF CANTERBURY AND YORK, D. 1567 To the first part of the question I say that confirmation is a sacrament of the New Testament.

BARBER, SOMETIME ADVOCATE IN THE ARCHES AND CHAPLAIN TO CRANMER I believe that it is not clear from scripture about the institution; but I think it was given to the church by apostolic men.

BELL, ARCHDEACON OF GLOUCESTER, LATER BISHOP OF WORCESTER, D. 1556 That confirmation is a sacrament of the New Testament to me appeared most true, not only by a decree of Melchiades, *de Consecrat. Dist., V. c. 2,* with others in the same place [i.e. the section in Gratian dealing with confirmation] and many other great and ancient authors: St Jerome *contr. Lucif.,* Basil, *de Sp. Sancto,* Euseb. in *Hist. Eccles.,* lib. vi, c. 34, but also by the universal consent and use of the holy catholic church; so receiving, observing and even from the beginning to this present time continuing: and, finally, for that meseemeth it is whole granted without controversy of this honourable Council.

And that furthermore it is institute by Christ, I take it; thinking verily that none other might institute a sacrament, as we here take and use the name of a sacrament to be a sensible sign, having an infallible assistance of grace of the Holy Ghost: and so hath both the sign and the very cause thereof.

Wolman Archdeacon of Sudbury and later Dean of Wells (d. 1537) took the conservative position, appealing to well-known passages from "Urban", "Melchiades", Rabanus Maurus, and Ambrose.

MARSHALL, ARCHDEACON OF NOTTINGHAM Confirmation is a sacrament of the new law instituted by Christ, and handed down to the church through the apostles.

CLIFF, CHANTER OF YORK, LATER DEAN OF CHESTER It is a sacrament of the new law, instituted by the apostles of Christ who handed it on.

EDMUNDS, MASTER OF PETERHOUSE, CAMBRIDGE, D. 1544 Confirmation is not a sacrament of the new law, instituted by Christ by any expressed word in holy scripture, but only by the tradition of the fathers.

DOWNES, CHANCELLOR OF YORK   Confirmation is a sacrament of the new law, instituted by Christ, handed down through the apostles.

MARMADUKE (SURNAME NOT GIVEN)   This is a sacrament of the New Testament, institute of Christ.

A NAMELESS DIVINE   That authority that it hath must needs be of the New Testament, or else it would have no place among Christian men, forsomuch as all ceremonies of the Old are abrogated. And as to the second, necessarily it followeth that needs it must have its institution of Christ. For the New Testament is only of Christ. The institution of Christ may be either by express scripture, or else by the authority of scripture it may be institute, though that the scripture by express words do not institute the same. And this appeareth not only by all the old fathers in divers matters, but also by the words of Melanchthon in his article of the baptism of children. When as he hath for the proving of the said article this formal rule, that is to say, Though that by express scripture it be not instituted, yet it is received and used by the authority of scripture, joining with the same the perpetual consent of the universal church: which in all things hath been at all times of a great estimation by the doctrine of all the fathers, as Melanchthon approves before, not dissenting from the old fathers, as he protests divers times.

The place of scripture that giveth authority to this sacrament seemeth to be the viiith chapt. of the Acts, as Bede expressly understandeth the same, and Rabanus after him, and Erasmus also.

Wherefore though it have not so great mystery, nor yet be not of so great necessity and virtue as the other sacraments are, yet is it reverently to be observed.

ROBERTSON, FELLOW OF MAGDALEN COLLEGE, OXFORD, LATER DEAN OF DURHAM [who was involved in the making of the 1549 Prayer Book but disapproved of it, welcomed the accession of Mary, resigned on the accession of Elizabeth]   That confirmation, consignation or the sacrament of chrism was instituted by Christ the authors Fabian, the martyr, and Clement, the companion of Paul, and Dionysius, the disciple of Paul, Augustine XV *de Trinitate*, cap. 26, Bede *Act.* 10, Cyprian in his sermon on the unction of chrism and other sacraments prove.

RICHARD SMITH, REGIUS PROFESSOR OF DIVINITY AT OXFORD, 1531–47 AND 1553–9, A WITNESS AGAINST CRANMER, D. 1563   I affirm that it is so, and that by the word of Christ written, Not the tables of stone, nor yet the skins of parchment, or any other semblable thing: but in the hearts of the apostles. The which strait after their Master's ascension used the said sacrament, and left it to the church without writing. For those apostles of Christ, fully and perfectly instructed by him, left sundry and many things to the church, not putting them in any manner of writing. The which universally received, and always used in the church, from that time even to these days, must and ought to be believed as firmly and stedfastly as any part of the gospel written; or else these articles were necessary to be ceased; which to defend is heretical.

BUCKMASTER, VICE-CHANCELLOR OF CAMBRIDGE, 1537, D. 1545

And as touching these two, that is to say, oil and balm, which we called before the matter of this sacrament, with the holy consecration of the same, which may be called the mystery of the sacrament, no doubt but that, as the most ancient doctrine doth write, the apostles of Christ by Christ's authority did institute and ordain the same; or else, to speak better, Christ did institute them by the apostles, although that in the beginning for a certain season he might dispense with them, that they should not need to use such matter, but only prayer and imposition of their hands upon such as they did confirm. And although mention of these and such other things, rites and ceremonies, which our mother, the church, useth not only in the ministration of this sacrament but also in many of the other is not had expressly in scripture, yet be all such to be observed and fulfilled by the order of apostolical tradition. For as St Augustine writeth in a certain place,[1] Those things be not mentioned in scripture which were commonly done, and yet by some things there they may be understanded in the word. Wherefore St Gregory, *Lib, 7. Registr. Ep. 16*, saith that the order of ancient custom and the canons of the church is an interpreter of all doubts that be not expressed in scripture.

Wherefore albeit all things concerning and appertaining unto this sacrament be not expressly had in scripture, yet ought we reverently and obediently to accept and receive the same, forasmuch as the church, that is to say, the whole multitude of Christian people, hath so allowed and received them hitherto.

The second question to which an answer was required was, What is the outward sign and invisible grace that is conferred in the same.

[1] *de Fide et Operibus.*

LEE   That the outward sign is consignation done by a bishop: and that the graces conferred in the sacrament be the graces called, The seven gifts of the Holy Ghost. . . . And to the second question answer may be made by the words of St Dionysius . . . [he then quotes Clement, Melchiades, and Urban, and the Council of Orleans] And so by the words of the same St Melchiades, among other things, doth appear that one special benefit of the sacrament of confirmation is ghostly strength to fight. Which effect is also shewed by divers other writers.

GOODRICH   The outward sign is imposition of hands, or the anointing with chrism, and the prayer. And yet it is not to be doubted but the receivers of this sacrament receive such graces as be necessary for them, according to the promise of Christ made unto the church and to the ministers of the same, even as it pleaseth him who distributes to each as he pleases, as saith St Paul.

LONGLAND   Imposition of hands. The sign of the cross on the forehead with the application also of chrism. Proof: imposition of hands is attested expressly in the Acts of the Apostles. As for signing with chrism, Fabian and Dionysius say that they have received it from the apostles by divine tradition.

CAPON   That the outward signs be the unctions with chrism and certain words thereunto appointed. The invisible graces promised by scripture we can find none: but by the doctors we find that thereby is given a ghostly strength to confess boldly faith and to resist the temptations of the adversaries.

STOKESLY   That the words *I sign thee with the sign of the holy cross and confirm thee*, etc., with the consignation with the cream, imposition of the hands of the prelates be the signs: and the increase of the gifts of the Holy Ghost, and especially of fortitude, to speak, shew, and defend the faith, and to suffer for the same in case need be, [be the invisible graces].

CRANMER   Secondly, these acts [a reference to Acts 8 and 19] were done by a special gift given to the apostles for the confirmation of God's word at that time.

WOTTON   To the second question I say that the outward sign of confirmation is the touching and marking of the forehead by the hand of the ministers to that sacrament deputed. And the invisible grace is a corroboration or a strengthening and encouraging of him that receiveth the said sacrament to resist his ghostly enemy, and the more willingly and boldly to confess the name and cross of Christ.

BARBER   I believe that imposition of the hand is the sign, that oil was added, as happens in baptism, but does not belong to the essence of the sacrament.

BELL   The outward sign of this sacrament is the sign of the cross in the child's forehead by the bishop's [hand] with holy cream, and the form of the words, viz. *I confirm thee*, etc. then spoken. . . . With sacred unction, according in all parts to some parts of the scripture. Where also is declared the invisible grace given thereby. And I believe verily the seven gifts of the Holy Ghost.

MARSHALL   It is given through imposition of hands, that is, consignation: it confers sevenfold grace, and especially strength, that sin may be resisted.

CLIFF   The external sign is imposition of the hands of the bishop who signs the person to be confirmed with the sign of the holy cross on the forehead with chrism.

EDMUNDS   Confirmation hath not any outward sign expressed by holy scripture. But doctors saith that the holy chrism and certain words said by the bishop, that is to say, *I sign thee with the sign of the cross, I confirm thee with the chrism of salvation in the name of the Father and of the Son and of the Holy Spirit*, be the outward sign.

DOWNES   And through it is conferred the sevenfold grace of the Holy Spirit, and especially strength, that we may resist sin. Its sign is imposition of hands and consignation.

MARMADUKE   The outward sign is imposition of hands, and the sign of the cross with holy oil in the forehead. And the graces invisible is the Holy Ghost, in whom is all graces and especially consolation and strength.

THE NAMELESS DIVINE   The outward sign is the imposition of the hand, for that is expressed in scripture. The oil or the chrism are the institutions of the fathers, as I suppose, for the good signification that oil hath in scripture, that is to say, comfort, gladness, the Holy Ghost, and the gifts of the Holy Ghost.

The invisible graces are gifts of the Holy Ghost; gifts of constancy, strength and such other: but in what measure is only in the knowledge of almighty God. The Holy Ghost, that is to say, gifts of the Holy Ghost, were given by the imposition of the hands at that time visible; as gifts of tongues, and such other. As at that time it was necessary to have external gifts and miracles to teach expressly and confirm the faith, which now are not necessary. The imposition of the hand with prayer of the bishop (as without fail in my opinion there was never imposition of hands without prayer), by virtue of God's word, giveth the former gifts.

And, as I suppose, to give a form of a sacrament, because there should not want an element, required peradventure in such a sacrament, as in baptism water, the fathers added oil.

But, I suppose, as in the sacrament of penance, witnessing so Melanchthon, the absolution which is done by imposition of the hand with the word, is the sacrament in that case; so in this case the imposition of the hand with the prayer of the minister is the sacrament.

ROBINSON   Prayer, imposition of hands, the sign of the cross made on the forehead with the addition also of chrism. What the sign is is taught by Augustine 2, *de Doctrina Christiana*, cap. 1. How the Holy Spirit is given through the prayer the same Augustine teaches, book 15, *de Trinitate*, cap. 26. This [imposition of hands] was of many kinds. For hands were laid on those to be confirmed, Acts 8. In the ordaining of presbyters, 1 Tim. 4. In the healing of the sick, Mark 16. And on heretics returning to the church; and on those corrected, as in Cyprian and Augustine. And this is an apostolic tradition. . . . That Christ or the apostles used the unction of chrism cannot be incontrovertibly proved or disproved, since it is not expressly mentioned in holy writ, although Fabian the Martyr and Dionysius assert that they received it from the apostles at their hands. John also testifies in his last chapter that there are many things which Jesus did which are not written. In addition the things done by the apostles which Luke describes in the Acts of the Apostles were done before the thirtieth year after the passion of Christ; moreover some of the apostles survived till after the fall of Jerusalem. On this [John] Damascene, Book 4, chapter 13, *Of the*

Orthodox Faith, says that many things were handed down by the apostles, which are not written, for example, praying to the east, etc. Cyprian also on the washing of the feet, Augustine to Januarius, Tertullian On the Soldier's Crown, bind us to the traditions of the apostles, to the universal councils duly assembled, to lawful and received customs, not less than to holy writ itself.

The force of the sacrament is the conferring of the grace of the Holy Spirit for strength and perseverance in the good, for fighting against evil, for extinguishing the tinder (of original sin), for the increase of grace, etc. [For this he finds support in Clement, Cyprian, Augustine, Origen, Chrysostom, and Theophylact. He then proceeds to refute Luther without mentioning him by name.] If any one objected that the gift of tongues and prophecy and the other gifts of the Holy Spirit, which were formerly given by the apostles, have ceased, and consequently grace is not now given through imposition of hands, let Augustine, book 3, *de Baptismo contra Donatistas*, give the answer in these words. . . .[1]

Among unwritten traditions necessary to salvation he included infant baptism, the banning of rebaptism for those baptized by heretics, "One Substance", the perpetual virginity of Mary, the baptism of the apostles.

SMITH   The outward sign is the imposition of the hands of the bishop, and the unction of cream used therein. The invisible grace is the sevenfold grace of the Holy Ghost, as wisdom, fear, with the rest; and increase of the grace, justification received by baptism, or the sacrament of penance, if the taker be in grace.

BUCKMASTER   The matter of this sacrament is twofold, the proximate and the remote. The proximate matter is the unction made on the forehead in the form of a cross with consecrated chrism. The remote matter is chrism composed of olive oil and balsam, consecrated specially by a bishop, or by another to whom such a consecration can be entrusted. . . . The form of this sacrament is this, *I sign thee with the sign of the cross, and confirm thee with the chrism of salvation, in the name of the Father and of the Son and of the Holy Spirit.* . . .

[For the inward graces of confirmation he quoted Rabanus Maurus and Urban] . . . that is to say, to have all those things which be profitable unto our health, and perfection of virtue.

[1] Above, p. 191.

The third question asked was, What promises be made that the said graces shall be received by this sacrament.

LEE ... that forsomuch as the seven graces be given in this sacrament, that these graces be his promise, by whose commandment the sacrament is institute. ...

GOODRICH Although that confirmation, as it is now used in the church, hath no special promise of God expressed in scripture thereto annexed, yet certain it is, that imposition of hands was a sacrament ministered of the apostles to them which were baptized, whereby they received the gifts of the Holy Ghost invisible, and to the confirmation of their faith, and strength of that which they had professed before in baptism. Which imposition of hands derived from the apostles' times was not only given to men of years and discretion, first examined by the bishop before the congregation of the articles of their faith and promptness to profess the same against all persecutors thereof, but also to infants and younglings, following the example of Christ, which put his holy hands upon the infants, prayed for them, and blessed them. ...

Longland found the promise of this sacrament in St Peter's quotation from Joel in Acts 2.

CAPON Promise made by scripture we find none. The doctors write that by this sacrament be received the graces above mentioned.

STOKESLY I answer that the facts and deeds that be expressed in the books of the apostles, with the effects ensuing, by the imposition of their hands upon them that before had received remission of their sins, joined with the promises of Christ made to his church, and the continual belief of the university of the same catholic church from the time of the apostles hitherto, without contradiction of any man (ignorants and suspects of heresy only excepted), maketh us, and in my opinion (without prejudice of other men's opinions) ought to suffice to make all men, that hath promised to believe the catholic church, assuredly to think that God hath made the promises of the said grace.

CRANMER The church useth chrism for the exterior sign, but the scripture maketh no mention thereof. What is the efficacy of this sacrament? The bishop in the name of the church doth invocate the

Holy Ghost to give strength and constancy with other spiritual gifts unto the person confirmed, so that the efficacy of this sacrament is of such value as is the prayer of the bishop made in the name of the church.

BARBER   I believe that a sure promise of grace does not appear in the scriptures. None the less I believe that the Holy Spirit is given, and I think it most pious so to believe. . . .

BELL   Meseemeth that the general promise that our Saviour made to his disciples might for an answer suffice every good Christian, although there were no other, as indeed many is. For the general promise is this . . . [the rest is missing].

MARSHALL   It has also a general promise to be received, by which Christ is present in his sacraments.

CLIFF   Through this sacrament the faithful soul is strengthened and comforted against spiritual enemies through the sevenfold grace of the Holy Spirit then poured into the confirmed.

EDMUNDS   Confirmation hath no promise of any invisible grace by Christ, by any expressed word in holy scripture. But doctors saith, By it is received strength to fight against the spiritual enemies. There be no promise of grace made by Christ to them that receive confirmation.

DOWNES   The general promise that Christ is present with those men who have been appointed by him.

MARMADUKE   Christ promiseth the church to be with them, and to assist them to the end of the world. And in the 8th cap. of the Acts was by the apostles given the Holy Ghost; and also in the 19th of the Acts. Which places and Christ's promise no Christian man need doubt, but ought to believe the graces and gifts of the Holy Ghost to be given in this sacrament.

THE NAMELESS DIVINE   I know none other promises than are made in the said viiith chapter of Acts, supposing the apostles executed that thing. By the which there were at that time apparent tokens of the gifts of the Holy Ghost, so taught by Christ their Master, that it might remain a perpetual doctrine to their successors in like manner to use the same.

SMITH This is not apertly put in writing, but taught the apostles by Christ and the church by them.

BUCKMASTER The promises made unto the receivers of this sacrament. The apostles laid their hands on the baptized, and they received the Holy Spirit, Acts 8. Which thing they never would have attempted but only by revelation and precept of the Holy Ghost. And so that sure hope, which they used in the ministering of this sacrament, doth openly shew and argue that the Holy Ghost had promised unto them that he would be ready to give his grace unto them which should be confirmed: upon whom for the same cause they should lay their hand. And so it appeareth that the Holy Ghost, which taught and also commanded the apostles to use this outward sign, did in like manner make a promise to the worthy receivers of the same.

These answers are fully discussed by S. L. Ollard, "Confirmation in the Anglican Communion", in *Confirmation or the Laying on of Hands* (London 1934), pp. 64–70. It will have been noticed how much more importance most of these divines attached to hand-laying than did the *Decree for the Armenians*.

Secondly, it is clear that of all the bishops and theologians who answered the questions it was Cranmer who expressed the most radical views. He could see no evidence in Scripture that confirmation was a sacrament instituted by our Lord, or that chrism was its duly appointed matter. He inclined to the Lutheran belief that the hand-laying in Acts 8 conferred a temporary gift which was subsequently withdrawn, and consequently that this passage of Scripture, much quoted by the conservatives, had nothing to do with the contemporary rite of confirmation.

Now it is known that he had in his library the *Trialogus* of Wycliffe and some of Luther's works. While abroad in part of 1531 and 1532 he met Osiander[1] and also Bucer; and the latter thought well enough of him to dedicate to him his *Metaphrases et Enarrationes in Ep. ad Rom.*, published in 1536. Nevertheless, although by 1537 Cranmer had as a consequence moved towards a Lutheran view of confirmation, he was still open to persuasion, because at the end of his answers appear the words, "This is my reply, saving always the judgment of more learned men and of the orthodox church".

---

[1] Above, p. 17.

43. *The Bishops' Book*[1]

THE SACRAMENT OF CONFIRMATION[2]

As touching the sacrament of confirmation, we think it convenient that all bishops and preachers shall instruct and teach the people committed to their spiritual charge how the apostles in the beginning of Christ's church, although they did certainly know and believe that all such as had duly received the sacrament of baptism were by virtue and efficacy thereof perfectly regenerated in Christ, perfectly incorporated and made the very members of his body, and had received full remission of their sins, and were replenished with abundance and plentifulness of the graces and gifts of the Holy Ghost; yet they used to go unto the people after they were baptized, and so by their prayer and laying of their hands upon them did give and confer unto them the Holy Ghost. And the said people did speak divers languages and prophesied to the intent that the consciences not only of them that had received baptism and professed Christ should be thereby the better ascertained, confirmed and established in Christ's religion, and so more constantly profess the same, but also that the consciences of other, which were out of the church and unbelievers, should the sooner be reduced thereby from their errors, and be brought into the right belief of Christ and his gospel.

Item, How the holy fathers of the primitive church, taking occasion and founding themselves upon the said acts and deeds of the apostles, and considering also that such as had once received the gifts and benefits of the Holy Ghost by the sacrament of baptism might and oftentimes did indeed by temptation, frailty, or otherwise by their own sin and malice lose and fall from the same again, thought it very expedient to ordain that all Christian people should after their baptism be presented to their bishops, to the intent that by their prayers and laying of their hands upon them, and consigning of them with the holy chrism, they should be confirmed, that is to say, they should receive such gifts of the Holy Ghost as whereby they should not only be so corroborated and established in the gifts and graces before received in

[1] Above, p. 73.   [2] Lloyd, op. cit., pp. 94ff.

221

baptism that they should not lightly fall again from the same, but should constantly retain them and persevere therein, and should also be made strong and hardy as well to confess boldly and manfully their faith before all the persecutors of the same, and to resist and fight against their ghostly enemies, the world, the devil and the flesh, as also to bear the cross of Christ, that is, to suffer and sustain patiently all the afflictions and adversities of this world, but also that they should attain increase and abundance of the other virtues and graces of the Holy Ghost.

Item, We think it convenient that all bishops and preachers should instruct and teach the people committed unto their spiritual charge that, although it be well done that men do present their children unto the bishop to receive at his hands the sacrament of confirmation, when they be of so tender age as commonly they be wont to do, yet it is not to be thought that there is any such necessity of confirmation of infants, but that they being baptized and dying innocent before they be confirmed shall be assured to attain everlasting life and salvation by the effect of the sacrament of baptism before received.

44. The Questionnaire of 1540

In 1540 a number of questions were addressed by order of the King to a group of bishops and theologians. They are published in Burnet's *History of the Reformation of the Church of England*, II (London 1841), pp. lxxxviii–cxxxv. The first six questions concerned the number of the sacraments.

1. What a sacrament is by the scripture.
2. What a sacrament is by the ancient authors.
3. How many sacraments there be by the scripture.
4. How many sacraments there be by the ancient authors.
5. Whether this word be and ought to be attributed to the seven only: and whether the seven sacraments be found in any of the old authors.
6. Whether the determinate number of seven sacraments be a doctrine either of the scripture or of the old authors, and to be taught.

The answers to these questions are relevant here only in so far as they show a growing sense that the medieval doctrine that there were seven sacraments, of which confirmation was the second, could not be justified from the use of the word "sacrament" in Scripture and the ancient Fathers.

The seventh question, more closely related to confirmation, asked, "What is found in scripture of the matter, nature, effect and virtue of such as we call the seven sacraments, so as, although the name be not there, yet the thing be in scripture or no, and in what wise spoken of?"

CRANMER   I find not in the scripture the matter, nature and effect of all these which we call the seven sacraments, but only of certain of them, as of baptism ... of Eucharistia ... of penance.... Of the matter, nature and effects of the other three, that is to say, confirmation, order and extreme unction, I read nothing in the scripture as they be taken for sacraments.

LEE   Of baptism we find in scripture the institution by the word of Christ: we find also that the matter of baptism is water, the effect and virtue is remission of sins. Of confirmation we find that the apostles did confirm those that were baptized by laying their hands upon them, and that the effect then was the coming of the Holy Ghost unto them upon whom the apostles laid their hands in a visible sign of the gift of divers languages, and therewith of ghostly strength to confess Christ, following upon the same.

HEATH, BISHOP OF ROCHESTER, 1540–4 The scripture teacheth of baptism, the sacrament of the altar, matrimony and penance manifestly: there be also in the scripture manifest examples of confirmation, viz. that it was done after baptism by the apostles by imposition of hands.

ALDRICH, BISHOP OF CARLISLE, 1537–56 Of confirmation we have in scripture that when the Samaritans by the preaching of Philip had received the word of God and were christened, the apostles hearing of the same sent Peter and John unto them . . . "this", saith Bede, "is the office and duty only of bishops." "And this manner and form", saith St Hierom, "as it is written in the Acts the church hath kept, that the bishop should go abroad to call for the grace of the Holy Ghost, and lay his hands upon them who had been christened by priests and deacons."

COX, HEADMASTER OF ETON, BISHOP OF ELY, 1559–80 I find in scripture of such things as we are to call sacraments: first, of baptism manifestly. Of Eucharistia manifestly. Of penance manifestly. Of matrimony manifestly. Of ordering, through the laying on of the hand and prayer, manifestly. It is also manifest that the apostles laid their hands upon them that were christened.

DAY, PROVOST OF KING'S COLLEGE, CAMBRIDGE, BISHOP OF CHICHESTER, 1543–56 Albeit the seven sacraments be not found in scripture expressed by name, yet the thing itself, that is, the matter, nature, effect, and virtue of them is found there. Of baptism in divers places; of the most holy communion; of matrimony; of absolution; of bishops, priests, and deacons . . . of laying the apostles' hands on them that were christened, which is a part of confirmation . . .

Oglethorpe, Fellow of Magdalen College, Oxford, Bishop of Carlisle, 1557–9, said that the nature, force, and effects of each of the sacraments was found in scripture "as the ancients have interpreted it".

REDMAYNE, LADY MARGARET PROFESSOR OF DIVINITY AT CAMBRIDGE As it appeareth in the articles which be drawn of the said seven sacraments.

EDGEWORTH, FELLOW OF ORIEL COLLEGE, OXFORD In scripture we find of the form of the sacraments, as the words sacramental: and the matter, as the element, oil, chrism; and the patient receiving the sacrament; and of the grace and increase of virtue given by them as the effects.

SYMMONS   The things are contained in scripture, as baptism, confirmation, eucharist, penance, extreme unction, order, although they have not there this name *Sacrament*, as matrimony hath; and every one of them hath his matter, nature, effect and virtue.

TRESHAM, CANON OF CHRIST CHURCH, OXFORD   I think the thing, the matter, the nature, the effect and virtue of them all be in the scripture, and all there institute by God's authority, for I think that no one man, neither the whole church, hath power to institute a sacrament, but that such institution pertaineth only to God.

LEIGHTON, POSSIBLY DEAN OF YORK, 1539–44   To the seventh I say that we may evidently find in scripture the substance of every one of the seven sacraments, the nature, effect, and virtue of the same; as of baptism, confirmation, penance, matrimony, and so forth of the rest. . . .

In conclusion, "In the seventh they do agree, saving this, that the bishop of St David's [Barlow, Bishop of St David's, 1536–48, of Bath and Wells, 1549–54] says that the nature, effect and virtue of these seven sacraments, only baptism, the sacrament of the altar, matrimony, penance are contained in the scripture. The other say that the nature and the virtue of all the seven be contained in the scripture."

The eighth question was Whether confirmation with chrism of them that be baptized be found in scripture.

CRANMER   Of confirmation with chrism, without which it is counted no sacrament, there is no mention in the scripture.

LEE   We find confirmation with imposition of hands in scripture, as before; with chrism we find not in the scripture, but yet we find chrismation with oil used even from the time of the apostles, and so taken as a tradition apostolic.

BONNER, BISHOP OF LONDON, 1540–9 and 1553–9   I find in scripture in many places concerning imposition of hands, which I think, considering the usage commonly and so long withal used, to be confirmation; and that with chrism, to supply the visible appearance of the Holy

Ghost, which Holy Ghost was so visibly seen in the primitive church; nevertheless for the perfect declaration of the verity hereof, I refer it to the judgment of men of higher knowledge in this faculty.

HEATH   Although confirmation be found in the scripture by example, as I said before, yet there is nothing written about chrism.

ALDRICH   The imposition of hands the holy doctors take for the same which we call confirmation, done upon them which were christened before, whereof is written in the Acts. And as for chrism it should seem by Cyprian, both as touching the confection and usage thereof, that it hath a great sound [ground] to be derived out of scripture, though it be not manifestly therein spoken of.

ROBERTSON FELLOW OF MAGDALEN COLLEGE, OXFORD   The thing and effect of confirmation are contained in scripture, namely, laying on of hands by the apostles upon the baptized, through which was given the Holy Spirit. About chrism we read nothing there, because during that time the Holy Spirit descended on the baptized with a visible sign. When that ceased to happen, the church began to use chrism in the place of the external sign.

COX   I find not in scripture that the apostles laying their hands upon them that were baptized, did anoint them with chrism.

DAY   Confirmation with chrism I read not in scripture, but imposition of hands upon the baptized I find there is, which ancient authors call confirmation; and inunction with chrism hath been used from the primitive church.

OGLETHORPE   Of imposition of hands with prayer there is express mention in the scriptures, and it is now called by the doctors by the usual name of confirmation. Holy chrism is an apostolic tradition, as is clear from the ancients.

REDMAYN   The question is not simple, but as if it were asked, Whether eucharist with unfermented wine be in the scripture, or baptism with salt. Imposition of the apostles' hands, in which was conferred the Holy Ghost for confirmation of them who were baptized, is found in scripture. Chrism is a tradition deduced from the apostles, as may be gathered by scripture, and by the old authors, and the mystery thereof is not to be despised.

EDGEWORTH   This sacrament is one, in the unity of integrity, as some others be: therefore it hath two parts, of which one, that is, imposition of hands, is taken Heb. vi and Acts viii. The other part, that is, chrism, is taken of the tradition of the fathers, and so used from the primitive church. See Cyprian, *Epist.*, *Lib.* i, *Ep.* 12.

SYMMONS   Confirmation is found in scripture, and confirmation with chrism is gathered from the old authors.

TRESHAM   I say confirmation is found in scripture, but this additament, with chrism, is not of the scripture, yet is it a very ancient tradition, as appeareth by Cyprian, *On the Unction of Chrism.*

LEIGHTON   To the eighth question I say that confirmation of them that be baptized is found in scripture, but with chrism it is not found in scripture, but it was used with chrism in the church soon after the apostles' time, as it may evidently appear by the cited authors.

COREN   The laying of the bishop's hands upon them that be christened, which is a part of confirmation, is plainly in scripture; and the unction with chrism, which is another part, hath been observed from the primitive church, and is called of St Austin, sacrament of chrism. Unction of the sick with oil and the prayer is grounded expressly in scripture.

Thus there is almost complete agreement that confirmation with the laying on of hands is scriptural, being derived from the laying on of hands in Acts 8, and that the use of chrism goes back to the primitive church, if not to the apostolic age itself; and the most radical view was expressed by Cranmer, who believed that of the seven sacraments only in the case of baptism, Eucharist, and penance could the matter, nature, and effect be found in Scripture. But the other scholars were noticeably more conservative than he in their views about confirmation.

45. The King's Book

The so-called *King's Book* was published in May 1543; above, p. 76. We include here the section on confirmation from T. A. Lacey's edition of 1932, pp. 77f, 82.

We read in holy scripture how the apostles in the beginning of the church, although they did certainly know and believe that all such as had duly received the sacrament of baptism were by virtue and efficacy thereof regenerated in Christ, perfectly incorporated and made the very members of his body, and had received full remission of their sins, and were endued with graces and gifts of the Holy Ghost; yet they went unto the people after they were baptized, and so, by their prayer and imposition of their hands upon them, the Holy Ghost was given and conferred unto them. And the said people did speak divers languages and prophesied; whereby not only they which had received baptism and professed Christ were the better confirmed and established in Christ's religion, and made more constant to confess the same; but also other which were out of the church and infidels might the sooner be reduced by such gifts and miracle from their errors, and be brought into the right belief of Christ and his gospel.

Whereupon the holy fathers of the primitive church, taking occasion and founding themselves upon the said acts and deeds of the apostles, and considering also that such as had once received the gifts and benefits of the Holy Ghost by the sacrament of baptism might, and oftentimes did indeed, by temptation, frailty or otherwise by their own sin and malice lose and fall from the same again, did use and observe, as it hath been hitherto by succession of ages continued, that all Christian people should after their baptism be presented to their bishops, to the intent that by their prayers and imposition of their hands upon them, and consigning them with the holy chrism, they should be confirmed, that is to say, they should receive such gifts of the Holy Ghost as whereby they should be so corroborated and established in the gifts and graces before received in baptism, that they should not lightly fall again from the same, but should constantly retain them, and persevere therein, and also be made stronger and hardier as well to confess boldly and manfully their faith before all the persecutors of the same, and to resist and fight against their ghostly enemies, the world, the devil and the flesh, as also to bear the cross of Christ, i.e. to suffer and sustain patiently all the affliction and adversities of this world, and finally that they should attain increase and abundance of virtues and graces of the Holy Ghost.

And although men ought not to contemn this sacrament, but should present their children unto the bishop to receive at his hands the sacrament of confirmation, yet it is not to be thought that there is any such necessity of confirmation of infants, but that they being baptized and dying innocents before they be confirmed, shall be assured to attain everlasting life and salvation by the effect of the sacrament of baptism received. . . .

[At the end of the section on the seven sacraments] The other two sacraments of confirmation and extreme unction, although they be not of such necessity but that without them men may be saved, yet, forasmuch as in the ministration of them, if they be worthily taken, men receive more abundantly ghostly strength, aid and comfort, they be very wholesome and profitable, and to be desired and reverently received.

46. Tyndale

The rite of confirmation was vigorously attacked by Tyndale in two of his works, in his *Obedience of a Christian Man*, published in 1527, and in his *Answer to the Dialogue of Sir Thomas More*, published in 1530. The excerpts which we have included from these two works are found in his *Works*, Parker Society, I, pp. 273–83 and II, pp. 71f.

(i) If confirmation have a promise, then it justifieth as far as the promise extendeth. If it have no promise, then is it not of God, as the bishops be not. The apostles and ministers of God preach God's word; and God's signs or sacraments signify God's word also, and put us in remembrance of the promises which God hath made unto us in Christ. Contrariwise, antichrist's bishops preach not; and their sacraments speak not; but as the disguised bishop's mum, so are their superstitious sacraments dumb. After that the bishops had left preaching, then feigned they this dumb ceremony of confirmation, to have somewhat at the leastway, whereby they might reign over their dioceses. They reserved unto themselves also the christening of bells, and conjuring or hallowing of churches and churchyards, and of altars and super-altars, and hallowing of chalices and so forth; whatsoever is of honour or profit, which confirmation and the other conjurations also, they have now committed to their suffragans, because they themselves have no leisure to minister such things, for their lusts and pleasures and abundance of all things, and for the cumbrance that they have in the king's matters and business of the realm. One keepeth the privy seal, another the great seal, the third is confessor, that is to say, a privy traitor and a secret Judas, he is president of the prince's council; he is an ambassador; another sort, of the king's secret council. Woe is unto the realms where they are of the council. As profitable are they, verily, unto the realms with their counsel as the wolves unto the sheep, or the foxes unto the geese.

They will say that the Holy Ghost is given through such ceremonies. If God had so promised, so should it be; but Paul saith, (Gal. iii) that the Spirit is received through preaching of the faith. And (Acts x) while Peter preached the faith, the Holy Ghost fell on Cornelius and on his household. How shall we say then to that which they will lay against us in the eighth chapter of the Acts of the Apostles, where Peter and John put their hands on the Samaritans, and the Holy Ghost came? I say that by putting, or with putting, or as they put their hands on them, the Holy Ghost came. Nevertheless, the putting on the hands did neither help nor hinder: for the text saith, They prayed for them that they might receive the Holy Ghost.

God had made the apostles a promise that he would with such miracles confirm their preaching, and move other to the faith (Mark, the last). The apostles, therefore, believed and prayed God to fulfil his promise; and God for his truth's sake even so did. So was it the prayer of faith that brought the Holy Ghost, as thou mayest see also in the last of James. "If any man be sick," saith James, "call the elders of the congregation, and let them pray over him, anointing him with oil in the name of the Lord, and the prayer of faith shall heal the sick." Where a promise is, there is faith bold to pray, and God true to give her petition. Putting on of hands is an indifferent thing. For the Holy Ghost came by preaching of the faith, and miracles were done at the prayer of the faith, as well without putting on of the hands as with, as thou seest in many places. Putting on of the hands was the manner of that nation, as it was to rend their clothes, and to put on sackcloth, and to sprinkle themselves with ashes and earth, when they heard of or saw any sorrowful thing, as it was Paul's manner to stretch out his hand when he preached; and as it is our manner to hold up our hands when we pray, and as some kiss their thumbnail and put it to their eyes, and as we put our hands on children's heads when we bless them, saying, "Christ bless thee, my son, and God make thee a good man"; which gestures neither help nor hinder. This mayest thou well see by the xiiith of the Acts, where the Holy Ghost commanded to separate Paul and Barnabas to go and preach. Then the other fasted and prayed, and put their hands on their heads, and sent them forth. They received not the Holy Ghost then by putting on of hands; but the other, as they put their hands upon their heads, prayed for them that God would go with them and strength them; and couraged them also, bidding them to be strong in God, and warned them to be faithful and diligent in the work of God and so forth.

ANOILING

Last of all cometh the anoiling, without promise and therefore without the Spirit and without profit, but altogether unfruitful and superstitious. The sacraments, which they have imagined, are all without

16—C.I.

promise, and therefore help not. For "whatsoever is not of faith is sin" Rom. xiv. Now without a promise can there be no faith. The sacraments which Christ himself ordained, which have also promises, and would save us if we knew them and believed them, them minister they in the Latin tongue. So are they also become as unfruitful as the other. . . .

That they call confirmation the people call bishoping. They think that if the bishop butter the child in the forehead, that it is safe. They think that the work maketh safe, and likewise suppose they of anoiling. Now is this false doctrine verily.

(ii) As for confirmation, it is no doubt but that it came this wise up, and that this was the use, which the word itself well declareth . . . For the succour and help of young children, baptized before the age of discretion, to know the law of God and faith of Christ, was confirmation instituted, that they should not be alway ignorant and faithless, but be taught the profession at their baptism. And this no doubt was the manner, as we may well gather by probable conjectures and evident tokens: when the children were six or seven years old, their elders brought them unto the priest or deacon in every parish, which officer taught the children what their baptism meant, and what they had professed therein, that is to wit, the law of God and their duty unto all degrees and the faith of our Saviour. And then, because it should not be neglect or left undone, an higher officer, as the archdeacon (for it hath not been, as I suppose, in the bishop's hands alway as now, neither were it meet), came about from parish to parish at times convenient; and the priests brought the children unto him, at eleven or twelve years old, before they were admitted to receive the sacrament of Christ's body haply; and he apposed them of the law of God and faith of Christ, and asked them whether they thought that law good, and whether their hearts were to follow it? And they answered, Yea. And he apposed them in the articles of our faith, and asked them whether they put their hope and trust in Christ, to be saved through his death and merits. And they answered, Yea. Then confirmed he their baptism, saying "I confirm you, that is, I denounce and declare by the authority of God's word and doctrine of Christ that ye be truly baptized within in your hearts and in your spirits, through professing the law of God and the faith of our Saviour, in the name of the Father, the Son and the Holy Ghost. Amen." Which manner I would to God for his tender mercy were in use this day. But after that the devil was

broken loose . . . because the labour seemed too tedious and painful to
appose the children one by one, they asked the priests that presented
them only, Whether the children were taught the profession of their
baptism. And they answered, Yea: and so upon their words they confirmed them without apposing. So when they no longer apposed them,
the priests no longer taught them, but committed the charge to their
godfathers and godmothers, and they to the father and mother, dis-
charging themselves by their own authority within half an hour. And
the father and mother taught them a monstrous Latin *Paternoster* and
an *Ave* and a creed . . . And in process, as the ignorance grew, they
brought them to confirmation straight from baptism, so that now
ofttimes they be volowed[1] and bishopped both in one day.

[1] I.e. baptized; above, p. 86.

47. *The Catechism of Justus Jonas*

Justus Jonas (1493–1555) was a friend of Luther, accompanying him to Worms in 1521, and later becoming professor of canon law at Wittenberg. He compiled a catechism, which was based chiefly on Luther's *Shorter Catechism*, and which was later translated into Latin. In 1548 there was published an English translation of the Latin version, sometimes known as Cranmer's Catechism,[1] although it is uncertain whether the work of translation was done by Cranmer himself or by somebody in his employ. But since he wrote a preface to it, in the form of a dedicatory letter to Edward VI, it would seem that Cranmer must have approved in the main of its contents.

It is in six sections:

(i) the ten commandments with a sermon on each of them;
(ii) the Apostles' Creed with three sermons;
(iii) the Lord's Prayer with a sermon on each clause;
(iv) an instruction on baptism;
(v) a sermon on the authority of the keys (i.e., penance);
(vi) the Lord's Supper.

On the number of the sacraments it said this:

... our Lord Jesus Christ instituted and annexed to the gospel three sacraments or holy seals of his covenant and league made with us ... the first of these is baptism, by the which we be born again to a new and heavenly life, and be received into God's church and congregation, which is the foundation and pillar of the truth. The second is absolution or the authority of the keys, whereby we be absolved from such sins as we be fallen into after our baptism. The third sacrament is the communion of the Lord's Supper, by the which we be fed and nourished and fortified in the faith of the gospel and knowledge of Christ. . . .[2]

Confirmation, therefore, is not regarded as a sacrament. But more important for the present purpose is a section in the preface which Cranmer himself wrote:

And I perceiving that your majesty by the advice of your most dear

---

[1] *A Short Introduction into Christian Religion being a Catechism set forth by Archbishop Cranmer in 1548*, ed. E. Burton. Oxford 1829.
[2] Ibid., p. 183.

uncle, my lord protector, and the rest of your grace's most honourable council, is most desirous to finish and bring to pass that your father did most godly begin, do think that there is nothing more necessary for the furtherance hereof than that it might be foreseen how the youth and tender age of your loving subjects be brought up and traded in the truth of God's holy word ... (there would be no need for so many laws, injunctions, and proclamations) if so great negligence of the education of the youth had not been so much suffered, and the necessary points and articles of our religion and profession omitted, of those whose office and bounden duty was to have most diligently instructed the youth in the same; or if the ancient and laudable ceremony of confirmation had continued in the old state, and been duly used of the ministers in time convenient, where an exact and strait examination was had of all such as were of full age, both of their professions that they made in baptism touching their belief and keeping of God's commandments, with a general solemn rehearsal of the said commandments and of all the articles of the faith. . . .[1]

---

[1] *Works*, Parker Society, II, p. 419. For other instances of the belief that this was the original state of confirmation before it became corrupted by later accretions see pp. 171, 175, 182f, 194, 258f.

48. Confirmation in the Prayer Book of 1549

The evidence which has been cited above proves that in the last years of Henry VIII there was considerable variety of opinion in the English Church as to the matter, form, and effect of confirmation, but that the radical opinions expressed by Cranmer were not widely held.

A passage in the Act of Uniformity of 1549 tells how the King had "appointed the archbishop of Canterbury and certain of the most learned and discreet bishops and other learned men of this realm to . . . draw and make one convenient and meet order, rite and fashion of common and open prayer and administration of the sacraments, to be had and used in his Majesty's realm of England and Wales".[1] It would seem from this that Cranmer himself was mainly responsible for the 1549 book, and consequently for its order of confirmation; and nobody now seems disposed to dispute this. In a letter which he later wrote to Queen Mary, Cranmer referred to a "good number of the best learned men reputed within this realm, some favouring the old, some the new learning, as they term it . . . gathered together at Windsor for the reformation of the service of the church".[2] Nobody now knows for certain the identity of those who assembled at Windsor. But if they were truly representative of the different shades of opinion, they must have engaged in long argument over confirmation, and cannot have reached unanimity.

The title of the service in the 1549 Prayer Book is "Confirmation, wherein is contained a catechism for children".

The retention of the term "confirmation" is in itself significant. Calvin and Zwingli had abandoned the rite in their churches. Many of the Lutheran churches had also abandoned it, while few of those who retained it retained also the ancient name for the rite, among those few being the *Brandenburg Church Order* of 1540; above, p. 182. Evidently the order of confirmation in the 1549 Book is intended to be regarded as a continuation, albeit in another language and in a revised form, of the rite which had borne that name in the West since the days of Faustus of Riez in the fifth century.

THE FIRST RUBRIC: THE FIRST PARAGRAPH

To the end that confirmation may be ministered to the more edifying of such as shall receive it (according to Saint Paul's doctrine, who teacheth that all things should be done in the church to the edification of the same) it is thought good that none hereafter shall be confirmed

---

[1] H. Gee and W. J. Hardy, *Documents Illustrative of English Church History* (1896), pp. 358ff; quoted by C. W. Dugmore in *The English Prayer Book 1549–1662* (1963), p. 9.
[2] *Remains*, Parker Society, p. 450; quoted by Dugmore, op. cit., pp. 9f.

but such as can say in their mother tongue the articles of the faith, the Lord's prayer and the ten commandments, and can also answer to such questions of this short catechism as the bishop (or such as he shall appoint) shall by his discretion appose them in. And this order is most convenient to be observed for divers considerations.

The emphasis on the need for edification recalls a passage in Cranmer's preface to the 1549 Book, where he complained of services in Latin, not understood of the people, "so that they have heard with their ears only, and their hearts, spirit and mind have not been edified thereby".

There were some recent precedents for the rule that children must be able to say the Creed, Lord's Prayer and Ten Commandments in English before they could be confirmed:

ROWLAND LEE'S INJUNCTIONS FOR COVENTRY AND LICHFIELD (c. 1537)   8. *Item*, That ye and every one of you do your diligence and endeavour yourselves to your best industries and labour to instruct and teach as well children as all other your people, both men and women, of that your parish the *Pater Noster*, *Ave* and creed and the ten commandments in English, and that ye or any of you do admit no man nor woman to receive the sacrament of the altar, until ye have heard them recite and declare at the least the same *Pater Noster*, *Ave* and creed in English without book.

THE SECOND ROYAL INJUNCTIONS OF HENRY VIII (1538)   5. *Item*, That ye shall in confessions every Lent examine every person that comes to confession unto you whether they can recite the articles of our faith, and the *Pater Noster* in English, and hear them say the same particularly; wherein if they be not perfect, ye shall declare to the same that every Christian person ought to know the same before they should receive the blessed sacrament of the altar . . .

CRANMER'S INJUNCTIONS FOR HEREFORD (1538)   7. *Item*, That ye, and every one of you, do not admit any young man or woman to receive the sacrament of the altar, which never received it before, until that he or she openly in the church, after mass or evensong upon the holy day, do recite in the vulgar tongue the *Pater Noster*, the creed and the ten commandments.

ROYAL INJUNCTIONS OF EDWARD VI (1547)   33. *Item*, Whether they have declared to their parishioners that they ought to know and under-

stand the *Pater Noster*, the articles of our faith and the ten commandments in English, before they should receive the blessed sacraments of
the altar.[1]

The *Sarum Manual* had included this rubric: "Likewise the godfathers should
be enjoined to teach the infant the Our Father and Hail Mary and I believe in
God."[2]

   The requirement that the bishop or such as he shall appoint shall question the
children in the catechism allows for the fact that most English dioceses were too
large for the bishop to have time to perform this task in person.[3]

   The expression "shall by his discretion appose them in" recalls some similar
words in Tyndale.[4]

THE FIRST RUBRIC: THE SECOND PARAGRAPH

First because that when children come to the years of discretion and
have learned what their godfathers and godmothers promised for them
in baptism, they may then themselves with their own mouth, and with
their own consent, openly before the church ratify and confess the
same, and also promise that by the grace of God they will evermore
endeavour themselves faithfully to observe and keep such things as
they by their own mouth and confession have assented unto.

The clause "come to years of discretion" has a history extending back to the
Fourth Council of the Lateran (1215), of which c. 21 said, "Every faithful person
of either sex, after he has come to years of discretion, shall alone duly confess
all his sins to his own priest at least once a year, and study, as best he may, to
perform the penance imposed upon him, reverently receiving the sacrament of
the eucharist at least at Easter."[5]

   The age at which children were thought to reach the age of discretion was
not defined by this council. Other councils which used the same phrase without
defining the age were Cahors, Rodez, and Tulli (1289) xvi,[6] Toulouse (1229)
c. 13,[7] Albi (1254) c. 29.[8] The *Statutes of John of Liège* (1287), V. 44. were more
explicit: "Children shall not be communicated before they are seen to have discretion of the faith, at about the age of ten."[9] This was repeated at the Council
of Cambrai (1300).[10] With these compare Council of Constance (1300), c. 7:
"But if the person to be confirmed is an adult, that is to say of fourteen years

---

   [1] W. H. Frere and W. M. Kennedy, *Visitation Articles and Injunctions of the Period of
the Reformation* (London 1910), II, pp. 21, 37, 66, 107.
   [2] See Fisher, op. cit., p. 175.
   [3] See also the *Consultation*, above, p. 196, and the *Brandenburg Church Order* of 1540,
above, p. 183.
   [4] Above, p. 232.
   [5] C. J. Hefele and H. Leclercq, *Histoire des Conciles* (Paris 1907, etc.), V, p. 1350.
   [6] P. Labbe, *Sanctorum Conciliorum et Decretorum Collectio nova*, Suppl. III (1749), p. 170.
   [7] Mansi 23.197.   [8] Mansi 23.840.   [9] Mansi 24.899.
   [10] J. Hartzheim, *Concilia Germaniae* (Cologne 1759, etc.), IV, p. 73.

or over, he shall first make his confession and then be confirmed",[1] and the Council of Bamberg (1496) tit. 23: "*item*, children lacking the use of reason, who cannot distinguish between physical and spiritual food shall on no account be admitted to the reception of the body of Christ, since to receive that actual devotion is required. But the Lord's body shall be given to those who begin to have discretion, even before they reach perfect age, as when they are at the age of eleven, or twelve or thirteen."[2]

The need for baptized infants as they grew older to receive instruction and to confess their faith in public and in person was stressed in all the German church orders and in the writings of the Bohemian Brethren[3] and Erasmus.[4] The expression "openly before the church" is found in Cranmer's Injunctions for the diocese of Hereford (1538).[5]

THE FIRST RUBRIC: THE THIRD PARAGRAPH

Secondly, forasmuch as confirmation is ministered to them that be baptized, that by imposition of hands and prayer they may receive strength and defence against all temptations to sin, and the assaults of the world, and the devil, it is most meet to be ministered when children come to that age, that partly by the frailty of their own flesh, partly by the assaults of the world and the devil, they begin to be in danger to fall into sin.

All this had been said at greater length in the *King's Book*,[6] except that there is here no suggestion that one of the purposes for which grace was given in confirmation was to enable those confirmed to confess boldly their faith before the world. The argument here put forward as an attempt to justify on theological grounds the refusal of confirmation to infants shows a singular unawareness of the practice of the primitive Church, where normally candidates of any age from infancy upwards were admitted not only to baptism but also to confirmation and communion,[7] and of the fact that this primitive practice has continued in the Eastern Church until the present day, and continued in the Western Church until the late Middle Ages, and gradually came to an end in the West for reasons quite other than a sense that confirmation candidates ought to be old enough to be able to make a personal profession of faith.[8]

THE FIRST RUBRIC: THE FOURTH PARAGRAPH

Thirdly, for that it is agreeable with the usage of the church in times past, whereby it was ordained that confirmation should be ministered to them that were of perfect age, that they being instructed in Christ's

---

[1] Mansi 25.31.   [2] Hartzheim, op. cit., V, p. 615.   [3] Above, pp. 166ff.
[4] Above, p. 169.   [5] Above, p. 237.   [6] Above, pp. 228f.
[7] See Hippolytus, *Apostolic Tradition*, 21, ed. B. Botte (Munster 1963), pp. 44–56; Whitaker, op. cit., pp. 2–7.
[8] See Fisher, op. cit., pp. 120–40.

religion should openly profess their faith, and promise to be obedient unto the will of God.

The claim is advanced that the rite of confirmation in the 1549 Book, where all candidates had to be old enough to be able to confess the faith in person, represents a return to the usage of the Church in times past.[1] The expression "of perfect age" Brightman thought[2] might be due to a misunderstanding of the canon law, where Gratian[3] quoted a possibly spurious canon of the Council of Orleans (511).[4] But Brightman considered it more likely that the rubric is based upon the *Consultation*[5] or perhaps upon the *Brandenburg Church Order* of 1540.[6] But neither of these authorities actually used the phrase "of perfect age". The Council of Cologne (1536), however, after referring to the subject of infant confirmation, expressed a preference for the ruling of the Council of Orleans, "Namely, that they come fasting to confirmation, of a perfect age".[7]

THE FIRST RUBRIC: THE FIFTH PARAGRAPH

And that no man shall think that any detriment shall come to children by deferring of their confirmation, he shall know for truth, that it is certain by God's word, that children being baptized (if they depart out of this life in their infancy) are undoubtedly saved.

All this had appeared in similar words in the *King's Book*,[8] where we find the same reluctance to pronounce upon the destiny of infants who die unbaptized. It was generally believed in the later Middle Ages that all infants who died unbaptized were undoubtedly deprived of eternal salvation.[9] Furthermore, this same stern doctrine, derived from Augustine, was clearly expressed in some *Articles about Religion*, issued in 1536 by the Convocation and published by the King's authority: "*Item*, that the promise of grace and everlasting life, which promise is adjoined unto this sacrament of light, pertaineth not only unto such as have the use of reason, but also to infants, innocents and children; and they ought therefore and must needs be baptized; and that by the sacrament of baptism they do also obtain remission of their sins, the grace and favour of God, and be made thereby the very sons and children of God, insomuch as infants and children dying in their infancy shall undoubtedly be saved thereby, and otherwise not."[10] This article was included in the *Bishops' Book* of 1537.[11] It is relevant here because of its last three words, which were deliberately omitted in the *King's Book* of 1540 and in the 1549 rubric; and the omission affords an insight into the mind of the English Church on this subject in 1549.

After the first rubric comes "A catechism, that is to say, an instruction to be

---

[1] But see below, pp. 295f.   [2] *The English Rite* (London 1915), p. 778.
[3] *de Consecr. Dist.* 5, c. 6; ed. Freidberg, p. 1414.
[4] Above, p. 185.   [5] Above, p. 195.   [6] Above, p. 182.
[7] Above, p. 185, where it is shown that the intention of the Council of Orleans has been misrepresented.
[8] Above, p. 229.   [9] See Fisher, op. cit., p. 112.
[10] D. Wilkins, *Concilia Magnae Britanniae et Hiberniae* (London 1737), III, p. 818.
[11] Above, pp. 73f.

learned of every child, before he be brought to be confirmed of the bishop". It is virtually the same as the catechism in the Prayer Book of 1662, except that the ten commandments are given in an abbreviated form, and there is no section on the sacraments. All other contemporary formularies of the faith included some teaching about the sacraments. The absence of any such teaching in the catechism of 1549 prompted Brightman to ask whether Cranmer did not know his own mind or whether it was impossible to find agreement at that time.[1] But so far as confirmation is concerned, if the bishops and theologians associated with Cranmer in the production of the 1549 Book were representatives of the various shades of opinion which were revealed in the questionnaire of 1540, agreement can hardly have been possible.

After the catechism there follows this rubric:

So soon as the children can say in their mother tongue the articles, the Lord's prayer, the ten commandments and also can answer to such questions of this short catechism as the bishop (or such as he shall appoint) shall by his discretion appose them in, then shall they be brought to the bishop by one that shall be his god-father or godmother, that every child may have a witness of his confirmation. And the bishop shall confirm them on this wise.

CONFIRMATION

Our help is in the name of the Lord.
Answer: Which hath made both heaven and earth.
Minister: Blessed is the name of the Lord.
Answer: Henceforth world without end.
Minister: The Lord be with you.
Answer: And with thy spirit.[2]

Let us pray.

Almighty and everliving God, who hast vouchsafed to regenerate these thy servants of water and the Holy Ghost, and hast given unto them forgiveness of all their sins, send down from heaven, we beseech thee, O Lord, upon them thy Holy Ghost, the Comforter, with the manifold gifts of grace, the spirit of wisdom and understanding, the spirit of counsel and ghostly strength, the spirit of knowledge and true godliness, and fulfil them, O Lord, with the spirit of thy holy fear.[3]
Answer: Amen.

[1] Op. cit., p. 786.
[2] These versicles and responses come from the *Sarum Manual*, ed. Collins, p. 167; Fisher, op. cit., p. 180.
[3] This prayer is a literal translation of the corresponding Latin prayer in the *Sarum Manual*, which is in turn derived from the sixth-century *Gelasian Sacramentary* (n. 451; ed. Mohlberg, p. 74; Whitaker, op. cit., p. 178). This is the prayer in which the purpose of the rite of confirmation is stated, namely, to send upon the baptized the Holy Spirit with his sevenfold gifts of grace. In the 1549 version a number of Amens, which appeared in the *Sarum* version, have been omitted, and the order in which the seven gifts are mentioned is different.

Minister: Sign them, O Lord, and mark them to be thine for ever, by the virtue of thy holy cross and passion. Confirm and strength them with the inward unction of thy Holy Ghost, mercifully unto everlasting life. Amen.

Then the bishop shall cross them in the forehead, and lay his hands[1] upon their heads, saying:

N., I sign thee with the sign of the cross, and lay my hand upon thee, in the name of the Father and of the Son and of the Holy Ghost. Amen.

And thus shall he do to every child one after another. And when he hath laid his hand upon every child, then shall he say:

The peace of the Lord abide with you.
Answer: And with thy spirit.[2]

Let us pray.

Almighty Everliving God, which makest us both to will and to do those things that be good and acceptable unto thy majesty, we make our humble supplications unto thee for these children, upon whom, after the example of thy holy apostles, we have laid our hands, *to certify them by this sign* of thy favour and gracious goodness toward them, *let thy fatherly hand,* we beseech thee, ever be over them, let thy Holy Spirit ever be with them, and so lead them in the knowledge and obedience of thy word, that in the end they may obtain life everlasting, through our Lord Jesus Christ, who with thee and the Holy Ghost liveth and reigneth, one God world without end. Amen.[3]

Then shall the bishop bless the children thus saying:

The blessing of God almighty, the Father, the Son and the Holy Ghost, be upon you, and remain with you for ever. Amen.

---

[1] The next rubric has "hand" in the singular. It had been the invariable custom in the West from the time of Tertullian at the end of the second century to impose only one hand.

[2] This represents as close a following of the *Sarum* rite as possible, now that chrism is no longer used. The *Sarum* forms were: "And sign them with the sign of the holy cross † and confirm them with the chrism of salvation unto life eternal. Amen. . . . I sign thee *N.* with the sign of the cross † and I confirm thee with the chrism of salvation, in the name of the Father † and of the Son † and of the Holy Ghost. † Amen. Peace be to thee." See Collins, op. cit., p. 167; Fisher, op. cit., pp. 180f.

[3] As the prayer which came at this point in the *Sarum Manual* referred to chrism, it has been omitted here. This prayer is a new composition, the words in italics being taken from the collect before the hand-laying in the *Consultation*. The claim is made that the imposition of hands is after the example of the apostles. While no particular passages of Scripture are cited in support of this claim, the conservative theologians who sat with Cranmer would certainly have seen here a reference to the laying on of hands in Acts 8.

The curate of every parish once in six weeks at the least upon warning by him given shall upon some Sunday or holy day half an hour before Evensong openly in the church instruct and examine so many children of his parish sent unto him as time will serve, and as he shall think convenient, in some part of this catechism. And all fathers, mothers, masters and dames shall cause their children, servants and prentices, which are not yet confirmed, to come to the church at the day appointed, and obediently hear and be ordered by the curate, until such time as they have learned all that is here appointed for them to learn.

And whensoever the bishop shall give knowledge for children to be brought afore him to any convenient place, for their confirmation, then shall the curate of every parish either bring or send in writing the names of all those children of his parish which can say the articles of their faith, the Lord's prayer and the ten commandments. And also how many of them can answer to the other questions contained in this catechism.

And there shall none be admitted to the holy communion, until such time as he be confirmed.[1]

---

[1] Since none could now be confirmed without having learnt the catechism, this rubric ensured that all communicants should have imbibed some instruction and should personally have confessed their faith before their first communion. It "fenced the altar" in so far as it excluded from communion children too young to be able to answer the questions in the catechism. Infant communion has always been permitted in the Eastern Church, and was permitted in the West also from at least the third century until the twelfth; see Fisher, op. cit., pp. 101–8. The intention of this rubric was that all baptized persons should learn the catechism and be confirmed, and so become eligible to communicate.

49. Bucer's Censura

The children on whom confirmation should be conferred are defined in the Book as those who can recite the articles of the faith, the Lord's prayer and the ten commandments, and can sufficiently answer to the questions of the shorter catechism. Now this at once demands careful consideration. For either it is a question of children at their confirmation making a serious confession of their faith, and a confession of such a kind as the church can fairly ratify, such as, for instance, she necessarily requires of those to whom baptism is given in adult age. Or it is thought enough if they merely recite the words of that confession.

If the latter is thought enough, it must be borne in mind how much God is repelled by all those who glorify him with words and their heart is far from him, and that the catechism of Christ was not drawn up in order that the catechised may reply in words only that they believe in God and wish to observe his commandments. For the Lord said, Teach them to observe, not only to relate, all that I have commanded you; and he requires worshippers who worship him in spirit and in truth. Furthermore, if a genuine confession of faith be required and a profession of obedience to Christ, such as indeed has to be required of all adults who by reason of their age can now hear the gospel, and, if they do not refuse the grace of the Holy Spirit, can also understand it, then certainly it will be far from enough to be able to recite it merely in the words which are in the catechism, and to remain still, as afterwards in the Book is stated, in danger of sin: but a confession is to be required of such a kind as can be judged to have proceeded not from the mouth or only from humanly devised teaching, but also may have such signs in life and conduct that it should be accepted by the churches as coming from a heart truly believing the gospel and the teaching of the Holy Spirit.

For although churches cannot see into the hearts of men, yet they must judge trees by their fruits. Hence in olden times adults who asked to be baptized, whom they used to call competents, were examined for a long time so that it might be known from the fruits of faith which are produced in the life and conduct of true believers, so far as men are able to ascertain about men, whether they seriously desired baptism and loved Christ the Lord.

For if the old leaven foolishly taken into the churches has to be purged out, in the fifth chapter of the first Epistle to the Corinthians, it must surely not be knowingly taken in: nor is it right to give anybody any chance to mock the divine majesty by a false confession of the mouth. If you believe, Philip said to the eunuch, with all your heart, you may be baptized. Nor from the fact that Philip baptized this eunuch immediately, as also Paul his gaoler at Philippi, in the sixteenth chapter of Acts, does it follow therefore that all and sundry are to be admitted into the fellowship of the church, as soon as they have with their voice confessed Christ. For these two, the eunuch and the gaoler, indubitably exhibited in that short time the signs of their faith, so that there was no need at all of a longer time in which to examine their faith. Then again these two ministers of Christ, Paul and Philip, were endowed with the spirit of discerning of spirits somewhat more than all of us commonly are.

Therefore so that no opportunity be given to mock God and the churches with vain words, and to confess in words a faith and desire to live to God which the heart does not feel, and so that a leaven may not be implanted in the churches which having been introduced must be purged out lest it spoil the whole lump, it is surely to be wished that children be not admitted to that public and solemn confession of faith and obedience to Christ before they have also demonstrated by their lives and conduct their faith and their intention of living to God.

So that, if they have carefully learnt their catechism, they may earnestly gather at the sacred assemblies: they may frequently and voluntarily call upon God, not compelled by others to do so, they may willingly both hear and speak about God. To their parents and all who give them good advice and teach them they may show themselves obedient: to their elders they may pay due deference: with their equals they may behave humanely: they may be affectionate to their relatives and sympathetic to all the unfortunate: they may be humble and modest: they may shrink from offending anybody: they may be truthful: they may be careful to learn those things which are put before them to learn, and they may be seen to have understanding and respect for the divine law and shame and fear of sin.

So in the case of those in whom these necessary signs of the new man and of true faith in Christ do not manifest themselves, I do not know whether that very public and solemn confession of faith in the church can be received with a good conscience; for these are the pillars and foundations of the truth. And it is evident that not a few children make a confession of this kind with no more understanding of the faith than some parrot uttering his Hallo. So it would be far better to keep among the catechumens those children who as yet show no or only meagre signs of the fear of God and faith in their lives and manners, and to instil into them the doctrine and knowledge of God, until not merely the works of the flesh but the fruits of the spirit of regeneration appear in them. For it will be enough for these, when they are trained in the catechism, thereafter to confess the things of Christ. And if all who are merely able to learn the words of the catechism and to recite them from memory were not so promiscuously admitted to the public confession of the faith and to the firm fellowship of Christ, but only those in whom some signs of regeneration reveal themselves, those slower ones, if indeed they have been born of God, would be the more aroused by the example of these who were deservedly put in front of them to learn in earnest the things of Christ.

Prayer is indeed rightly made over children of any age, whatever faith they have, while they allow themselves to be taught the gospel of Christ. They are also rightly admitted to the common prayers and praises of God which they equally with the others offer to God, so that out of the mouth of babes and sucklings God may perfect praise to himself. But as for making a public confession of faith in the church of Christ, and that one in which the covenant of salvation with God is to be confirmed by knowing and consenting people, as is proposed in the Book, and ratifying that confession publicly in the churches of Christ, I certainly do not see how that can be allowed, since no sound argument is adduced for believing that to be a confession of the faith which is in the confessor, and a confession of a true understanding of the gospel, and not some vain copying of words, which the children have repeated at length because they merely recite them from memory, although in their hearts they perceive nothing of their meaning. Indeed in every administration of the holy things of Christ care must be taken that some holy thing of the Lord is not thrown to the dogs, and that the pearls of the kingdom of Christ are not scattered to the swine, and that the leaven of Satan is not knowingly mixed into the lump of Christ, and wolves are not put among his sheep, and finally that there are not included among those that worship God in spirit and in truth those who honour God with their lips only but their heart is far from him. For even if the utmost care be taken that the assembly of the children of

God be not contaminated and disturbed by the children of the devil, nevertheless while men sleep the devil sows enough tares among the Lord's wheat. But it is evident that God wished his people to dwell alone, without the company of wicked Gentiles, lest they should learn their works. Hence also he strictly commands that they should be cut out and as it were purged out by fire from among his people, who have openly degenerated from it into impiety. He is holy himself and rightly demands that we also be holy.

And how preferable this would be and how much better would be the state of Christianity, if to the table of the Lord and to the full communion of Christ there were only admitted those who according to the rule of God's word can from the fruits of their lives be recognized as members of Christ, and be led by the Spirit of Christ, by whom are led all who are true children of God. The works of the flesh are evident, and the fruits of the Spirit are not concealed. The others should be included among the catechumens until they allow themselves to be catechized, and until the Lord himself grants them surely to receive his regeneration offered in baptism, and also to make progress in their life. For so the just discipline and fellowship of Christ could be preserved, and there would be some semblance of a true church, and that vehement denunciation of the Lord would be avoided, in which God denounces everyone of the wicked who feigns piety by his outward religious acts, saying, Why dost thou preach my ceremonies and take my covenant in thy lips, although thou hatest discipline and castest my words behind thy back? If thou sawest a thief, thou wouldest run with him, etc. [Ps. 50.16f].

Surely no inconvenience to the state and to civil concord can possibly be expected from this separation of the true people of God from those who declare in fact that they are not yet of that people. For in the first place this division is commanded by God, who cannot command anything but what is salutary: nor can his so often repeated promise fail that those will in the end fare best and most happily who fashion their lives in all things according to his word. Moreover, philosophers also have observed that those states function in the most desirable way, in which everyone is esteemed for his own worth, and the honours due to good men are not given to bad men; but Satan, who is effectual in unbelievers and holds wicked men enslaved to his pleasure, cannot in wicked and impious people be more surely guarded against, and also more powerfully driven away from the children of God, than when these latter join themselves as closely as possible to God, and separate

17—C.I.

themselves from every brother who walks disobediently, and cast away all the filth of wicked men and do not touch an unclean person, and hold as Gentiles and publicans, as they are, all who do not hear the church of God calling them to the death of sins and to the life of virtues. For then God adopts his children and makes himself their God and Father, dwells and is found in the midst of them, and makes them formidable and invincible to all evil people, and to be in favour with all men, even with those not altogether lost. And God is delighted not by the number of his people but by their piety.

So fervent prayer is to be made to God that he would grant that these things be truly recognized and perceived by all who are of the episcopal order, and have the care of parishes, so that with all their might they may address themselves to the recovery of this discipline, and in accordance with those ways which God has prescribed—for neither men nor angels will think of better ones—whereby they may some time present a perfect people to the Son of God, the chief shepherd. But this matter requires much care and trouble, so that everyone may submit himself completely and utterly to this gentle yoke of the Lord. But many think this too difficult: nor are there lacking people who dare to blaspheme saying that those things are impossible in this world of ours, as if now there are no Christians left, or our Lord Jesus Christ, who received from the Father all power in heaven and in earth, and is ever most loving to his own, now either will not or cannot enable his people to observe all that he has commanded, and to realize that his commandments are not grievous, if only we ministers and people did not deliberately scorn God's beneficence offered to us, and were willing to pray and even take great care that we might work out our salvation with fear and trembling. Here may our only Saviour, the resurrection and the life, grant us to recognize in time the time of our visitation and the things which belong to true and eternal peace for us.

XVIII

ON THE CATECHISING OF THOSE TO BE CONFIRMED

After the description of this ceremony some rubrics are appended about the time of catechizing, about the presentation of children for confirmation and about the minister of this ceremony, and one that nobody not yet confirmed may be admitted to the holy communion.

As regards the first rubric, it is surely too long to defer the teaching of the catechism till every sixth Sunday. For who could learn any art, however easy, if it were not taught him more often than one day in every sixth week. Now no art at all is more difficult than this art of living to God, since man is born lost in sins. On the whole, therefore, the catechism ought to be expounded and taught on every festal day: the slowness in learning the things of God, innate in all men, demands that; and the days associated with the divine name are particularly to be kept holy to God and spent in religious exercises. Let games and jestings have their own days, and not be mixed with religious things.

In Germany there are not a few churches in which on two days every week besides Sundays the catechism is gone through with the children.

The second rubric also must be enforced with the greatest strictness, that all parents, masters, and mistresses should urge their children and family to present themselves at the right times at the catechizings. But this rubric is presently limited to those only who have been confirmed. But who doubts that young people need catechizing until they have acquired a full knowledge of religion? Now they are to be confirmed who can merely recite the words of the catechism. I would wish, therefore, for the omission of the parenthesis "which are not confirmed" and in its place the insertion of this rubric, that adolescents and all young people, male and female, should attend the catechizing until they are so proficient in the doctrine of Christ that they may be excused by their pastor from the requirements of this rubric. Nor are those somewhat few words, which are prescribed in the Book, to be asked and answered to as if they were the entire catechism of Christ: but catechumens ought to be placed in various classes, and all the mysteries of Christ which it is necessary to believe should with such method, diligence, and power be explained and elucidated, commended and instilled into them, as will enable each to make the quicker and fuller progress and to observe whatever the Lord has commanded.

The minister of this ceremony is defined as the bishop or he whom the bishop shall depute for this purpose. But it would have been desirable that the bishops should undertake this ministration: and it would be especially fitting that this should be performed by them when they visited their churches, which they ought to do every year. But if they cannot achieve that, they must certainly take care to depute other men firmly taught and inspired about the kingdom of God to visit each church every year, and diligently enquire how the sacred ministrations are presented to the people and received by them: or their conduct . . . [something is missing from the text] that it may be corrected, and both ministers and people may be strengthened and advanced in the faith and life of Christ.

And that occasion when the churches are thus visited and restored in the religion of Christ will be very suitable also for the solemn administration of confirmation to those who have made sufficient progress in the catechism of our faith. By this episcopal diligence the people would be very much stirred to become proficient in all the true and efficacious knowledge of Christ: and the bishops of ancient times truly showed this diligence with great zeal for their churches: which also in Germany the superintendents, who are accustomed to perform the office of bishops in our churches, have faithfully reproduced.

Finally, it is here ordered that nobody be admitted to the holy communion, unless he has been confirmed. This rubric will be extremely salutary, if none are solemnly confirmed except those who have confirmed the confession of their mouth with a congruous manner of life, and can be seen also from their conduct to be making confession of their own and not another's faith.

50. Confirmation in the Prayer Book of 1552

The order of confirmation in the Prayer Book of 1552 was identical with that in the 1549 Book from the introductory rubrics as far as the rubric at the end of the catechism, with the one exception that in 1552 the ten commandments were given in full. But drastic changes were made in the second half of the rite, the confirmation proper. Hence to avoid repetition, only the second part is given here.

CONFIRMATION

Our help is in the name of the Lord.
Answer: Which hath made both heaven and earth.
Minister: Blessed is the name of the Lord.
Answer: Henceforth world without end.
Minister: Lord, hear our prayer.[1]
Answer: And let our cry come unto thee.

Let us pray.

Almighty and everliving God, who hast vouchsafed to regenerate these thy servants by water and the Holy Ghost, and hast given unto them forgiveness of all their sins, strengthen[2] them, we beseech thee, O Lord, with the Holy Ghost, the Comforter, and daily increase in them thy manifold gifts of grace, the spirit of wisdom and understanding, the spirit of counsel and ghostly strength, the spirit of knowledge and true godliness: and fulfil them, O Lord, with the spirit of thy holy fear. Amen.

Then the bishop shall lay his hand upon every child severally, saying:

Defend, O Lord, this child with thy heavenly grace, that he may continue thine for ever, and daily increase in thy Holy Spirit more and more,[3] until he come unto thy everlasting kingdom. Amen.

Then shall the bishop say:

Let us pray.

Almighty everliving God, which makest us both to will and to do

[1] 1549: "The Lord be with you ..."
[2] 1549: "Send down from heaven ... upon them ..."
[3] See a prayer in the Strassburg rite of baptism, above, p. 39.

251

those things that be good and acceptable unto thy majesty, we make our humble supplications unto thee for these children, upon whom, after the example of thy holy apostles, we have laid our hands, to certify them by this sign of thy favour and gracious goodness toward them: let thy fatherly hand, we beseech thee, ever be over them, let thy Holy Spirit ever be with them, and so lead them in the knowledge and obedience of thy word, that in the end they may obtain the everlasting life, through our Lord Jesus Christ, who with thee and the Holy Ghost liveth and reigneth one God, world without end. Amen.

Then the bishop shall bless the children thus saying:

The blessing of God almighty, the Father, the Son and the Holy Ghost, be upon you, and remain with you for ever. Amen.

The curate of every parish, or some other at his appointment, shall diligently upon Sundays and holy days[1] half an hour before Evensong, openly in the church instruct and examine so many children of his parish sent unto him as the time will serve, and as he shall think convenient, in some part of this catechism.

And all fathers, mothers, masters and dames shall cause their children, servants and prentices, which have not learned their catechism[2] to come to the church at the time appointed, and obediently to hear and be ordered by the curate, until such time as they have learned all that is here appointed for them to learn. And whensoever the bishop shall give knowledge for children to be brought afore him to any convenient place for their confirmation, then shall the curate of every parish either bring, or send in writing, the names of all those children of his parish which can say the articles of their faith, the Lord's prayer and the ten commandments: and also how many of them can answer to the other questions contained in this catechism.

And there shall none be admitted to the holy communion, until such time as he can say the catechism[3] and be confirmed.

The 1549 order of confirmation, far more conservative than any Lutheran rite, had closely followed that in the *Sarum Manual*, with the one great exception that chrism was no longer used and some consequential alterations had to be made in some of the prayers. The changes made in 1552 represent a move away from the position taken in 1549 and in a Lutheran direction. First the signing of the forehead and the *pax* were discontinued. Secondly, and most significantly, the 1552 order omitted the prayer, "Sign them, O Lord . . ." with its clause, "confirm and strengthen them with the inward unction of the Holy Ghost". Closely related with this is the change of one word in the prayer for the sevenfold Spirit, where "send down from heaven . . . thy Holy Ghost . . ." becomes "strengthen them with the Holy Ghost". Again, the prayer "Defend, O Lord . . .", said by the bishop over each candidate as he confirmed him, was a prayer which did not necessarily imply that there was any objective gift of

[1] Bucer had criticized the 1549 rubric, which had only asked for the teaching of the catechism on one Sunday in six; above, pp. 248f.

[2] 1549: "which are not yet confirmed".

[3] 1549 did not have "as he can say the catechism and". The greater emphasis in 1552 on the need to know the catechism well was due to Bucer's criticism in the *Censura*; above, p. 249.

the Holy Spirit conferred at that moment. Indeed Cosin commented on this prayer, "And this prayer seems to be rather a prayer that may be said by any minister, than a confirmation that was reserved only to the bishop."[1] It is a prayer which can appropriately be used on many occasions besides that of confirmation itself. The prayer is based upon phrases in the long collect which Bucer compiled for the *Consultation*,[2] where we read, "increase in them the gift of the Spirit that ever going forward in the knowledge and obedience of the gospel . . . they may continue to the end . . . that thou wilt defend them with thy almighty right hand . . .".

Thus, whereas the hand-laying with prayer in the rite of 1549 could be interpreted, and no doubt was so interpreted, if not by Cranmer himself at least by a number of his fellow-divines, as a means of grace wherein the Holy Spirit was sacramentally imparted, the changes made in 1552 have the combined effect of making such an interpretation, if not impossible, at any rate more difficult.

[1] *Works*, V, Parker Society, p. 489.   [2] Above, p. 202.

51. Calvin and Confirmation

Calvin condemned confirmation in the most vigorous and unrestrained language. He wrote:

I hasten to declare that I am certainly not of the number of those who think that confirmation, as observed under the Roman papacy, is an idle ceremony, inasmuch as I regard it as one of the most deadly wiles of Satan. Let us remember that this pretended sacrament is nowhere recommended in scripture, either under this name or with this ritual, or this signification.[1]

But where is the word of God [he demanded] which promises the presence of the Holy Spirit in this ceremony? They cannot allege a single iota. How, then, will they assure us that their chrism is the vessel of the Holy Spirit? We see oil, a thick and viscous liquid, and we see nothing besides. Augustine says, "Let the word be added to the element, and it will become a sacrament." Let the Romanists produce the word, if they wish us to contemplate in the oil anything beyond the oil itself.[2]

... even if they could prove themselves to imitate the apostles in the imposition of hands, ... whence do they derive their oil, which they call the oil of salvation? Who has taught them to seek salvation in oil? Who has taught them to attribute to it the property of imparting spiritual strength?[3]

In particularly violent terms Calvin assailed the use of chrism.

And with this they joined detestable blasphemy, because they said that sins were only forgiven by baptism, and that the Spirit of regeneration is given by that rotten oil which they presumed to bring in without the word of God.[4]

---

[1] *Tracts containing Antidote to the Council of Trent; Antidote to the Canons on Confirmation,* tr. H. Beveridge (Edinburgh 1851), p. 183.
[2] *Institutes of the Christian Religion* IV.19.5, tr. John Allen, ed. Benjamin B. Warfield (Presbyterian Board of Christian Education, Philadelphia 1936), II, p. 606.
[3] Ibid., IV.19.7, ed. cit., p. 608.
[4] *Comm. in Acts* 8.16, in *Works,* ed. H. Beveridge (Edinburgh 1844), p. 340. Calvin's criticism is unfair. The "confirmation prayer" in the Latin rite began, "Almighty and

The question is, whether oil, the moment after they have been pleased to call it chrism, receives, at the will of man, a new and secret virtue of the Spirit? Oil is not mentioned by any ancient Christian writer, nay, not even by any one of that middle age wherein numerous errors abounded.[1] Let them do what they may, therefore, they will gain nothing by denying that they insult the Spirit of God when they transfer his virtue to filthy oil.[2]

Confirmation [Calvin says] is oil polluted with the falsehood of the devil, to darken and deceive the minds of the simple.[3]

Another criticism is that confirmation detracts from baptism.

But the Papists are worthy of no pardon, who being not content with the ancient rite, durst thrust in rotten and filthy anointing, that it might be not only a confirmation of baptism, but also a more worthy sacrament, whereby they imagine that the faithful are made perfect who were before only half perfect, whereby those are armed against the battle, who before had their sins only forgiven them.[4] For they have not been afraid to spew out these horrible blasphemies.[5]

... they declare that the Spirit is given in baptism for innocence, in confirmation for increase of grace, that baptism is sufficient for those who were instantly to die, but by confirmation those who are to prove victorious are armed so as to be able to sustain the contest. Thus a half of the efficacy of baptism is lopt off, as if it were said in vain, that in baptism the old man is crucified, in order that we may walk in newness of life.[6]

That which was truly given in baptism he falsely asserts to be given in confirmation, with the crafty design of seducing us unawares from baptism. Who can doubt, now, that this is the doctrine of Satan, which severs from baptism the promises which belong to that sacrament, and transfers them to something else? It is now discovered on what kind

---

everlasting God, who hast vouchsafed to regenerate these thy servants by water and the Holy Ghost . . .". This is a clear reference to the grace conferred in baptism. Although the gift of the sevenfold Spirit was associated with the chrismation, the Holy Spirit was still regarded as the author of the regeneration imparted at the font.
  [1] This is a wildly inaccurate assertion. Every Western rite of initiation from the time of Tertullian at the end of the second century included an anointing with oil after the act of baptism; and the Fathers frequently referred to it. See Whitaker, op. cit., pp. 6, 8, 96, 101, 111, 133, 142, 152, 178, 194, 202, 210.
  [2] *Antidote to the Canons on Confirmation* III, ed. cit., p. 184.
  [3] *Institutes* IV.19.8, ed. cit., p. 609.   [4] Above, pp. 160, 162.
  [5] *Comm. in Acts* 19.1–7, ed. cit., II, p. 211.
  [6] *Antidote to the Canons on Confirmation* III, ed. cit., p. 183.

of a formulation this famous unction rests. The word of God is, "that as many as have been baptized into Christ have put on Christ, with his gifts".[1]

Sacrilegious mouth, dost thou dare to place an unction, which is only defiled with thy fetid breath, and enchanted by the muttering of a few words, on a level with the sacrament of Christ, and to compare it with water sanctified by the word of God?[2]

That spurious confirmation . . . they deck out like a harlot, with great splendour of ceremonies and gorgeous shows without number; nay, in their wish to adorn it, they speak of it in terms of execrable blasphemy, when they give out that it is a sacrament of greater dignity than baptism, and call those only half Christians who have not been be-smeared with their oil.[3] Meanwhile, the whole proceeding consists of nothing but theatrical gesticulations, and rather the wanton sporting of apes without any skill in imitation.[4]

The rule that only bishops may confirm was condemned by Calvin as un-scriptural.

Of a truth the horned and mitred herd are worthy of such a privilege. For what could they do, seeing they are no fitter to execute the episcopal office than hogs are to sing? Verily I do not envy them; only let them confine their impurities to their taverns, and keep them out of the church of God. But how, pray, will they prove that this office is more befitting bishops than other priests, unless that it hath so pleased some unknown authors? If a reason be sought from scripture, all confess that it makes no distinction between a bishop and a presbyter. Then Paul is enjoined to receive imposition of hands from Ananias who was one of the disciples. If imposition of hands is their confirma-tion, why do they not charge God with violating orders, and so pro-faning a mystery by confounding presbyter and bishop?[5]

But if any one inquire of them how such a prerogative has been conferred on bishops, what reason will they assign but their own pleasure? They allege that the apostles alone exercised that right, being the sole dispensers of the Holy Spirit. Are bishops the only apostles; or are they apostles at all? . . . why do they not on the same principle

---

[1] *Institutes* IV.19.8, ed. cit., p. 609.   [2] Ibid., IV.19.10, ed. cit., p. 610.
[3] Above, p. 160.
[4] *Catechism of Geneva, Dedication:* in *Tracts and Treatises on the Doctrine and Worship of the Church by John Calvin*, tr. H. Beveridge (Edinburgh 1849), II, p. 36.
[5] *Antidote to the Canons on Confirmation*, ed. cit., p. 184.

contend that none but bishops ought to touch the sacrament of the blood in the Lord's supper, which they refuse to the laity, because the Lord, as they say, only gave it to the apostles?[1]

Calvin hotly denied that Acts 8.17, the passage usually quoted in defence of the rule of episcopal confirmation, had anything to do with confirmation.

... we must not deny but that the Samaritans, who had put on Christ, indeed, in baptism, had also his Spirit given them, and surely Luke speaketh not in this place of the common grace of the Spirit, whereby God doth regenerate us, that we may be his children, but of those singular gifts wherewith God would have certain embued at the beginning of the gospel to beautify Christ's kingdom ... forasmuch as the Samaritans were already endued with the Spirit of adoption, the excellent graces of the Spirit are heaped upon them, in which God showed to his church, for a time as it were, the visible presence of his Spirit, that he might establish for ever the authority of his gospel, and also testify that his Spirit shall be always the governor and director of the faithful.[2]

... they are not afraid to break out into their sacrilegious speech, that they are but half Christians upon whom the hands have not been as yet laid. This is not tolerable now, because, whereas this was a sign which lasted only for a time, they made it a continual law in the church, as if they had the Spirit in readiness to give to whomsoever they would ... but even they themselves are enforced to grant that the church was beautified for a time only with these gifts; whereupon it followeth that the laying on of hands which the apostles used had an end when the effect ceased.[3]

Now, I do not conceive that the imposition of hands concealed any higher ministry, but am of opinion that this ceremony was employed by them as an external expression of their commending, and, as it were, presenting to God the person upon whom they laid their hands. If the ministry which was then executed by the apostles were still continued in the church, imposition of hands ought also to be still observed; but since such grace is no longer conferred, of what use is the imposition of hands?[4]

Such were Calvin's views on the contemporary Latin rite of confirmation. But he believed that confirmation had once existed in a pure form before the Papists

[1] *Institutes* IV.19.11, ed. cit., pp. 610f.   [2] *Comm. in Acts* 8.16, ed. cit., pp. 338f.
[3] Ibid., p. 339; for a similar argument by Luther see above, p. 172.
[4] *Institutes* IV.19.6, ed. cit., p. 607.

had debased it. Such a belief, however erroneous, was widely held among the Reformers;[1] and Calvin presumably did not realize on what unsure ground it rested.

In a section of the *Institutes* found in the original edition published in 1536, Calvin wrote:

I sincerely wish that we retained the custom, which I have stated was practised among the ancients before this abortive image of a sacrament made its appearance. For it was not such a confirmation as the Romanists pretend, which cannot be mentioned without injury to baptism; but a catechetical exercise, in which children or youths used to deliver an account of their faith in the presence of the church.[2]

In the revised edition of 1543 Calvin wrote at greater length:

It was an ancient custom in the church for the children of Christians, after they were come to years of discretion, to be presented to the bishop in order to fulfil that duty which was required of adults who offered themselves to baptism. For such persons were placed among the catechumens, till, being duly instructed in the mysteries of Christianity, they were called to make a confession of their faith before the bishop and all the people. Therefore those who had been baptized in their infancy, because they had not then made such a confession of faith before the church, at the close of childhood or the commencement of adolescence, were again presented by their parents, and were examined by the bishop according to the form of the catechism which was then in common use. That this exercise, which deserved to be regarded as sacred and solemn, might have the greater dignity and reverence, they also practised the ceremony of imposition of hands. Thus the youth, after having given satisfaction respecting his faith, was dismissed with a solemn benediction. This custom is frequently mentioned by the ancient writers.[3]

Whereas the men of old time did use laying on of hands, that they might confirm the profession of faith in those who were grown up, I do not mislike it; so that no man think that the grace of the Spirit is annexed to such a ceremony, as doth Jerome against the Luciferians.[4]

We also should like to see that rite everywhere restored by which the

---

[1] Above, pp. 171, 175, 182f, 194.   [2] *Institutes* IV.19.13, ed. cit., p. 612.
[3] Ibid., IV.19.4, ed. cit., p. 605.   [4] *Comm. in Acts* 19.1–7, ed. cit., p. 211.

young are presented to God, after giving forth a confession of their faith. This would be a not unbecoming approval of their catechism.[1]

In the second passage quoted from the *Institutes* Calvin asserted that this practice was frequently mentioned by ancient writers. But in support of this claim he only cited statements by Leo I and Jerome,[2] neither of which in fact proved his point. Leo was writing not about people who had been baptized in infancy and were now old enough to confess their faith in person, but about persons who had been baptized, not necessarily in infancy, in heretical sects, and wished to enter the catholic church,[3] and Jerome was referring to the visits paid by bishops to remote country districts to lay hands on those whom the local presbyters had baptized, but had not laid hands upon them because they were not competent to do so.[4] The reason why these persons had not received the hand-laying at their baptism was not because they were considered too young to receive it, but because there was no bishop present to administer it at their baptism. Nor is there any reason to assume that all these persons had in fact been baptized in infancy.

In actual fact the practice of the ancient Church does not support Calvin's claim at all. The *Apostolic Tradition of Hippolytus* (c. A.D. 217) and the sixth-century *Gelasian Sacramentary*, for example, show that, when infants were baptized, they were confirmed and communicated immediately afterwards;[5] but if there were no bishop present, the confirmation had to be omitted and deferred until his next visitation, which need not have been many years later. There was a public confession of the faith in the primitive baptismal liturgies; but this formed part of the catechumenate before baptism, being commonly known as the *redditio symboli*. Adult candidates confessed their faith in person and infants through their sponsors.

There is one passage in the New Testament which seemed to Calvin to afford scriptural evidence for his alleged purer form of confirmation. In his *Commentary on Hebrews*, first published in 1549, Calvin wrote:

He here refers to a catechism commonly used. It is hence a probable conjecture that this Epistle was written, not immediately after the promulgation of the gospel, but when they had some kind of polity established in the churches, such as this, that the catechumen made a confession of his faith before he was admitted to baptism. . . . With baptism he connects the laying on of hands; for as there were two sorts of catechumens, so there were two rites. There were heathens who came not to baptism until they made a profession of their faith. Then as to these, the catechizing was wont to precede baptism. But the children of the faithful, as they were adopted from the womb, and belonged to the body of the church by right of the promise, were baptized in infancy: but after the time of infancy, they having been

---

[1] *The True Method of Giving Peace and of Reforming the Church*, tr. H. Beveridge (Edinburgh 1851), III, p. 288.

[2] *Institutes* IV.19.4, ed. cit., p. 605.   [3] *Ep.* 159.6f, *P.L.* 54.1138f.

[4] *Dial. c. Lucif.* 9; *P.L.* 23.164f.   [5] See Whitaker, op. cit., pp. 5f, 157–78.

instructed in the faith presented themselves as catechumens, which as to them took place after baptism: but another symbol was then added, the laying on of hands.

This one passage abundantly testifies that this rite had its beginning from the apostles, which afterwards, however, was turned into superstition, as the world almost always degenerates into corruptions, even with regard to the best institutions.... Wherefore the pure institution at this day ought to be retained, but the superstition ought to be removed.[1]

Calvin's interpretation of Hebrews 6.1f is quite untenable. He believed the author of Hebrews to be St Paul. But there is no evidence that St Paul or any other New Testament writer knew of the practice of infant baptism, or, if they did, that they had it in mind when they wrote about baptism. All the other references to baptism in the New Testament presuppose that the subjects of baptism were adults. To suppose that the author of Hebrews 6.1f had infants in mind at the moment of writing is an altogether gratuitous assumption. Moreover, if it was normal to lay hands on the baptized, there is no evidence that infants, if any, who were admitted to baptism were debarred from receiving the laying on of hands by reason of their age. The practice of the early Church lends no support to such an hypothesis. In short, Calvin's theory of a primitive and pure form of confirmation consisting in a personal and public confession of the faith and a solemn blessing cannot be justified by appeal either to Scripture or to primitive tradition.

Now, however much Calvin wished his imaginary primitive rite of confirmation to be restored, he did not restore it in the church of Geneva. In his baptism service he required infants as soon as possible to be instructed in the faith and in the Christian way of life. But he provided no ceremony for children when they were examined in the faith and satisfied their examiners.

Similarly Knox dispensed with any rite of confirmation. The *Book of Discipline* required children to receive instruction, forbidding them to be admitted to communion until they could say the Lord's Prayer, the Creed, and the Ten Commandments.[2]

So also Zwingli compiled no rite of confirmation to be used in Zurich. He denied that confirmation was a sacrament:

Christ left to us only two sacraments, baptism and the Lord's supper. ... The other sacraments are rather ceremonies, for they initiate nothing in the church of God. Wherefore they are deservedly abolished, for they have not been instituted by God. ...[3]

He believed that confirmation had its origin when it became common for infants to be baptized, apparently sharing the Reformers' views about a purer form of this rite in primitive times.[4]

[1] *Commentaries on the Epistle of Paul the Apostle to the Hebrews*, tr. J. Owen (Edinburgh 1853), pp. 131–4.
[2] Above, p. 125.   [3] *de Vera et Falsa Religione*, ed. cit., pp. 201f.   [4] Ibid., p. 302.

Bibliography

Agenda (*secundum imperialem ecclesiam et dyocesim Bambergensem*). 1491.

H. Beveridge, *Tracts and Treatises on the Doctrine and Worship of the Church by John Calvin*. Edinburgh and London, reprinted in U.S.A. 1958.

The Book of Common Prayer, printed by Whitchurch, March 1549. London 1844.

The Book of Common Prayer and Administration of the Sacraments and other Rites and ceremonies in the Church of England. Published by Whitchurch. London 1552.

A. Boudinhon, Art., "Decretals", in *Encyclopaedia Britannica*, 11th edn, VII, pp. 915ff.

F. E. Brightman, *The English Rite*. London 1915.

G. W. Bromiley, *Baptism and the Anglican Reformers*. London 1953.

—— *Thomas Cranmer Theologian*. London 1956.

M. Bucer, *Scripta Anglicana fere omnia*. Basle 1577.

J. F. Buddeus, *Supplementum Epistolarum Martini Lutheri*. Halae 1701.

E. Burbidge, *T. Cranmer, An Account of his Library*. 1892.

G. Burnet, *A History of the Reformation of the Church of England*. London 1841.

E. Burton, *A Short Introduction into Christian Religion being a Catechism set forth by Archbishop Cranmer in 1548*. Oxford 1829.

J. Calvin, *Commentaries on the Acts of the Apostles*, ed. H. Beveridge. Edinburgh 1844.

—— *Commentaries on the Epistle of Paul the Apostle to the Hebrews*, ed. J. Owen. Edinburgh 1853.

—— *Institutes of the Christian Religion*, tr. J. Allen. Philadelphia and London 1935.

—— *Works*. Corpus Reformatorum, vols. 34, 49.

—— *Works*, I, II, III, tr. H. Beveridge. Edinburgh 1844, etc.

F. H. Chase, *Confirmation in the Apostolic Age*. London 1909.

A. J. Collins, *Manuale ad usum percelebris ecclesiae Sarisburiensis*. London 1950.

Cologne, Chapter of, *Antididagma*. Paris 1549.

—— *Canones Concilii Provincialis Coloniensis*. 1537.

A. Comenius, *Historia Fratrum Bohemorum*. Halae 1702.

J. Cosin, *Works*. Parker Society, V.

T. Cranmer, *Works*. Parker Society, I, II.

K. B. Cully, *Confirmation: History, Doctrine and Practice*. Greenwich 1962.

J. Daniélou, *Bible et Liturgie*. Paris 1958.

E. H. Davenport, *The False Decretals*. Oxford 1916.

J. G. Davies, *The Spirit, the Church and the Sacraments*. London 1954.

J. Daye, *see* Hermann.

G. Dix, *The Shape of the Liturgy*. London 1943.

C. W. Dugmore, "The First Ten Years, 1549–59" in *The English Prayer Book 1549–1662*. London 1963.
Enchiridion Christianae Religionis. Cologne 1538.
E. Evans, *Tertullian's Homily on Baptism*. London 1964.
J. D. C. Fisher, *Christian Initiation: Baptism in the Medieval West*. London 1965.
W. H. Frere and W. M. Kennedy, *Visitation Articles and Injunctions of the Period of the Reformation*, II. London 1910.
A. Friedberg, *Decretum Magistri Gratiani*. Leipzig 1879.
T. Fuller, *Church History of Britain*, ed. J. S. Brewer, III. Oxford 1845.
H. Gee and W. J. Hardy, *Documents Illustrative of English Church History*. 1896.
W. Goode, *The Doctrine of the Church of England as to the Effects of Baptism in the case of Infants*. London 1849.
J. Hartzheim, *Concilia Germaniae*, IV. Cologne 1759.
C. J. Hefele and H. Leclercq, *Histoire des Conciles*, V. Paris 1907.
Henry VIII, *Assertio Septem Sacramentorum*, ed. L. O'Donovan. New York 1908.
Hermann (of Wied), *Einfaltigs Bedencken*. Cologne 1543.
—— *Simplex et Pia Deliberatio*. 1545.
—— *A Simple and Religious Consultation*, tr. J. Daye. 1547 and 1548.
P. Hinschius, *Decretales Pseudo-Isidorianae*. Leipzig 1863.
C. Hopf, *Martin Bucer and the English Reformation*. Oxford 1946.
F. Hubert, *Die Strassburger Liturgischen Ordnungen in Zeitalter der Reformation*. Gottingen 1900.
B. J. Kidd, *Documents Illustrative of the Continental Reformation*. Oxford 1911.
J. Knox, *Works* I–IV, ed. D. Laing. Edinburgh 1846, etc.
T. A. Lacey, *A Necessary Doctrine and Erudition for any Christian Man*. London 1932.
B. Leeming, "The False Decretals, Faustus of Riez and the Psuedo-Eusebius" in *Studia Patristica*, II, part 2. Oxford 1955.
—— *Principles of Sacramental Theology*. London 1956.
T. M. Lindsay, *A History of the Reformation*. Edinburgh 1934.
C. Lloyd, *Formularies of the Faith, put forth by authority during the reign of Henry VIII*. Oxford 1856.
W. Lockton, "The Age for Confirmation" in *Church Quarterly Review*. April 1925.
C. E. Luthardt, *Zeitschrift fur kirchliche Wissenschaft und kirkliches leben*, X. Leipzig 1889.
M. Luther, *D. Martin Luthers Werke*, Band X–XII. Weimar 1907.
—— *Primary Works*, ed. H. Wace and C. A. Buckheim. London 1896.
Luther's Works, vol. 53. Philadelphia 1965.
W. D. Maxwell, *The Liturgical Portions of the Genevan Service Book*. London 1965.
L. L. Mitchell, *Baptismal Anointing*. London 1966.
D. Moody, *Baptism: Foundation for Christian Unity*. Philadelphia 1967.
S. L. Ollard, "Confirmation in the Anglican Communion" in *Confirmation or the Laying on of Hands*. London 1934.
Ordo Romanus 11 and *Ordo 50*, ed. M. Andrieu, *Les Ordines Romani du Haut Moyen Age*, II and V. Louvain 1948 and 1961.

A. Osiander, *Ordnung wie man tauffet bisher in Latein gehalten verteucht*. Nürnberg 1524.

P. F. Palmer, *Sacraments and Worship*. London 1957.

J. Pohle, *The Sacraments*, ed. A. Preuss. St Louis and London 1946.

F. M. Powicke and C. R. Cheney, *Councils and Synods, with other Documents relating to the English Church*. Oxford 1964.

F. Procter, *A History of the Book of Common Prayer*. London 1870.

—— *A New History of the Book of Common Prayer*, revised and rewritten by W. H. Frere. London 1965.

A. C. Repp, *Confirmation in the Lutheran Church*. St Louis 1964.

A. L. Richter, *Die Evangelischen Kirchenordnungen*. Weimar 1846 and 1871.

G. Rietschel, *Lehrbuch der Liturgie*. Berlin 1909.

Rituale Romanum (secundum consuetudinem Romanae Curiae). 1487.

Rituale Romanum (secundum Curiam Romanam). 1520.

Sacramentarium Fuldense Saeculi X, ed. G. Richter and A. Schonfelder. Fulda 1912.

E. Sehling, *Die Evangelischen Kirchenordnungen des XVI Jahrhunderts*. Leipzig 1902, etc.

A. Souter, "Observations on the Pseudo-Eusebian Collection of Gallican Sermons" in *Journal of Theological Studies*, XLI. 1940.

G. W. Sprott, *The Book of Common Order*. Edinburgh and London 1901.

J. Strype, *Ecclesiastical Memorials*, I.

L. S. Thornton, *Confirmation: Its Place in the Baptismal Mystery*. London 1951.

W. Tyndale, *Works*. Parker Society, I, II.

L. A. Van Buchem, *L'Homélie Pseudo-Eusébienne de Pentecôte*. Nijmegen 1967.

L. Vischer, *Ye are Baptized*. 1964.

J. Warns, *Baptism*, tr. G. H. Lang. London 1957.

W. M. S. West, "The Anabaptists and the Rise of the Baptist Movement" in E. Gilmore, ed., *Christian Baptism*. London 1960.

E. C. Whitaker, *Documents of the Baptismal Liturgy*. London 1960.

—— *The Baptismal Liturgy*. London 1965.

D. Wilkins, *Concilia Magnae Britanniae et Hiberniae*, III. London 1737.

B. L. Woolf, *Reformation Writings of Martin Luther*, I. London 1946.

J. Wycliffe, *Trialogus*, ed. G. Lechler. Oxford 1869.

J. Ysebaert, *Greek Baptismal Terminology*. Nijmegen 1962.

U. Zwingli, *Works*. Corpus Reformatorum, vols. 88–94.

INDEXES

Index of Proper Names

Index of Subjects

About the Liturgical Institute

The Liturgical Institute, founded in 2000 by His Eminence Francis Cardinal George of Chicago, offers a variety of options for education in Liturgical Studies. A unified, rites-based core curriculum constitutes the foundation of the program, providing integrated and balanced studies toward the advancement of the renewal promoted by the Second Vatican Council. The musical, artistic, and architectural dimensions of worship are given particular emphasis in the curriculum. Institute students are encouraged to participate in its "liturgical heart" of daily Mass and Morning and Evening Prayer. The academic program of the Institute serves a diverse, international student population—laity, religious, and clergy—who are preparing for service in parishes, dioceses, and religious communities. Personalized mentoring is provided in view of each student's ministerial and professional goals. The Institute is housed on the campus of the University of St. Mary of the Lake/Mundelein Seminary, which offers the largest priestly formation program in the United States and is the center of the permanent diaconate and lay ministry training programs of the Archdiocese of Chicago. In addition, the University has the distinction of being the first chartered institution of higher learning in Chicago (1844), and one of only seven pontifical faculties in North America.

For more information about the Liturgical Institute and its programs, contact: usml.edu/liturgicalinstitute. Phone: 847-837-4542. E-mail: litinst@usml.edu.

Msgr. Reynold Hillenbrand
1904-1979

Monsignor Reynold Hillenbrand, ordained a priest by Cardinal George Mundelein in 1929, was Rector of St. Mary of the Lake Seminary from 1936 to 1944.

He was a leading figure in the liturgical and social action movement in the United States during the 1930s and worked to promote active, intelligent, and informed participation in the Church's liturgy.

He believed that a reconstruction of society would occur as a result of the renewal of the Christian spirit, whose source and center is the liturgy.

Hillenbrand taught that, since the ultimate purpose of Catholic action is to Christianize society, the renewal of the liturgy must undoubtedly play the key role in achieving this goal.

Hillenbrand Books strives to reflect the spirit of Monsignor Reynold Hillenbrand's pioneering work by making available innovative and scholarly resources that advance the liturgical and sacramental life of the Church.